S Christopher

The rose of Venice

S Christopher

The rose of Venice

ISBN/EAN: 9783741163654

Manufactured in Europe, USA, Canada, Australia, Japa

Cover: Foto ©Andreas Hilbeck / pixelio.de

Manufactured and distributed by brebook publishing software
(www.brebook.com)

S Christopher

The rose of Venice

THE ROSE OF VENICE.

"Know ye the land where the cypress and myrtle
Are emblems of deeds that are done in their clime,
Where the rage of the vulture, the love of the turtle,
Now melt into sorrow, now madden to crime?"

BYRON—*Bride of Abydos.*

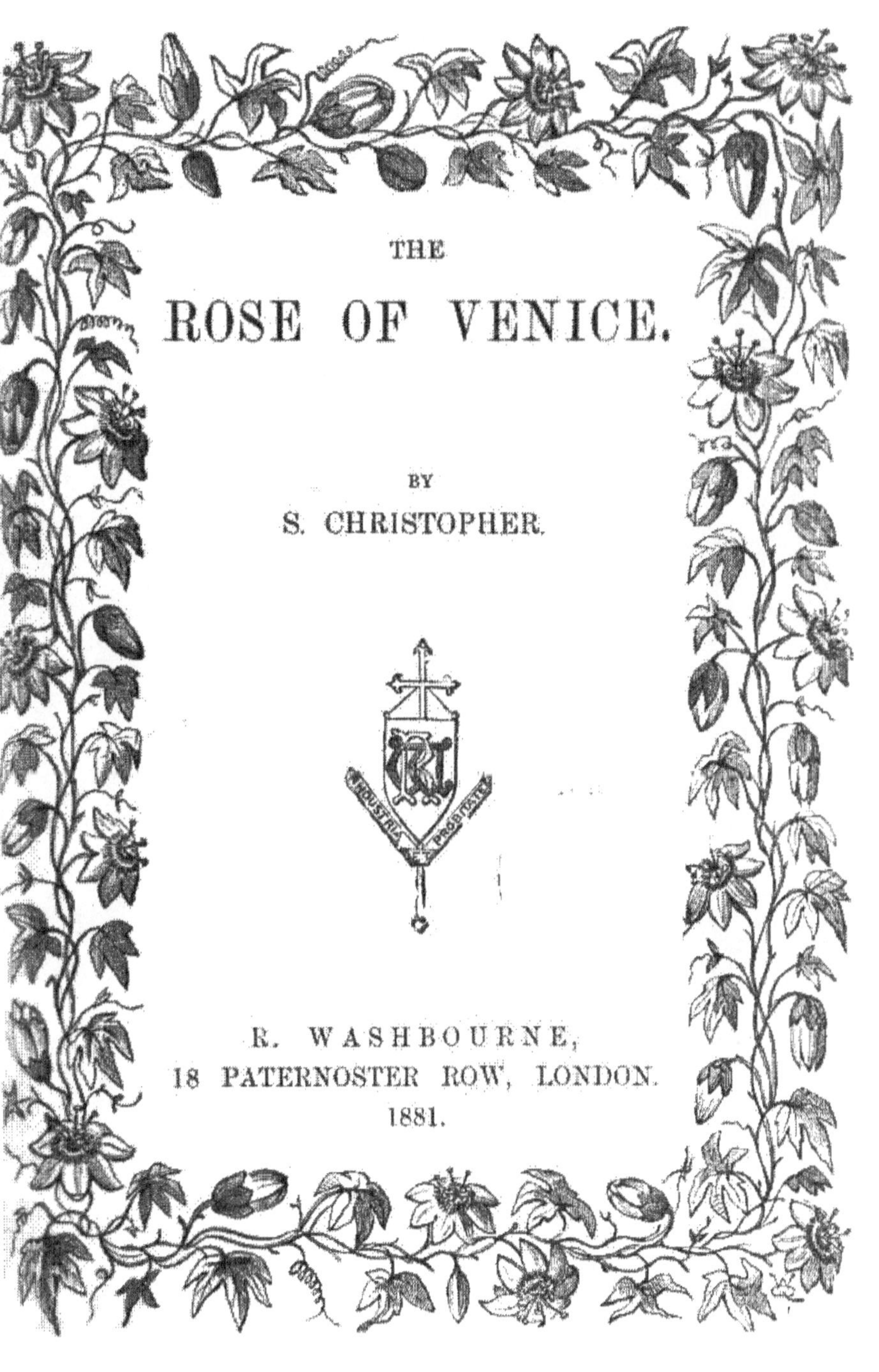

THE ROSE OF VENICE.

BY

S. CHRISTOPHER.

R. WASHBOURNE,
18 PATERNOSTER ROW, LONDON.
1881.

PREFACE.

THOUGH we are aware that prefaces are rarely if ever read, we cannot abstain from noticing what perhaps will be considered the greatest fault in the following pages, and explain the reason of it.

The only historical character in the whole narrative is that of the heroic and unfortunate Antonio Foscarini. It will seem strange, therefore, that he is not the principal actor in the drama; that he makes his appearance in a somewhat commonplace manner, just to love for a short time and die. We have done so purposely, and we have been actuated in so doing by our unconquerable aversion to what is termed "an historical novel;" being convinced that truth is thereby made subservient to the author's imagination, and persons with a superficial knowledge of history allowed to form the most erroneous judgment respecting individuals, events, and customs.

Why, therefore, may be asked, introduce an historical character at all?

In our case it has been *a matter of feeling*, if we may

so express ourselves, having always felt the greatest admiration for the man who could prefer death to the vile act of purchasing life by causing a slur to be attached to the name of the woman he loved. Besides provided one keeps faithful to history, and to what is known respecting the character of the individual called in to act his or her part, no detriment can possibly be caused to the reader. But perhaps it will be further observed, that in describing the love of Antonio Foscarini we have not entirely kept to history, inasmuch as nothing is known respecting the woman who inspired him with so great and holy an attachment. Exactly so; but where nothing certain is known the author may be allowed entire liberty in the creations of his imagination; and furthermore, it is in perfect accordance with the nobleness of Foscarini's character, and with his willingness to meet death, to imagine that a pure and devout girl, unable to control her own destiny, and bestow her hand on whom she chose, *alone* could inspire him with such heroic devotion.

To the Catholic reader we next state, that the letter supposed to have been written in the beginning of the seventeenth century, faithfully describes the cause of the small success met with by Protestants in bringing about a religious change in Italy; and will, we trust, be perused with pleasure. The description also of the famous image of the Volto Santo (Holy Face) of Lucca, is perfectly true.

THE ROSE OF VENICE.

PART I.

CHAPTER I.

THE LOVERS.

OUR story opens on the 5th of May, 1590.

In a small square, in a quiet part of Venice, stood a youth and maiden: the patrician Marco Centofoglia, and Rosalia Leoni, the daughter of a Sicilian merchant.

"Rosalia," said Marco, "Rosalia, my first, my only love—for never shall I love another woman as I do you—Rosalia, my own beautiful betrothed, when will you seal my happiness by allowing me to ask your hand of your austere father?"

"Not yet, Marco; you know my father has forbidden my having any further intercourse with you."

"I know it but too well. Your father has Sicilian obstinacy in his character."

"My father does not believe a proud Venetian nobleman would marry the daughter of a Sicilian merchant."

"Do you think me proud, Rosalia?"

"No, indeed."

"Do you suspect I could ever be false?"

"No; I would sooner think I could be false myself. I would swear by all that is most sacred—I would lay my head on the block before I could for one moment suspect that you, the best of men, the truest of gentlemen, would prove faithless to the girl who has trusted in you."

"Rosalia, I have never seen you look more beautiful than this evening. I feel as though it were asking too much of me to tell me to delay calling you my bride."

"Marco, have patience. Pity me. Mine is a difficult task. I must strive with great caution to overcome my father's prejudices."

"Obstinate man!"

"Speak not thus. He is an honourable man."

"Can anything be more honourable than my proposals? I would even promise never to go to his house, not to see you any more till the day fixed for our marriage, provided he gave his consent."

"But you never told me so before. I will broach the subject to him this very evening, and endeavour to make him trust in your honourable intentions."

"Fail not to do so, my beloved Rosalia. Pray, entreat, implore, don't give up till he answers 'yes,' and seals my happiness. And now, methinks it is getting too late for you to be out alone. We must part. The day after to-morrow at the usual hour we will meet again. Oh, may it be my happy lot to hear you say, 'I can be yours for life!'"

He kissed her hand and disappeared.

About two years before the date of this interview, Giovanni Leoni, a Sicilian merchant, had arrived in Venice. He was a widower with an only daughter, whose mother had died at the earliest stage of her infancy. He settled near the Rialto, where he carried on an apparently flourishing business. His habits were strange, very strange. The hours of business once over, he shunned intercourse with the rest of mankind, except with his most beloved daughter. He was miserly where his own comfort was in question, but to his child, on whom his whole soul was centred, he was liberal in the extreme. She wanted nothing her station could require. He took the most paternal care of her, save that he enforced upon her also his solitary mode of life, insisted on her knowing no one, and passing her life at home. He had caused her to be instructed, considering her position and the times, tolerably well; for Rosalia could read very well, write pretty well, and was expert in all kinds of needlework.

Notwithstanding, however, his jealous care, Rosalia was endowed with too much beauty to pass unnoticed. Her figure was the most beautiful that could be seen in

Venice. Her features, though not entirely regular, resembled those enchanting descriptions which travellers give of Eastern women, especially of natives of the environs of Bethlehem in Palestine. Her eyes, once seen, could never be forgotten—large, black, sparkling. She doted on her father, but the buoyancy of youth prevented her from strictly obeying his orders. She knew herself beautiful. Whenever she went out she saw every eye turned on her. In time the desire of admiration superseded the duty of obedience; and often to her father's remonstrances that she strolled about too much, that he would not allow her to walk in the streets of Venice alone, she framed the excuse that a particular skein of silk was needed for her embroidery, that she had forgotten something the day before, and had been obliged to buy it now, etc., etc.

On the occasion of one of these pretended shopping excursions she met on the Piazza S. Marco a fair-haired, gentlemanly young man, who looked at her fixedly. She took no notice of him; it was nothing strange to be looked at; she thought it her due, and continued her walk homewards. On entering her door, she discovered the same gentlemanly figure had followed her; he then loitered awhile opposite the house. From that day for some weeks did the identical youth follow her in her walks, visit that street, look up at her window. Unconsciously those visits and looks entirely occupied her thoughts. The fair-haired young man was ever present to her mind, and brightened her dreams.

One evening, passing under her window, and emboldened by the shade of advanced twilight, he bowed and smiled. She returned the bow, and accompanied it with a smile. Two or three days afterwards a few words were exchanged between them. Then words of love were uttered, and finally the promise of an everlasting affection was sworn by both parties, both sincerely and firmly believing they were necessary to each other's happiness.

They were the very opposite of each other in person and in character, but this difference only served to enhance their love. Rosalia Leoni was dark, passionate, vehement. Marco Centofoglia fair, gentle, sedate, and by nature inclined to be calculating. Now, however, blinded by admiration and love, he did not calculate the difference of birth between himself and the daughter of a second-rate merchant, finding a good excuse for this forgetfulness, in his own eyes at least, by the knowledge that his very small means made it difficult for him to form a suitable alliance in his own rank of life. He was descended from one of the noblest and richest families of Venice. His grandfather had left two sons, both equally well provided for.

One, Marco's father, a spendthrift, had squandered all his property, had well-nigh lost his fame, and died, leaving his only son with nothing save his mother's portion, which was very small. The other, still living, of thrifty habits, had increased instead of diminished his portion, and had even bought of his brother the half of their ancestral palace, which had fallen to his share.

He had an only son, but he was married, and had a child, so it was not likely Marco could ever inherit his uncle's fortune. He lived in an humble manner, his dress alone vieing with that of the elegant youths of his time and rank.

It was generally thought that Rosalia's father was richer than he chose to admit; even his own daughter had fallen into this notion. What harm could there be in his loving her? His uncle and cousin would most assuredly refuse to see him and his bride, but he did not care for that. They had taken little notice of him, and had acted towards him as rich relations generally act towards poorer ones, viz. with neglect.

Consequently, they had no right to expect that he should consult their likes or dislikes concerning his marriage. Lastly and chiefly, love spoke strong and loud, and succeeded in persuading him that once married everyone who saw Rosalia's surpassing beauty, would envy instead of blaming him for his disregard of received opinions and customs.

He asked her hand, and she readily acquiesced, for she loved him as woman alone can love. It was all-absorbing. She lived, she breathed for him alone! She would have died the worst of deaths to spare him a little pain, or trifling sorrow.

She fancied her father would be as delighted as herself at the patrician's offer, and with almost childish joy she related to him her whole adventure, from the first moment she had set eyes on Marco Centofoglia, to that in which he had made her an offer of marriage. To her surprise and grief her parent, far from being flattered at the unlooked-for offer, answered her sternly:

"Rosalia, you have disobeyed my orders. You have spoken with a stranger, forgetful of my repeated injunctions. You have believed his false vows of love. Do you imagine a proud nobleman, and a Venetian noble above all, would ever marry the daughter of a middle-class merchant like me? He admires you, foolish child, and talks of marriage in order to blind me as well as you. But he does not know my cunning is a match for his, and my knowledge of the world and experience greater than his. I not only refuse his false offer, but from this moment I forbid your speaking with him again."

"Father—pray—father—hear me!" answered Rosalia, falteringly.

"Silence! Not another word," replied her father, with increased sternness. "You either obey, or I leave Venice and take you back to Sicily. Beware! I have warned you."

Giovanni Leoni may have had great experience of the world as far as man goes, he certainly evinced very little as regards woman's heart, and still less as regarded his daughter's character. To insist on Rosalia's giving up Marco Centofoglia was like commanding the flowing tide to ebb; the one was as impossible as the other. She made up her mind to disobey her father, and continue her intercourse with her lover. It must be said, however, to her credit, that she hoped to succeed in persuading her reluctant parent to believe that Marco's intentions were loyal.

She met him the next day at the usual place of appointment, related what had passed between her father and herself, and readily acceded to his entreaties to continue to meet him at least three times a week. They only changed the spot, as it did not appear prudent to hold their meetings in the same place. They chose a more solitary one, and there, eluding Leoni's vigilance, who, it must be owned, overrated his child's sense of duty and fear of displeasing him, they met, and talked, and planned how best to succeed in overcoming the old man's reluctance.

It is on the occasion of one of these meetings that our chapter opens.

As soon as Rosalia reached her home, she set about superintending the preparations for supper. As this was the only meal her father could enjoy in peace, she always strove to order it according to his liking.

She had great taste in adorning a room, though Leoni preferred a shabby state of disorder to a neat and pretty apartment, and consequently did not appreciate her talents, she nevertheless managed so to dispose their humble furniture, and ornament the window-sill, stands, and tables with flowers and flower-pots—her peculiar care, and which reminded her of her sunny isle—that their dining-room, which served also as sitting-room, always looked cheerful and pleasant.

But while she seemed intent on giving orders to a very young servant-maid, her whole mind was bent on finding out the best way of broaching to her father the question he had forbidden her to mention again.

By the time Leoni had eaten his supper, and had placed himself in an easy-chair, enjoying rest after many hours of toil and anxiety, Rosalia thought she had hit on the surest way of testing whether her father was still firmly opposed to her marriage.

"Father," said she, looking at him tenderly, "whenever I marry you will come and live with me. I could not part from you."

"Don't fear, my child, parting from me; marriage is not so easy a thing."

"It is easy for others, why should it be difficult for me? Am I uglier or poorer than many?" and Rosalia looked archly at her father.

"I cannot answer for beauty, for I will not make you vain. As for riches, it is a mistaken idea. I am a poor man, and you will be a poor woman."

"That is no reason why I should not marry."

"Dear child, I am tired; don't worry me with nonsense about marriage," said Leoni, rather peevishly.

"Father, I thought there was no harm in saying this, as there certainly is no harm in wishing to be married."

"In your case there is."

"Why so, father?" and Rosalia looked almost alarmed.

"Because it is contrary to my wish."

"Am I never to marry, then?"

"Never."

"Never? Really never?" Rosalia grew pale.

"Never, so long as I live. Afterwards you may do as you please."

"But I shall be too old then to marry, as I trust you will live to a very old age. Nay," she added, fixing her beautiful eyes on the old man tenderly, "I hope you will survive *me*."

Leoni was moved by her affection for him; he cast a loving look on her, answering:

"And I hope that I may never be deprived of my dear daughter's soothing care. Child, I shall not live long," and he looked sad.

"Do not say so, my father. Are you ill? Tell me. I will try everything in my power to restore your health."

"I am not exactly ill; but, Rosalia, if you love me, don't talk about marriage again."

"Father, if it is to hurt your feelings, I will not," and the poor girl sighed from her very soul; "only tell me the reason—do tell me."

"On my death-bed I will tell you."

"Why on your death-bed? Why not now?"

There was an earnestness in her voice and manner that struck Leoni. Wishing to cut the matter short and hear no more about it, he assumed a stern look:

"On my death-bed, I repeat. And from this moment till then, never upon any account let me hear the word 'marriage' again from your lips."

Leoni arose and went into his room.

"It is over," thought poor Rosalia; "my dreams of happiness are over," and she did not close her eyes all night.

The sun's bright rays brought a little balm to her aching heart, for they encouraged hope to appear again, and persuaded her events might change; she might succeed at last in persuading her father to relent.

At the appointed place and hour she met her lover, and told him word for word the conversation she had had with her father. He listened attentively, was silent a little while, as if to collect his thoughts, then looking her full in the face, said:

"Rosalia, do you love me?"

"More than life," and her eyes sparkled with greater kindness.

"As much as your soul?"

"More."

Rosalia did not know what she said; she only knew she loved.

"Will you abide by all I tell you?"

"By all."

"Then fly with me. Let us go to Tuscany. Once out of the reach of the Lion of St. Mark, you will be free. We will marry there. We will seal our happiness, and after a few months return to Venice man and wife. Your father will then be reconciled; and if he is not, so much the worse for him. He will have no right to interfere."

Oh, how perplexing were poor Rosalia's thoughts!

She had just said she would abide by all her lover told her, and now a cruel suspicion flashed across her mind. Who knew but that her father might be right in distrusting the sincerity of Marco's proposal? If he really intended to make her his wife, would he allow the future mother of his children to elope, bearing the slur ever attending the name of her who quits the paternal roof, to entrust her honour even to an honourable man? And then what would her father do? He had said he should not live long. The grief caused by her elopement might cost him his life! And then, and perhaps most of all, a sense of womanly modesty—for Rosalia was innately virtuous—made her shrink from such a proposal. No; she would have committed her life to him, but not her honour; she therefore, as if looking into vacancy, and with a deep flush on her cheeks, answered:

"Marco! do you wish to have a good wife?"

"In wishing to marry you I prove, beyond the possibility of doubt, that I wish to have the best of wives."

"Then remember, that a bad daughter cannot make a good wife."

"Is that an answer to what I have proposed, my dearest?"

"It is, Marco. If you wish me now to disobey my poor old father, could you afterwards expect me to obey you, as a dutiful wife should? If you wish me to leave him, sickly as he says he is, do you think I should be a fit companion to comfort you in sickness or in sorrow?"

"Rosalia!"—and Marco fixed an inquiring, serious look upon her—"Rosalia! do you, or do you not love me? I ask you for the last time—speak the whole truth."

"Marco, I love you as woman has never loved. Why ask me so often," and a tear glistened in her beauteous eyes, "as though you did not believe me? Ah! Marco, would that it were in my power to convince you! I adore you, and shall do so to the last moment of my life."

"Then why begin to moralise when I propose the *only* means left us in order to be united for ever?"

"But it is not the *only* means. I may still be able to persuade my father. Marco! love me — love me always; but do not propose what is not right for a daughter—for a woman——"

There was an imploring expression in her sparkling eyes, which Marco could not resist. Interrupting her, he took her hand, kissed it; then pressing her to his heart, said:

"I love you—I shall love you till death—after death. I call St. Mark to witness the sincerity of my love, the purity of my intentions."

Marco Centofoglia felt as he spoke. He did not lie. Oh that wealth had never been his portion on earth!

Rosalia withdrew her hand, returned his vows of love, and after having settled with him the next day and hour of meeting, went back to her home.

CHAPTER II.

A CHANGE OF FORTUNE.

ON entering his house Marco Centofoglia received a summons sent in great haste from his uncle. He felt almost amazed. His cold relative had taken no notice of him for many months, and now of a sudden sent a pressing message.

What could it mean? Had he, perhaps by means of some spy, of which there was no lack in Venice, heard of his love-making with a merchant's daughter? Had some one overheard his passionate exclamations of love, or his proposals of marriage? But, no; it could not be. He had been cautious. He had never spoken in a loud voice; and as for stopping to talk to a girl, that was no extraordinary event in a young man's life, and not worth repeating to the old nobleman, who would most certainly have called anyone a fool who had given himself the trouble of coming and talking such nonsense to him. What could it mean, then? Marco was at a loss to guess. He hastened to obey, and soon found himself within the precincts of his ancestors' old palace. He thought the servants looked odd. They bowed to him profoundly; they seemed to wish to tell him some news, but respect kept them silent. The maggiordomo accosted him with a woeful countenance, and led him to the hall. He paused; and Marco said with earnestness—rather assumed, it must be acknowledged:

"Pietro, how is my uncle?"

The maggiordomo did not answer. Marco continued:

"And my cousin, and the Signora Teresa, and the child?"

"Ah! Signor Marco——" he stopped.

"Well, what? You look horror-struck. What is the matter?"

"Yesterday we feared nothing——" he stopped again.

"Something has happened, then?"

"Too truly. My poor master!"

"Is he ill?"

"He is not well; but that is not all."

"Is he in danger?"

"No. He is in an agony of grief, and . . . and . . . the poor lady . . . ."

"Is in danger, perhaps?"

"No, Signor Marco; she is a widow, and childless!"

Marco could not answer, not because he felt much grieved, but because the announcement of a person's demise, even if it is one for whom one cares little, is apt to strike one with surprise, if with nothing else. In

Marco's bosom it wrought, furthermore, a perfect revolution.

"Ah! my poor cousin!" said he at last.

"He is not to be pitied. He died like a saint. It is my master—and most of all the poor lady. She has lost *all*."

Pietro laid a long stress on the last word.

"How did it happen? And why was I not apprised before? However, my uncle . . ." He did not finish the sentence, thinking it more prudent; but he meant to say, "However, my uncle never wished to have me much about him."

"It was so sudden; but this morning, who could have imagined such a catastrophe!"

"Tell me how it happened. My poor cousin!"

"He was taken ill about a week ago. It was nothing strange; he was subject to fever. Three days after his sickness increased, but no immediate danger was apprehended. Unfortunately his little boy caught the fever, and being a sickly child he died last night. His poor mother could not suppress her tears, even in her sick husband's room, and he insisted on knowing the cause. The lady, fearing lest he should think she was alarmed for him, told him the little boy was ill. He insisted on seeing him, and ordered him to be brought in. As there was no way of pacifying him, they said the child was asleep. 'Well,' said he, 'bring him here to me asleep; I will have him!' You must know, Signor Marco, as of course you do know, that my young master—may his soul rest in peace!"—the maggiordomo turned his eyes upwards, and gave vent to a deep sigh—" my young master could not be contradicted, and it has cost him his life. He could not. It made him ill. I have always heard he was so from an infant. It was therefore devised by my master, the Signora Teresa, the physicians, and Father Romualdo—who, you know, is a most holy man—to lay the infant on a pillow, cover him up, and let his wet-nurse take him in to his father, saying he was asleep. I happened to hear of all this. I said, 'The Signor Gustavo will discover all; he will embrace the child, and feel the icy coldness of death.'"

Here the maggiordomo gave himself a certain air of importance as if he meant to say, "Am I not a clever fellow?"

"It turned out as I said. The child was brought in. It had died only a few hours before, and looked so lovely. The lady hid herself behind the nurse in order that the Signor Gustavo might not see her agony. I stood by, and though my heart was breaking, and I was trembling all over, foreseeing the result, I strove to smile, and pretended to tell the bystanders to keep quiet, in order not to awake him, for you must know it had been settled that I should play this part, and most unwillingly did I obey. But the wet-nurse, Signor Marco, helped to make matters much worse. You know she is a peasant; thinking—*I* say so at at least—more of the pay and presents she had lost than of the child and its poor bereaved parents, she had been drowned in tears since the infant had breathed its last. She had been warned not to cry, to be calm. She obeyed till she reached the sick man's bed, and then, whether she really felt grieved or pretended it, she began to distort her face, as people generally do when they are going to burst out crying. I was aware of it, and endeavoured to push her a little on one side, but the Signor Gustavo had guessed all. In a moment he almost sprang out of bed, caught the nurse's arm—she declares he pinched her most severely—and taking his child, pressed it to his breast, uttering such words of agony—that—I cannot repeat them, though they still ring in my ears. He then reproached us all for having deceived him; and, to make short of it, grew so much worse that the physicians pronounced him dying. He had always been a delicate man, as nervous as a woman; a trifle upset him. But he died like a saint, and the Signora Teresa is alone to be pitied."

To this long account, which the maggiordomo might have given in a few words, Marco's sole reply was:

"My poor dear cousin! So young!"

"Death does not regard youth, Signor Marco. The old and the young alike must die. And now, Signor Marco, you are the heir," continued Pietro in a lower voice, accompanied by a most profound inclination of his whole person, as if he meant to make his obeisance, and imply his most willing services had already begun.

"Tush, man! who can think of *that* now, in this

house of mourning? Not I, assuredly. I care not for it."

Did Marco speak the truth? We dare not affirm it. Man is frail, and the prospect of so much prosperity could not but be most pleasing to him. He added:

"Where is my uncle? Show me in to him."

"He gave orders that you should wait a little, and that I should relate all to you, as he cannot speak on the subject."

"You have told me all, I think," said Marco, in an almost imploring tone, as if to say, "Pray say nothing more, you have said enough;" then he added: "Can I see the Signora Teresa?"

"She refuses visitors. She is like one stunned. Think what her sufferings must be, Signor Marco: she has lost *all.*"

"True. I do pity her. I shall wait, therefore, here till my uncle can see me."

Saying these last words he sat down, and the maggiordomo left the hall.

He did not wait long. His uncle ordered him to be shown into his bedroom.

He found the old nobleman in an easy-chair, his head resting on the back of it, deathly pale, his eyes staring into vacancy.

By a movement of his hand he welcomed his nephew, and beckoned to a chair that was near, on which Marco seated himself, quite at a loss to find any appropriate phrase of condolence.

The old patrician was the first to speak.

"Marco," said he, without looking at him, "you are now my nearest relation, and my—my——" The afflicted father meant to say heir, but could not utter the word. "I have sent for you that you may in a certain degree superintend those sad offices towards the departed, which in my agony of grief I am totally incapable of attending to myself; and, furthermore, that you may somehow or other console poor Teresa, who already says she means to retire to a convent."

"Dear uncle, I am at your service."

"I knew you would do all in your power to comfort me. From the birth of my beloved son I strove, I schemed to leave him the richest man in Venice. I had succeeded in every plan, and lo! when I thought of quitting him, he leaves me. Even his child has been taken! I am desolate!"

And the proud patrician, unmindful of other's woes, wept like a child for his own.

Marco did not know what to say or do in order to stop that burst of grief, so he had recourse to the best expedient in all such cases, viz., to let the old man weep unchecked, for, after all, it is the wisest course to pursue, since where grief is great, it relieves for awhile the poor heart, to let it shed copious tears.

Again the old man was the first to speak.

"Take up your abode at once in my house, my dear nephew. You will then be with me whenever I require you."

"I will do as you bid me, dear uncle. I have said

already I am at your service. Perhaps you wish now to be quiet, and so I had better leave you."

"No—yes," said the patrician, hesitating. "I have sent for Father Romualdo, and——"

"I understand. I shall just go home for a minute, and return to pass this night here."

"What do you mean by this night? I have said you are to remain here always. Ring the bell."

Marco rang, and the maggiordomo appeared.

"Pietro," said his master, shutting his eyes, "my nephew takes up his abode in my palace. Order the suite of apartments in the left wing to be prepared for him. He is to be obeyed, and considered as if he were my——"

The old nobleman could not finish the sentence; he hid his face, and wept again aloud.

"*Illustrissimo*, death pays no regard to youth. The young and the old, all must die. I will see that your orders be duly obeyed."

He bowed and left the room behind Marco.

That same night saw Marco Centofoglia, the hitherto despised, neglected relation, installed in the princely palace of his ancestors, and treated with all the respect due to the nephew of the proud owner. That same night beheld the hitherto poor young man, who had striven hard to get on in life with his limited means, the heir of the richest man in Venice!

In the morning the mere thought of such a change would have been next to madness. In the evening it was the truest reality.

In the midst of so much and such unlooked-for prosperity did Marco think of his humble betrothed? He did, and rejoiced in the prospect of her happiness as much as in that of his own.

When the day came for the longed-for meeting—the cousins, father and child, had been already laid in the family vault, and Marco was less busy giving orders, receiving visits, paying accounts, etc., etc.—he found himself before the time appointed at the usual place. He saw Rosalia coming, and ran to meet her, longing to tell her the change in his fortune. But Rosalia knew it already. Everybody in Venice knew it, and a sad foreboding oppressed the poor girl's heart.

"Rosalia, my dearest, all objections to our wedding are removed. I am rich now. I am powerful. Riches and power overcome all difficulties. Even if your father persists in refusing his consent, I can force him. Oh, Rosalia! how happy we shall be!" and Marco Centofoglia pressed her to his heart.

"Marco, forgive me, I cannot help it, but my heart aches. Will you love me *now* as you did before?"

Rosalia looked sad.

"You mistrust me, then? You think vile money can have the power of changing Marco Centofoglia's heart? I love you more instead of less. I love you with my whole soul!"

When prosperity first visits man, it is apt to produce the very contrary effects from those to which it unfortunately gives birth at a later period. In the beginning the man is happy; he is also better. His heart seems to enlarge towards all mankind, to yearn after what is right and good and noble. His spirits also are elated, every object, therefore, appears clothed in brighter colours. He does not reflect much, and in those moments he hardly needs it. The healthiest part of his nature is uppermost. He loves everyone, and plans benefiting every creature that may be in need of his help. He says, "I will not act like such an one. I will be superior to such another." But let a comparatively short time elapse, and prosperity has done its work. The worst part of man's character then comes to the surface, and pride, egotism, worldliness, are left to set themselves to work to frustrate all the good resolutions that had flourished for a moment under the bright sun of man's better nature.

"Believe me," Marco continued, with increasing vehemence, "believe me, one thought alone hath pervaded my mind during these days that have beheld so great a change in my fortune, the thought of you. As I have walked through those superb, spacious halls, through galleries where luxury and art seem to vie with each other in order to produce all that is most beautiful, it is *you* that have been always before my eyes. I have thought and repeated to myself, 'Rosalia will be here like a queen in her realm. What man now living in Venice can boast such a bride? She will grace this palace with her stately, elegant figure. Her eyes will shine with a brighter lustre as she gazes on all this splendour and hears from my lips, "'Tis thine."' And now, after I have longed to see you, to tell you all, I hear that your heart aches; you speak as though you did not believe me, and, let me add, did not love me."

Marco stopped, and seemed overcome with sadness.

Rosalia had never taken her large, expressive eyes from off him. She drank in deep all he said, felt a voluptuous ecstasy in hearing him again assure her he loved her as before, and had thought of her alone, and answered in the tenderest tone:

"Marco, forgive me. Yes, forgive me. I did not mistrust you, but I felt a sorrow—a something I cannot explain. I care not for riches, nor for splendour. You are my wealth, and the brightness of my soul—my only thought on earth. You have assured me you love me as before. It is enough for me. I am happy again. Oh, so happy! Let me only always hear those words from your lips; hearing them, death would be sweeter than the most prosperous of lives deprived of their beloved sound."

Rosalia looked supremely beautiful; like one of those unrivalled faces Oriental bards dream of as lying on a bed of roses, under a canopy of jessamine and orange blossoms—the houris in their voluptuous paradise!

Marco felt the influence of that beauty, beside which the loveliest of his countrywomen would have looked void of charm; more eloquent did he become, and still fonder words did he utter, to dispel the cloud from that beautiful brow. He succeeded. Rosalia's drooping spirit completely revived; the lovers parted happier than before, loving each other more than ever.

CHAPTER III.

THE CHOICE.

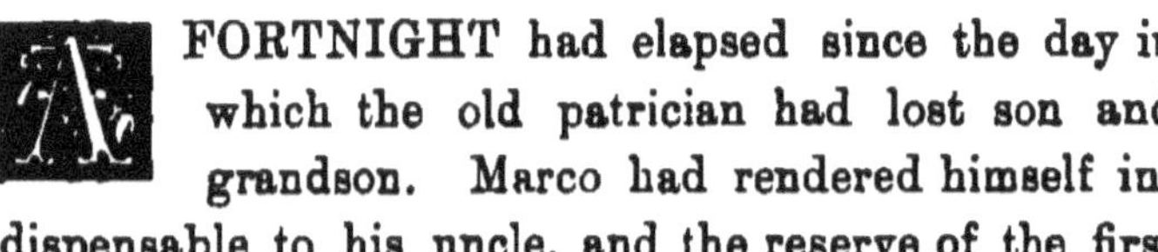

A FORTNIGHT had elapsed since the day in which the old patrician had lost son and grandson. Marco had rendered himself indispensable to his uncle, and the reserve of the first days having worn off, he had succeeded in restoring a little calm to the unhappy father's bereaved heart. The Signora Teresa he had seen little of; but on the few times when they had met in the old nobleman's bedroom, there had been great cordiality between them.

His uncle's health, however, had sensibly failed since the day of his double loss; and this, together with his advanced age, brought forcibly to his mind the conviction that he must soon leave his riches in other people's hands.

The uncle and nephew were sitting together. The old nobleman felt more feeble. He had had a long conference with Father Romualdo, the precise purport of which was not known, but we may guess it by listening to the one that followed very soon afterwards.

The old nobleman began abruptly:

"Marco—you know that you are now my heir!"

"Dear uncle, I know I am such only through your goodness."

"You are right; it is through my goodness, for you must know that I am not obliged to leave you anything. I can dispose of my property as I please."

"Of course you can. I have never thought to the contrary."

"Marco, do you think it is worth while to be rich and powerful!"

"To a certain extent it is; but I do not believe that riches and power can make a sensible man perfectly happy."

"Then you are a fool."

"Dear uncle—you—know——" Marco hesitated.

"I know what you mean to say. Riches and power cannot prevent afflictions. I know that too well. But then it is the doom of man to die. I tell you, wealth and power are a great blessing."

The old man spoke as the worldly-minded always speak. Marco did not like to contradict what he had said before, viz., that riches and power are not the only means of happiness; but the difference he had noticed in the manner of *all* his friends and acquaintances, the degree of command he had acquired wherever he went, the ready obedience he met with in all places, were most pleasing—made him feel his importance, and made him happy. He therefore concluded within himself that riches and power are conducive to earthly happiness, that every one must feel it; but no one—himself included—liked to acknowledge it.

The old nobleman continued:

"It is the trite way of philosophers to declare that riches and power are not worth seeking after; that man must not sacrifice to them his feelings and inclinations; that all ends, and such like stuff. I am now old, and have lived long enough to see that money is considered the universal panacea; so much so, that I should like to place any one of these dreamy philosophers in the position of succeeding to a large fortune, and see how many of them would refuse it. Not one. I would wager my head on it."

He felt rather exhausted, and stopped speaking. Marco fixed his eyes on him without answering. An odd thought was coming across his mind. Perhaps his uncle meant to add some disagreeable clause in his will.

Having rested a few minutes, and sipped a glass of the best wine the island of Cyprus could produce, the old noble resumed:

"I have not spoken thus far without a meaning. Are you one of these philosophers who would willingly give up riches, power, consideration, comfort? Answer me sincerely."

"I can't tell. It depends——"

"Say at once, without further hesitation—would you prefer being rich, or poor?"

"I had rather be rich."

"Well and wisely spoken. Now answer me again,

with equal conclusiveness. Will you, or will you not, be my heir?"

"That does not depend on me."

"Boy—it does."

Marco's heart beat as a school-boy's does at his first examination.

"Now listen to the conditions. Teresa, my dearest son's widow, is the daughter of the greatest friend I ever had. I loved him as a brother—much more than I did your father. On his deathbed—she was then only five years old—he entrusted her to me. I placed her in a convent; took care of her small property, increased it, and when she was sixteen years of age I presented her to my son as his bride. I have always loved her, and treated her as a daughter. How happy we have all been together! It was destined that at eighteen she should be a widow and childless. In her overwhelming grief she declares she will return to the convent, where she was brought up, and there take the veil. I cannot part with her. As it was decreed my own child's children should not inherit my fortune, I choose her children bearing my name to enjoy it. I also wish to benefit my brother's son, if he will agree to my conditions, which are as follows: You marry my daughter-in-law, Terêsa Zeno, and forthwith you are acknowledged as my legitimate heir, or——"

"Uncle——" put in Marco, in a supplicating voice.

"Don't interrupt me—or if you do not, you at once leave my house and return to what you were before!

I give you twenty-four hours to reflect upon it. Choose. Do you understand?" he added, seeing Marco did not answer.

"I do, uncle," said Marco, when he had so far recovered from the unexpected blow as to be able to speak. "But I was thinking I am not the only one to be consulted in this matter. Are you sure the Signora Teresa will consent to become my wife?"

"How void of all knowledge of the customs of the world you are! Who thinks of consulting women about their inclinations! One may give way to them as far as relates to a dress, a picture, even a party of pleasure; but marriage—that is the affair for man, and man *alone*."

"As for that, I don't know, uncle. I think it regards women also. They may love or hate."

"Nonsense—nonsense! Let us see what you will say if ever you have a daughter who refuses the husband you have decided on for her."

"I should feel in duty bound to respect her inclinations."

Ah, Marco, how frail is the human heart! Twenty-five years later that very same room was to witness another violation of woman's dearest right, and how didst thou act then?

"And more idiot you! In the meantime respect your own welfare, and decide to your own advantage. Leave me to think about Teresa;—besides, she is so mild and obedient. . . . . I feel weaker now. Call Pietro, and retire to rest."

Marco obeyed as far as regarded calling Pietro, and going to bed; but as for resting, it was out of the question. He tossed about in his bed like one in a burning fever. There was no alternative left him—he must either abandon Rosalia, or renounce the wealthy heritage.

"How can I," thought he, "accept the condition my tyrannical uncle forces upon me? Can I give up my bride—her whom I dote upon, and marry a woman for whom I care not? Even if I could be brought to consent, have I the right to break another's heart? Rosalia would surely die at the mere suggestion of such a thing. She would give up her life for me. Am I to be so base as not to give up houses, lands, pelf for her? After all, I shall always be a gentleman. I shall not be rich, but I can be happy. Yes, to-morrow I will tell my uncle frankly I cannot accept his conditions, and at once quit his house. And then, when Rosalia has learned the sacrifice I have made for her, will she again refuse fleeing with me? No. She will not, I am sure—but suppose she does! Am I always to be thwarted in my plans and schemes? . . . How happy I have been these few days! How my friends envy me! I am everywhere called the rich heir . . . How can I give up all, and be laughed at for it? And return to be a nobody! . . . My courage fails me at the very thought. Was ever a man placed in such perplexity?"

Marco turned and turned again in his bed, and thought more and more. At length, when the first rays of the morning sun entered his room, and his eyelids were closing in sleep, he came to this resolution: "Rosalia loves me more than life. I will recount all to her, and will leave her the arbiter of my fate. I know what her fond heart will say: 'Accept the condition laid upon you by your uncle; be happy, and forget me.' Then, though I shall suffer—though it will well-nigh break my heart, with her consent I can obey my uncle's wishes. Tyrant that he is, he thinks only of himself!" concluded Marco, and fell asleep, without perceiving that he also was beginning to think only of himself.

It is in man, or rather in the imperfection of man's education, that when too weak to make the sacrifices which conscience dictates, he should hit on plans and schemes that border on the verge of insanity. A species of torpor comes over him, and he follows almost without being aware of it, the paths of evil and injustice, goaded on by that fiend, egotism, which whispers in his willing ears, "You cannot help it. 'Tis the only way left you."

As soon as awake, without looking into the depths of woman's heart, without reflecting that Rosalia would give her life to save his, but would never give her consent to his becoming another woman's husband, and would sooner see him beg his bread by her side than that he should press another to his heart, Marco rose, dressed, and hurried under her window.

She had happened to go out, and she returned just as he found himself there.

"Rosalia," said he in a whisper, "I must speak with you. I have something most important to tell you, which refers to my welfare. Come this evening to the usual place of meeting; come earlier if you can."

"It suffices that you wish to tell me something which concerns yourself; your loving Rosalia will not fail to obey."

Saying this, she entered her house.

Wondering in her own mind what he could wish to tell her, Rosalia decided that of course he was tired of waiting, and would fix the day on which he should demand her hand of her father.

Marco, labouring under a sort of dreaminess, feeling what he would not acknowledge, even to himself, viz. that in *his* heart the love of wealth superseded love for his betrothed, passed the remaining hours which separated him from the one fixed for the meeting, in hearing and answering imaginary questions.

Before the appointed hour they were both at the usual spot.

"Events have changed for me since we last met," began Marco, looking sad.

"If your heart is unchanged, I care not," answered Rosalia, smiling and holding out her hand to him.

He took her hand. She felt his trembled—yes, trembled—for anticipation and reality are widely different.

"What sad news have you in store for me?" said she, inquiringly.

"I had best say all at once," thought Marco. "I can't suffer this any longer." And pressing her hand firmly in his, he replied:

"Rosalia, my future happiness is in your keeping."

"'Tis safe, then;" and she looked bewitching.

At any other moment Marco would have pressed her to his heart; now he seemed only to wish to have his disclosure over.

"I was so happy," said he; "but man is not born to happiness. Yesterday evening, at the very moment when I was arranging within myself how to induce your father to give his consent, my tyrannical uncle told me—he told me——"

Marco related his uncle's propositions and the choice laid before him, and finished by adding:

"Now, Rosalia, choose for me. Say what you wish. Am I to be poor or rich? powerful or weak—laughed at and pitied, or envied and honoured?"

The last words Rosalia did not so much as hear; even if she had heard them she would not have understood them. What to her were riches, power, envy? Love, love alone was what she cared for. She answered:

"We can be as happy without riches as with them, Marco. Let your tyrannical uncle leave his wealth to whom he likes. Have we not got the true wealth—love?"

"You do not understand me, Rosalia," replied Marco timidly. "I must return to what I was, or——"

"Or marry another woman? I understand that. But

you do not love another woman. You have vowed to me you love me only; therefore give up that other woman, and your uncle's riches, and——"

"Rosalia, poverty—is——"—"staring me in the face," he would have said.

"Poverty?" cried the infatuated girl, "poverty? There is no poverty where there is love. If I but see you I think myself rich. Can *you*, Marco, waver?"

Her eyes flashed. Marco almost feared.

"Marco, I can die for you, but see you another woman's husband, never, never!"

Marco now thought of his last anchor of salvation.

"Then, Rosalia, be just. You have chosen poverty for me, at least don't deprive me any longer of domestic joy. Returning to my former condition, I cannot insist on your father's bestowing his consent to our union; therefore promise to fly with me to become at once my wife."

"Marco, a——"

Rosalia sighed, and held down her head.

"No, Rosalia," said Marco, resolutely, "I have no time to wait. This evening I must inform my uncle of my choice, and this evening you must tell me yours. Either fly with me, or forget me. Choose."

A sudden thought struck Rosalia.

"Has he plotted all this in order to induce me to run away with him?"

She fixed her large, speaking eyes on him, and said, smiling:

"Marco, you are clever, but I am cleverer than you."

"Rosalia," and Marco looked serious, determined—"Rosalia, I take St. Mark to witness that I speak what I mean. Either fly with me or I must marry another woman."

"I will fly with you. I will go with you anywhere. I will leave father, *all*, but I cannot let you marry another."

"'Tis settled?"

"Yes, settled. Let me know the day, the hour."

"As soon as I can."

Marco kissed her hand, and left her. He felt he had outwitted himself. All he had planned had proved useless. He must again decide for himself. He loitered awhile on the Piazza S. Marco. He was weary of thought. A friend accosted him.

"Signor Marco," said he, "I have been out of Venice this month; I have just returned and have heard of your good luck. The whole town speaks of it. You are known by the name of the rich young patrician. Was there ever so happy, so fortunate a man!"

Other friends approached; flattery and compliments resounded in Marco's ears. To the respectful obeisances of his acquaintance he returned gracious bows. Intoxicated by the prospect of prosperity he felt he could not brave adversity.

The hour having arrived for his evening talk with his uncle, he entered his gondola, and found himself in a few minutes opposite the stately mansion.

"I cannot give up all," said he, as he looked upwards. "I cannot return to my former insignificance," continued he, as he enjoyed the respect and attentions shown him by porters, men-servants, etc.

He entered his uncle's room, and without further thought—for he strove not to think lest he should demur—said:

"Uncle, I have reflected. I will marry the Signora Teresa. I will be to you a dutiful son."

The old man sighed, took his nephew's proffered hand, and answered:

"I am glad. I see you are wise, and deserve to become the depository of the treasures I have hoarded up for my heirs. To-morrow I will speak with Teresa, and in a few months you will be man and wife."

CHAPTER IV.

THE MARRIAGE.

THE next day it was the unconscious Teresa's turn to bend to the old noble's will. He sent for her, and as soon as she had seated herself beside him, he began.

"My dearest child, is it still your intention to shut yourself up in a nunnery?"

"Yes, my father, it is."

"But," he took her hand in both his, "it is not my intention to let you go. I cannot part from you."

"Dear father, I am so unhappy. I feel it is the only comfort left me. You know I have never been fond of the amusements and pleasures of the world."

"Teresa, that may be; but I wish to leave your children my heirs."

"I do not understand you, father."

"You will soon. I wish you to marry my nephew Marco, and live with me always."

Teresa was a docile creature who had never opposed the will of anyone. She was below the middle height, but well proportioned, fair, with chestnut hair; her features were small and regular, her eyes blue, with little expression in them; her whole countenance denoting a total absence of self-reliance, a passiveness that nothing could shake. But now, for the first time in her life, she started, looked frightened, shrank in her chair, and muttered almost inaudibly:

"Father, I cannot marry the Signor Marco; I cannot love him."

"It is immaterial that you do not love him *now*. You will love him when you are married to him."

"I feel I never shall. I wish to go to a convent, and there end my days."

"Nonsense! talking of ending days at eighteen! Wait till you are eighty, then talk in this way. I love you as though you were my own daughter, and I cannot live without your company."

"You would get accustomed to my absence, my dear father."

"No, my child, I should not. You will break my heart. I am old now. I require a tender hand about me. I have always loved you, but I suppose you have never loved me."

The old man assumed a woeful countenance.

"I have, my dear father; I have, and still do love you as a devoted daughter should love a kind parent."

"Teresa, a devoted daughter who loves her parent does not oppose his will."

"Then, if I cannot convince you otherwise, I will

give up the idea of a convent. I will stay with you, and lead a retired and holy life."

"That cannot be. Two young persons like Marco and yourself cannot live together under the same roof without affording ample food to the bitter tongue of scandal."

"Could not Signor Marco leave the house?" Teresa ventured to say in a timid manner, not daring to look at her father-in-law, and seemingly occupied in twisting her pretty fingers, which she held in her lap.

"Teresa, you forget he is my nephew, my heir. How can I forbid him the house? The whole town would say, 'The patrician Centofoglia has gone mad. He has turned his nephew out, and keeps his daughter-in-law,' and—and—who knows what more besides?"

"Then, my father, I could leave the house, and come and see you every day. I could go and live with my old aunt."

"No, Teresa, you shall not leave my house. I never expected you would oppose my wish. You will make me ill. I am old now, child; I am bereaved of my only son. I have no comfort, no hope on earth. I meant to have a young couple again about me, and infants playing on my knee. It would have cheered me. It might have lengthened my days; instead of this, your unkindness will bring me to my grave."

The old man wept; that is to say, he wiped his eyes and made the grimaces which precede and accompany weeping. He knew it was the best course to pursue with any hope of success.

"Ah, Teresa!" continued he, "I have loved you—I have taken care of you—in order to be repaid thus. You may return to your apartments now—and—and leave me to die."

"No, no, my father. I will never leave you. Don't weep on my account. You will wound my poor breaking heart more deeply." Teresa threw herself on her knees, leaning her elbows on the old man's knees, and holding his hands in hers. "I will obey you, as a dutiful daughter should do. I will marry your nephew whenever you like."

The cunning patrician pressed her small head to his heart. His plan had succeeded. Nothing now remained but to send for Marco, and fix the day for their nuptials.

Teresa rose from her knees, and, obeying his request, ordered Marco to be immediately summoned.

In the silence of the night Marco's thoughts had been sad. He had loved, and still loved, Rosalia. He stifled that love, but could not entirely give up thinking of her. Futhermore, he feared her. The fire of her flashing eyes made him aware of the fire of the soul that spoke through them. To tell Rosalia he had obeyed his uncle's request was impossible. There was but one course left him, viz. to continue to see her, arranging their interviews at longer intervals on the plea of business. Then part from her, saying he was going to be absent a short time, in the meantime marry out of Venice, and pass a few months travelling, or in the country. Hearing of his marriage, Rosalia would be sure to forget him. Full of this plan, he entered his uncle's room.

The latter at once introduced Teresa to him as his bride, and after the most insipid compliments on each side—neither cared for the other at all—the old relative opened the preliminaries of marriage. Having expressed his wish that it should take place very soon, but in the most private manner, out of respect to his son's memory, he turned to Marco, saying:

"Now, my nephew, give me your opinion; as for Teresa, I know she will abide by what you say."

Teresa bowed her head in assent.

"I think, my dear uncle, that the first thing to be thought of is decorum. I therefore advise leaving Venice a short time before the day fixed for the wedding, and going to Treviso. After our union I advise staying a few months in the country, or wherever it may be more convenient to you, my dear uncle. By the time we return the precise date of our marriage will be forgotten, and the talk it may have caused will be silenced; for it must be said that it does not show proper feeling, or deference to the usages of people in our station, for a widow to marry again so soon after her husband's death."

"You are right, Marco, quite right. I see more and more every day how worthy you are of becoming my heir. Let us fix the wedding for this day two months. About a week before it we will go to Treviso, and afterwards to a castle I possess in the mountains of Friuli, where we will pass the rest of the summer and the autumn, and be back in Venice for Martinmas."

He felt so happy at finding all had turned out according to his most sanguine wishes, that his affliction began to diminish sensibly, and his health to improve immensely.

Teresa appeared to be, and was, utterly indifferent to everything. She did not love Marco, and felt assured she never could do so. She had submitted for the old man's sake, and now thought the best way was to swallow the bitter pill as well as she could without dwelling too much upon it. She passed the greater part of her time at church, and in visiting the poor.

Marco acted as he had made up his mind to act. He met Rosalia as he had done heretofore. A pang of remorse pierced his heart each time, but he endeavoured, and succeeded, in healing the wound as soon as he was out of her sight. He fixed their meetings at rarer intervals, saying that pressing business, and the necessity of making his uncle as favourable as he could towards him, were the cause.

The fond and trusting Rosalia believed him, and during the last meeting they had, on the very eve of his departure from Venice, she, smiling fondly, said to him:

"I guessed that all you told me about the choice forced upon you by your uncle was a made-up story in order to induce me to fly with you. Ah, Marco! you should not have treated me so. You extorted a promise from me which I ought not to have given; and you wait so patiently until I can obtain my father's consent. I thank you, and love you the more for it. Alas! my poor father is growing very unwell, and I fear that soon . . . there will not be . . . to ask his consent."

Rosalia looked unhappy. Marco felt the pang of keen remorse again. He did not know what to answer, and in a woeful voice said:

"Rosalia, I leave to-morrow. I am obliged to go away for a little while to superintend some property my uncle possesses at a distance. If I do not write, don't worry about me. Strive to forget me——"

"Forget you!"

Rosalia's eyes flashed upon Marco.

"I mean for the time I shall be away," replied he, in order to calm her.

"I shall never forget you. Marco, you look pale. What is the matter?" she added anxiously.

"I am not very well. The night air seems to give me a chill. The change will do me good. Farewell, Rosalia."

He kissed her hand. His lips were cold. In a moment he had disappeared.

Strange were Rosalia's thoughts, and stranger still would they have been, but when she returned home she found her father much worse. This occupied her exclusively, and together with her full and innocent reliance on Marco's word, drove all doubt as to his fidelity from her mind.

Marco returned home. His face had not recovered

from its ashy paleness. His uncle and his bride elect inquired what was the matter. He answered that he felt rather ill, but should be well in the morning.

The next morning he was quite well.

The party left for Treviso, and eight days afterwards, in a small chapel of the palace they had taken, and in the most private manner possible, Marco Centofoglia and Teresa Zeno were pronounced man and wife.

CHAPTER V.

A FORLORN CREATURE.

TRULY forlorn is she! It is midnight, and Rosalia is sitting alone beside her father's corpse.

In the morning she had learned the common talk in Venice, viz. that Marco Centofoglia, the rich heir, had married his cousin's widow. She could not doubt the veracity of an announcement that flew from mouth to mouth. She recalled to her mind her last interview with her faithless lover. She remembered those ominous words, "Strive to forget me," and she thought how foolish she had been not to notice them before. She had gone out to procure some delicacy which she fancied her father would have liked, and had thus heard the appalling news. In spite of it, she returned home quite calm. At first she did not realise the intensity of the blow. We never do. It is the reaction which crushes us. The physician came, and would not leave until he had spoken with her. He told her that her father would not live to see the night; he was dying. And added, that it was her duty to call in a minister of the Church.

Giovanni Leoni had brought up his daughter according to his own tenets, that is, with a total disregard to the outward forms of religion. He had at times talked to her of the Supreme Being, but had prohibited her from ever entering a church. She had obeyed as a general rule, but on occasions of great solemnity, when she had heard the organ pealing, and the priests chanting, she had entered a church; yet, alas! uninstructed in the love of holy things, her mind had been pleased, but her heart had remained untouched. Now, however, learning that her father was hourly approaching his end, a strange fear took possession of her. She thought of his eternal welfare, and asked him as cautiously as possible whether he would like to see a priest.

Giovanni Leoni looked at her fiercely, and summoning his remaining strength, answered:

"I mean to die as I have lived. I suppose the physician has told you my end is near, and given you this advice?"

Rosalia did not answer.

"Speak out boldly, child; I ask it for your good."

Rosalia bowed her head, and a tear fell on her lap. The dying man saw it.

"Yes," said he, "the hour is come, and I am glad I have been made aware of it. Rosalia, come nearer to me; but first shut the door."

Rosalia obeyed. The old man took her hand, or rather griped it with his thin, worn fingers, that had acquired the appearance of huge claws.

"Rosalia, my business has not prospered of late. Perhaps my delicate health may have been the cause, as it has prevented my being always on my guard against the infernal rapacity of man. I fear you will have to earn your bread, unless it be your lot to meet with less deceit in the world than I have."

Rosalia's mind reverted to Marco's recent betrayal, and she drew a long, deep sigh.

"You know I am in partnership, and you are acquainted with my partner. He is perhaps the most honest man I ever knew. I think he will help you. You may trust him. And now draw still nearer." The old man seemed to exhaust the little strength left him in order to pull his daughter even closer to his bed. "Listen attentively. I told you not long ago that on my deathbed I would tell you why I could not consent to your marriage. The moment is come—and——" The old man spoke in a whisper. He spoke long and earnestly. Rosalia became still paler; she trembled like a leaf shaken by the wind. He concluded: "Now you know all, act accordingly; but—don't curse the memory of the father who has loved *you* alone in the world. I am dying, and can speak no more——"

These last words were uttered in so faint a voice they were almost inaudible.

A minute after he had swooned, and within three hours he breathed his last.

The neighbours, and even the young maid-servant, knowing that Leoni had refused the consolations of the Church, felt a perfect dread at the very thought of approaching the room where he lay dead. They would have nothing to do with the corpse of one whom they considered in the light of a Jew or a heretic, and the wretched Rosalia was left to sit up alone beside the remains of her departed parent.

She had arranged the room, and dressed the body of the old man in his best clothes. A small lamp was burning, reflecting its glimmering light on the deathly paleness of the face of the corpse, and on that equally pale, yet so intensely beautiful, of the forlorn young woman. She wept not. Her heart ached at the sight of her dead father; but there was a keener grief there—yes, keener.

"Ah!" thought she, "my poor father! How he loved me! I have lost my best friend, but *that* friend loved *me* to the last. *The other* said he loved me, but his vows were false. What I thought a trick was the plain truth. He has preferred money to love. No; it is not for the sake of wealth that he has forsaken me. He who has once felt true love cares not for riches. He loved her; indeed he loves her. Oh, my heart, would thou couldst break at once, and in breaking stifle thy throbbing for ever! How can I bear this agony! I can't—I can't!"

The reaction was coming. Rosalia felt a sensation resembling madness seize her brain. Her head ached. Her whole body felt sore. She was burning hot; her temples beat quickly. When she rose she was obliged to sit down again. Her head swam. The room whirled round her. The table and chairs moved in a hideous dance. She thought she heard awful cries, then of a sudden a voice, a beloved voice, whisper words of love; but not to her—to a young woman in costly array. She shrank aside, and her head fell on—her father's face. The icy coldness of death seemed to bring her back to her senses. But consciousness lasted only an instant. The horrid fancies came again, and again left her, till at early dawn she heard the heavy steps of the men come to carry her father to his last resting-place. She let them enter, did not so much as move, saw them take up his body, lay it on a bier, and depart with it. Then she fell on the empty bed, and knew nothing further. She remained in that state some hours. No one thought of going in to see about her.

When she recovered she felt a strange heaviness; she could hardly move a step. She made an effort, left the room, called the maid-servant, told her she was too ill to sit up, and went to her own room to bed. A high fever supervened, accompanied by incessant delirium. The same physician who had attended her father, her little maid-servant, and a respectable neighbour, wife of a noble lady's agent, took care of the poor sufferer, the two latter nursing her tenderly.

Her delirium was of the wildest sort. As the doctor and the nurses attributed her illness to the affliction which her father's loss had caused her, they were not surprised, and believed all she said was the working of a fevered brain. And so it truly was, except that every word she uttered had a meaning in the agony she was enduring owing to Marco's betrayal of her fondest affections.

At times she fancied she saw him, poor and sick, and in her grief she would scream: "Recover, recover quickly. I cannot behold your sufferings; or if you cannot recover, let me die with you." When she fancied he was going to put a ring on her finger, she would smile and say, "I am so happy! Yes, you are mine. I am going to be your wife. You will stay with me, and never leave me."

Suddenly she thought she saw a beautiful room brilliantly lighted, and on a sofa a fair lady; then Marco enter, place himself by her side, and throwing his arms around her, press her to his heart. She would then insist on rising from her bed, and in the most passionate accents exclaim, "Take away those lights! She is sitting waiting for him. He is come. There he is; he embraces her—another woman—not me—another! Let me go, I will throttle her! I will tear her eyes out! I will be revenged!" Again his loving form would approach her, and he would utter the tender words he used to repeat, and again she would look happy.

In this manner twenty-one days went by. The crisis then came. It was favourable. The fever left her, and she slowly recovered. But what a miserable wreck was she! A shadow of her former self, barely recognisable! She looked fifty. The beauty of her features had disappeared. The extremity to which her illness had reduced her made her look as thin as a lath. The greater part of her luxuriant raven hair had fallen off, and the little left was tinged with grey. Her face might have been taken for that of a skeleton, but that, instead of empty sockets, a pair of large black eyes—larger than before—would at times gleam ferociously. Her very voice had changed. She rarely spoke, shunned the company of everyone, even that of her formerly kind nurses. She sat in a corner of her room looking straight before her, like a tigress crouching ere she pounces on her prey. She could not recollect all the scenes that had floated across her fevered brain during her illness; but they had left impressions which lingered in her memory, like the notions of an ill-remembered dream, making her believe that Marco was happy in the love of another, and this she could not endure.

Rosalia was by nature jealous. Had her lover abandoned her without having wedded another woman she would have grieved, but would have borne the affront quietly, would even have recovered from its effect, and perhaps have forgiven him. But the thought that when she imagined he loved her only, and talked to her only of love, he was in truth loving another; that he could so despise and scorn her fond and devoted attachment, so coolly leave her for ever, to marry another, and say to *her*, "Strive to forget me,"—those fatal words were ever ringing in her ears—this was more than many a woman could have borne, and most certainly more than Rosalia could.

But what was she to do? Against the powerful heir of the noble family Centofoglia, what could the sorrow-stricken and poverty-stricken Rosalia Leoni do? What? Let hatred, or rather frenzy, predominate where love formerly held empire, and it will end by devising something. "I feel I hate him, I feel I abhor him," she said to herself as she sat brooding in that same corner of the room. "I will vow my soul to the fiend; I will serve the demon, provided he help me to be revenged."

Some kindly feeling towards the man she had well-nigh adored would at times enter her heart, a sense of affliction, of intense distress would come over her; but she stifled both by the fiendish glee of revenge to which she wholly dedicated—except for a short interval—the remainder of her life.

Whilst thus brooding over her wrongs, she thought little of her worldly interests, not minding them. She implicitly trusted her late father's partner. He was an honest man, but had no capacity for business. His former gains had been owing, in a great measure, to Leoni's sagacity. This Leoni himself had not discovered, or he would most likely not have advised his daughter's continuing in the business, unless the bad opinion he entertained of mankind in general made him over-partial to his partner, whom he had reasons to consider an honest man, and induced him to believe it was a quality sufficient to ensure success in trade. It is a glorious gift truly, the brighter because its light does not often illuminate the dark paths of human affairs, but alas ! 'tis not the only one needed; but too often the honest, ingenuous man sinks, whilst the dishonest and crafty one floats proudly on.

About three months after Leoni's demise his partner failed. The small fortune Rosalia possessed was lost in his failure, and she was left to plod on through life as well as she could. During the space of three short months she had been deprived of everything held dear on earth : lover, father, fortune. She cared little for the loss of the last. "Would this had been all !" she kept repeating to herself. When the little money she had in the house was exhausted, she set about selling different objects she judged of least use; then came the turn of more useful things, then of the necessary ones, until Rosalia found herself in an empty house, with a miserable mattress to lie on, a change of linen, and the gown she wore, literally with nothing else.

She seemed, however, callous to everything, till hunger came. Nothing prompts to activity like the feeling of hunger. She woke from her lethargy, her one habitual thought, revenge, gave place to the thought of procuring herself food. She knew she must now exert herself in order to earn her daily bread, and she set about thinking how to procure a situation as companion to a rich lady, as nurse, or even as a superior lady's-maid. But she knew very few people, and none who could help her in that way. At last she hit upon her neighbour, the agent's wife; she fancied that she was the very person needed: furthermore, she had experienced in her illness what a kindly person she was, and consequently felt less shy to go and relate her misfortunes to her.

She went to her at once. As soon as the good woman saw her she guessed the poor, forlorn creature wished to ask some favour, and for that very reason, after having kissed her on both cheeks, said, holding her hand in both hers, in the kindest manner:

"How glad I am to see you, Rosalia; only I should have preferred seeing you looking better and stouter."

They now seated themselves on a sort of couch.

"Say, rather, my good and kind Signora Maria, that it is a wonder I am alive."

"Ah! it is true; you have had a serious illness."

"That is not all. . . . My heart has broken . . . and . . . and——"

"I know all," replied the good woman, hastily; "I know all. My poor child, do you not know that misfortunes have a great liking for the number three?"

Rosalia thought to herself, "Then she really knows all."

She was, however, soon relieved, for the Signora Maria continued:

"You have lost your poor father, you have been ill, and you have lost your——"

She hesitated. Rosalia came to her aid:

"My fortune; but for this I care little."

"That is right. Besides you will earn another. In the meantime, I offer you my house. Come and stay with me."

Rosalia's heart felt softened. A few tears glistened in her eyes. "How sweet is kindness!" thought she. "What a balm it is to the afflicted heart!"

"My dearest Signora Maria, how can I adequately thank you? But I cannot come and be a burthen to you. You would be sufficiently kind if you would speak to your husband about me; ask him to try to procure me a situation in some good family. I would take one as companion . . . as——"

"I understand all. I will speak to Leonardo this very evening. He is the factotum of a noble and rich lady, the Contessa Sofia Bernardi. Whenever he speaks he is listened to. He directs everyone and everything in that house. He will recommend you to the contessa, and she will speak to her friends; it is the easiest thing imaginable."

"But," thought the kind-hearted Signora Maria, "if I do not insist on the poor creature's coming to stay with me, by the time the place is obtained she will be starved to death." So, looking at her, she added:

"I insist on a condition to all this, and unless you agree to it I will not say a word for you—mind, not a single word. You must come this very day to stay with me, and you will remain here till the situation is found. Promise to do so."

"I . . . do . . . promise." Rosalia's emotion prevented her from speaking calmly. "But allow me, my dearest Signora Maria, to put in a little tiny condition."

"Well, let me hear what you can possibly have to say."

"Let me at least work for you. I am skilful with my needle. Let me help you in all your domestic occupations. Let me do your shopping for you, whatever errands you may require."

"Very well. Oh yes! I promise to ask you to do many things for me. Are you satisfied now?"

"I am. I thank you so much, so very much! I shall never be able to repay your kindness."

"Yes, you can repay it by cheering up a little, and letting me see you happier."

"Alas!" Rosalia sighed. It was the only answer she could give.

After having again thanked her good friend, she left her to return home to pack her few things.

That same evening saw her established in her new temporary home. The change did her good. Here she could not, as in her own home, sit apart from everyone brooding over her lover's faithless conduct. She was forced to mix in company, and this, added to the great kindness of her host and hostess, softened the tone of her mind, and prevented her from always encouraging the thirst for revenge.

This favourable state was doomed to last a very short time.

CHAPTER VI.

THE THREAT.

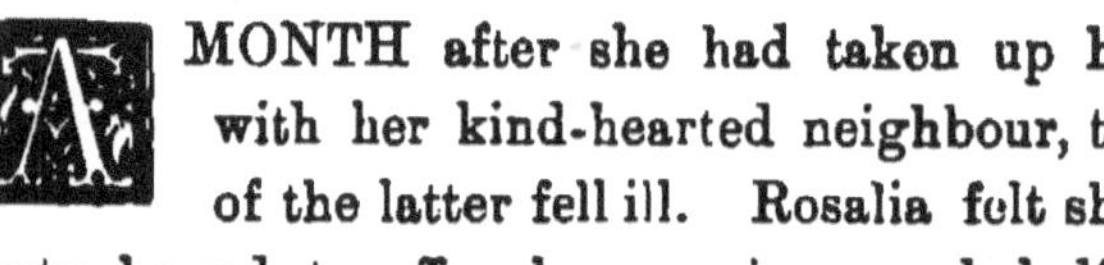

A MONTH after she had taken up her abode with her kind-hearted neighbour, the sister of the latter fell ill. Rosalia felt she was in duty bound to offer her services on behalf of her. They were readily accepted, and she entered forthwith upon her new office of nurse. Her nights were not always passed with the invalid, but every five or six days she returned home to have a good night's rest.

One evening, when it was nearly dark, she was slowly walking home. Her way led her through a small, unfrequented square, on one side of which stood a large church. The church was open, and on the steps leading up to it a man was sauntering about as if waiting for some one to leave the sacred edifice. The small street to which she was bound was opposite the church, and in order to avoid crossing the square, she ascended the steps, thus approaching close to the loiterer, whom she speedily recognised, and staggering backwards, well-nigh fell to the ground. Then, as if seized by a sudden fit of frenzy, her eyes flashing, her teeth chattering, she threw herself on the unconscious person, and holding, or rather grasping, his arms, said in ill-articulated accents:

"Traitor! Threefold traitor! Monster! Why does the earth not open and swallow thee up? Thou thought to crush a worm under thy feet, but it is Rosalia . . . Rosalia . . . " and loosing her hold she madly struck her breast. "It is Rosalia Leoni thou hast abandoned for another woman."

Marco, for it was he, was taken by surprise, and did not recognise who it was that dared thus attack a Venetian nobleman. Rosalia's words made him aware that that enraged virago was his once beautiful betrothed. He staggered in his turn, and grew ashy pale.

The fit suddenly left Rosalia; she now was pale and calm. She laid her hand on Marco's. Her touch was deathly. She looked fixedly at him; then, with the smile of a fiend meditating evil, said:

"Marco, you will never see me again, but beware and fear, for I have vowed my life to vengeance, and sooner or later I *will* be revenged."

Having said these words she disappeared.

Marco had almost recovered his presence of mind, but remorse tortured him. He saw how Rosalia was changed, and knew the cause. He wished to speak a word of comfort to her, and turning round quickly, said:

"Rosalia, I loved *you* only, and *you* only do I now love."

She did not hear his words, being already out of

sight. One moment had sufficed to destroy anew and for ever the peace of her wretched heart, and the desire of revenge having entered into it with greater fury, was henceforth to be her constant companion for the rest of her life. Apparently, however, she continued calm. Her manner was courteous, her actions were obliging. She acquired such a habit of controlling her feelings, that even a narrow observer would never have imagined what lurked in her soul.

Six weeks after the unlooked-for meeting with her lover, the kind Signora Maria announced to her that she thought a suitable situation had been found for her in the household of the Contessa Sofia Bernardi. Her husband himself would introduce her to that lady, and the following morning was appointed for the interview.

Rosalia's clothes had now become so shabby that she felt ashamed to appear before a noble lady in such mean attire, and, worst of all, she was too proud to acknowledge it and ask her good friend's help; so on the morrow she rose very early and set about cleaning and brushing her old gown and shawl, in order, as she said, to look at least clean and neat. But whilst thus occupied how sad were her thoughts!

"I must now become dependent on the will of others. Ah! this is the realm in which I was to be a queen! But——" and here Rosalia swore . . . her usual oath. . . . It was evil taking firmer hold on her benighted mind and forlorn heart.

Twelve o'clock was the appointed hour. A few minutes before the time she set out, accompanied by the agent. Rosalia had never entered a large palace. All she saw was so new to her that it bewildered her, and her bewilderment lessened the mortification she would otherwise have endured. On their way her companion took care to apprise her that she was going to be introduced to one of the most learned ladies in Venice; consequently she was not surprised at being shown into a small room where the display which distinguished the apartments she had passed through was totally wanting. Bookshelves which almost reached the ceiling supplied the place on the walls of costly pictures and damask hangings. A table, covered with books and pamphlets, stood in the centre of the room, beside which was an arm-chair occupied by a young woman, rather plain than otherwise, but of most distinguished presence. A few chairs completed the furniture of the study, for such it was, of the noble and most learned Contessa Sofia Bernardi—the lady seated in the arm-chair. She was reading; on hearing the door open she turned towards it, but did not put down her book. She nodded kindly to her man of business, and with a more distant bow returned Rosalia's profound curtsey. She then motioned with her hand, or rather with the book she held in it, to two chairs, on which her visitors seated themselves. After having closely examined Rosalia, she said:

"What is your age?"

"I am three-and-twenty, most noble signora."

The Contessa Sofia Bernardi started, and the book fell on her lap. She took it up again.

"Impossible! I suppose you mean three-and-forty?"

"Most learned signora," said the agent—and then Rosalia remembered he had warned her it was the lady's favourite appellation, the one by which all favours were generally obtained—"she is only three-and-twenty, but has been very ill——"

"St. Mark help me!" replied the contessa, her eyes wide open—hitherto they had been half closed—and looking alarmed. "Perhaps she is not blessed with good health. You know, Signor Leonardo, it is the principal, and *most necessary* qualification in a dependent. I could not have an invalid in the house, it would affect my nerves;" and she closed her eyes.

Leonardo's answer induced her partly to open them again.

"Her illness was brought on by her father's death, but she is a very healthy young woman."

"Ah! she looks anything but young."

"Misfortunes make us look older," humbly put in Rosalia.

"That is true. Where were you born?"

"At Girgento, in Sicily."

"Ah!" exclaimed the contessa with enthusiasm; "the ancient Agrigentum. Yes, yes, I understand. Superb ruins! Most interesting! Yes, I think she will suit me very well," she continued, turning towards her agent, and speaking in a tone of delight. "To be sure, Agrigentum."

Then turning towards Rosalia, she added:

"At present I will engage you as my companion, so

that at times when I wish to think without interruption you will accompany me in my gondola, and when I am tired of reading myself you will read to me. Your principal occupation will be needlework. When my little boy returns home—he is now out at nurse on the Berici hills—you will have the entire charge of him. The Signor Leonardo has spoken highly of you, and I am satisfied with his recommendation. He will tell you the other conditions, salary, etc., etc. Yes, the ruins of Agrigentum—most interesting. I hope to visit them some day ere I die. It will be most useful for me to have a native of the place with me."

These last words the Contessa Sofia Bernardi spoke to herself in an audible voice. It would have been equivalent to losing her rank if she had said thus much directly to her dependent, the first time she saw her.

Meanwhile, from the depth of her heart, Rosalia said to herself:

"Oh, blessed ruins of Agrigentum that have given me bread!"

She then attempted by thanks to express her satisfaction, but the contessa cut them short: she nodded as before. The applicants understood it as their dismissal, and obeyed.

Within three days from this interview Rosalia Leoni was finally established in the house of the most learned Contessa Sofia Bernardi.

CHAPTER VII.

JOY AND SORROW.

ON the fatal evening when Rosalia unexpectedly saw Marco, the latter had accompanied his wife to church. She was in daily expectation of becoming again a mother, and a son was ardently desired by all the three relatives. As her prayers were prolonged beyond the usual time, her husband grew tired of waiting; and having told her she would find him outside the church, had taken to loitering about in order to while away the time.

A few minutes after Rosalia had left him Teresa appeared on the church-steps. Her husband went up to her, and they both returned home.

Instances of man and wife caring so little for each other as Marco Centofoglia and Teresa Zeno did were very rare. The consequence was, the presence of the greatest coldness in their mutual intercourse, an icy coldness which precluded every idea of real happiness. This indifference to each other made them desire each other's company as little as possible, and they would most undoubtedly have carried their wish into effect had not the absolute necessity of keeping up appearances, at least during the first year of their marriage, and Marco's anxiety not to be suspected of having married his cousin's widow from mere interest—we always fear others will suspect what our conscience tells us is the truth—induced them to make a point of being seen together at times, especially at all religious ceremonials.

A few days after that evening Teresa gave birth to a beautiful boy. The joyful news was echoed from mouth to mouth throughout the palace and neighbourhood. The old patrician's heart palpitated with gratified pride. There was no fear his hoarded treasures would pass into strange hands; there was another heir to the wealthy house of Centofoglia. The christening took place with all the splendour and pomp pride and vanity could devise. The grandfather stood sponsor to the new-born babe, which was christened Gustavo, after his son.

The delicate health of its namesake, and that of his child, made the whole family most anxious that little Gustavo should grow up as healthy and as robust as possible. A wet-nurse in the house was Teresa's ardent wish, but her father-in-law observed that his grandson had had a wet-nurse in the house, and a fever of two days' duration had carried him off. He therefore strongly urged that the child should be sent to the most distant part of the Berici Hills, where he possessed a large estate, and that his wet-nurse should be one of his own peasants. The curato of the parish and his sister would be entrusted with the charge of visiting the baby at least twice a week.

Marco made no objection to this arrangement; he was as utterly passive as if the child were not his own; not from indifference, but out of deference to his uncle's wishes, as he made it a rule never to contradict him. Teresa obeyed, how unwillingly her own poor heart alone could tell. She thought Providence had had pity on her, and had given her an object to love, to fondle, to take care of. Her whole soul was centred on her boy. But what could she do? There was no help for her. She had never had a will of her own. She knew or fancied all resistance useless, so she gave her tacit consent, and the nurse came to fetch the child. She was accompanied by the curate's sister. A great number of presents were made to both. Advice, warnings, even threats were profusely showered on them regarding the bringing up of the infant; and finally the little heir quitted his ancestor's superb palace for the peasant's humble cot.

A year passed, during which the fond parents often visited their child, and even passed some months in the country to be near him. The time was approaching for the infant's return home, and all the preparations which affection dictates and wealth procures had been made in order to welcome the little heir. A lady in reduced circumstances had been appointed his nurse, as Teresa thought that by this means her boy would acquire more polite manners. The warmest apartment in the palace had been chosen for the nursery. To prevent the infant from being hurt, either when falling or in throwing himself about, the floor was covered with a thick carpet, and the walls hung up to a certain height with the softest hangings. His little bed was so beautifully carved it might have been considered a *chef d'œuvre*. His little quilts had been embroidered by Teresa's own hands, who in this pleasing occupation had whiled away the long months of separation from her little idol. His clothes were all ready, and were remarkable for their costly elegance. All was fond expectation and joy in the palace Centofoglia.

A week before the long-desired arrival a person hitherto unknown to any of the household arrived in breathless haste, saying he bore a letter for the maggiordomo. Pietro soon appeared, and the individual having put a letter into his hand, disappeared.

Pietro scrutinised the address; he had never seen the handwriting before. He opened it with some trepidation, and saw it was from the curate of the village of ——— where Gustavo was being nursed. He then read as follows:

"SIGNOR PIETRO,

"I have thought it prudent to address to you the awful news I have to communicate, as I am sure you will contrive to disclose it cautiously to the noble Signor Marco Centofoglia, and to his illustrious and sainted lady. At twilight yesterday the nurse was returning home with the little child in her arms, when she stopped in a field about a quarter of a mile from her cottage to gather some herbs for her supper. She put the infant on the ground, as was her custom, but, unfortunate wretch! she placed him near a wood which borders one side of the field, and went on gathering her herbs. When she had sufficient she returned to the place where she had left the child, but he had disappeared. She looked around, and could see him nowhere. Night was coming on, so she feared to enter the wood, and returned home in a state bordering on madness. In broken accents she related her misfortune. Her husband, all his male relations, and neighbours took lanterns and searched the neighbouring fields and the wood. They returned this morning, but instead of the poor child they brought a few fragments of his clothes, which they had found scattered about in the furthest part of the wood. It is supposed a wolf carried the child away and has eaten it up. The nurse declares she heard no cries, but the poor wretch speaks incoherently, and if she continues in this state must be placed in a madhouse.

"Do me the favour, Signor Pietro, to assure your noble masters that I and my sister are not blamable in this sad affair, as we have always faithfully obeyed the injunctions given us, and performed our duty to the utmost of our power.

"I beg you will present my devoted respects to the illustrious Signor Paolo Centofoglia, to the not less illustrious Signor Marco, and to the noble Signora

Teresa, for whom I invoke resignation from our glorious saint,

" And believe me your devoted

" DON FRANCESCO PAOLI.

" P.S. No one in the whole village would carry my letter, fearing to be the bearer of such terrible news. At length I found a bold young man who has undertaken to remit it to you on condition of not waiting for an answer."

If ever man was placed in a perplexing situation Pietro was that man. He stood there motionless, with the letter in his left hand, grasping his coat tightly with his right, as if he imagined it would fall off his back. At last a happy thought came to his relief.

" I will take the letter to Father Romualdo, and consult with him what I had best do."

He accordingly went to the neighbouring Dominican convent where the friar lived, and giving his name with some importance, asked to speak with the reverend Father. He was introduced without difficulty into the latter's cell, and at once disclosed his troubles.

Father Romualdo listened attentively, neither evinced great surprise nor grief, and on being pressed by Pietro to give his advice, calmly said:

" For my part, I think the Signor Marco ought to be apprised instantly of this sad occurrence, as the sooner the necessary steps are taken to endeavour to discover something else concerning the poor child, the better chance there is of success."

"I think so too. Would you, Father, undertake to announce the awful news?"

"Why . . . Pietro . . . you see I am not well. I cannot go to the palace at present, but go *yourself* and ask to speak privately with the Signor Marco, and tell him all."

"I don't know how to begin."

"You need not begin. Ask him to read the letter, telling him beforehand there is bad news, but that the case may not be hopeless. Mind that he is not standing when you tell him, as he might have a fit, for though he has never shown much affection for the child, still he is its father. Should I feel better this evening I will not fail to go and endeavour to comfort the Signora Teresa."

Pietro saw plainly that Father Romualdo made his ill-health a plea in order not to be the bearer of such afflicting news to the family Centofoglia; he therefore took leave, and returned to the palace. He went straight into Marco's apartment; finding him alone, and seated perusing some law papers, he shut the door carefully and approached him.

"Signor, I have a letter to give you which contains sad news, but it is my duty not to hide it from you, as if prompt measures are taken, all may yet be well."

Having said these words he tremblingly put the letter into Marco's hand.

Marco perceived the maggiordomo's agitation, and said:

"Why, man, what is the matter? you tremble."

Pietro did not answer, and placed himself behind his master's chair.

Marco read the missive; then rising, said in a tone of suppressed agony:

"Make haste, Pietro; prepare to leave with me for the Berici Hills. I shall tell my wife that the dear child is ill, and we are going to see him. I trust our promptitude will be crowned with success. An hour hence I leave the palace."

Having assumed a calmer aspect Marco went into his wife's room, and told her he was going to see their child, who was not very well.

"I will go with you, Marco," said Teresa, turning pale.

"No, my dear, I cannot allow you to expose yourself to the fatigue of a journey."

"But I *will*. I have never, Marco, had a will of my own, but now I hear my child is ill I *will* go, and you shall not prevent it."

Marco did not answer, but went to apprise his uncle of the sad misfortune, and tell him of Teresa's resolution. The old patrician did not think it a hopeless case, he believed the child could not have been eaten up by wolves, but had been lost in the wood.

"By ordering a proper search we shall find him, Marco, I have no doubt of it, but Teresa must not go. She must obey. What are these airs? She forgets herself. I will go with you to her room, and you will see she will be persuaded."

The uncle and nephew went to Teresa's room, made use of every argument, had even recourse at last to threats—all proved useless. Teresa defended her cause fearlessly, and ended by saying:

"Make no farther opposition, my dear father; say nothing more, Marco—go I *will*. I am a mother. I have given up too much, but now my boy is ill," Teresa evinced in her voice and manner the resolution of despair,—"and I call St. Mark to witness the truth of what I say—I will either go to my sick child or throw myself into the sea."

Opposing her will was of no avail, and she was allowed to accompany her husband. He took the precaution of delaying their departure, and in the meantime a messenger was despatched in great haste with orders to apprise the curate that the travellers would alight at his house in order to prevent Teresa's learning the catastrophe until a proper search had been made in the wood, and all the adjacent fields.

The coach with the agitated parents stopped at a small inn at an insignificant place, some miles beyond Mestra, for the purpose of changing horses. They found a travelling coach waiting there for the same purpose. As it had arrived first, Marco and Teresa were obliged to wait their turn, and witness the hurrying to and fro of the postillions, coachmen, servants, and stable-boys, who were endeavouring to be as quick as possible, but only contriving to lose more time by the confusion they made. Inside the coach were a lady, two other women, and a man. One of the women held something that looked like a bundle carefully in her arms. It was a child, so covered up that it no longer possessed its natural form, indeed, it was a wonder it was not suffocated. The curiosity of the lady and her women was excited at seeing another coach, and they looked through the windows at its occupants. The woman, however, who held the child soon grew tired of this occupation, and covering and wrapping her hapless charge more carefully, on the plea that stopping so long might cause it to catch cold, she leaned back, turning her face to the opposite side.

Marco foamed at the delay. Both he and Teresa continually put their heads out of the coach-door, anxious to see the party leave. At last they heard the cracking of the whip, and the cry of the postillion. The noise of the wheels came next; then, to their great relief, they saw the coach whirl rapidly away.

"Whose was that accursed coach?" said Marco to Pietro, who had come to the coach-door to announce that the horses would now be changed instantly, and they could leave within a few minutes.

"It was the Contessa Sofia Bernardi's, who is going to Lucca for a short time with her little son, his nurse, her lady's-maid, and her agent," answered Pietro.

"How happy she is with her child by her side!" said poor Teresa, sighing deeply.

Without further interruption they arrived at the curate's dwelling. They had some trouble to persuade

Teresa not to run to the nurse's cottage. She was more docile to the good priest's earnest entreaties to take a little rest before going, and in the meantime a troop of men was organised to scour in separate parties the wood, the adjacent fields and villages. Large sums of money were promised to whoever should bring back the child, or his little corpse. Every effort proved useless. Nothing had been seen or heard of the poor infant, and it was unanimously decided that a wild beast had eaten him up.

The sad news was then disclosed to the unhappy mother. She had suspected her child was gone. When she learned its afflicting end she calmly answered:

"I deserve this punishment. I had vowed my life to retirement and devotion in a convent. I had the weakness to break these holy resolutions, and now let the remainder of my days be passed in remorse and sorrow."

CHAPTER VIII.

A LEARNED LADY'S OPINION ON A QUESTION ALWAYS NEW.

THE coach that carried the Contessa Sofia Bernardi through her very pleasant journey entered the old and interesting town of Lucca. The contessa had travelled by long stages. She was very tired, and thankful to find herself settled in a fine old palace in a quiet street.

The precise reason of her removal to Lucca was not known. She had said she meant to return to her native city shortly, but in her own mind she had fully determined never to see it again.

A deep mystery enshrouded the contessa, and was the cause of much that was strange in her conduct. She was an only child, and had inherited the large fortune and title of Count Bernardi, her father. By her own choice she retained her maiden name. She had, no one knew why, married a merchant neither wealthy nor handsome, and had had a little boy whom she had confided to a peasant to be nursed on the Berici Hills. Her husband was separated from her. She said he had gone to the East, and had settled there. Whether he had met his death there was not known; but it is certain no one, not even his wife, ever heard anything more about him.

A few days before leaving Venice she sent Rosalia, who had succeeded in becoming a great favourite, to fetch her little boy. It had been arranged that with the infant she should await the contessa's arrival at Mestri, and thence all should start together for Lucca.

When the contessa saw her little boy, it was with maternal pride that she exclaimed:

"How beautiful he is! 'Tis true I never saw him during the whole time he was on the Berici Hills, but I never thought he would have grown so fair, with such lovely blue eyes, and light golden hair. He is not much like me, and is certainly most unlike his father."

"Children change in a wonderful way, Signora Contessa," answered Rosalia, timidly.

"That is very true," replied the contessa; "but why do you keep him wrapped up in that way, Rosalia? Instead of looking like a child he looks like a huge bundle of clothes."

"I keep him wrapped up lest he should catch cold. He has been used to much clothing, and is new to travelling. These precautions will not be necessary when we reach Lucca."

"Very well. I leave you to do as you like. You will take charge of him until he is old enough to have a tutor; I can spare him but little of my time; my books engross it almost entirely."

As she had not deemed it prudent to travel without a trustworthy man-servant, she had asked her agent to accompany her, which he had readily done; and he not only took every possible care of her and her female attendants during the journey, but he also superintended the establishment of her household at Lucca. When he judged his services were no longer required he left for Venice, the contessa having previously charged him to sell her palace there, and forward the proceeds of the sale for investment in a Florentine bank. It was equivalent to saying "I do not intend to return," but we do not know whether such a thought occurred to the worthy man, who, on his arrival in Venice, assiduously applied himself to the task of accomplishing his lady's commission; but some years were destined to elapse before he could conclude the business satisfactorily.

Rosalia noticed that the contessa looked much more cheerful after her arrival at Lucca; she mixed more in society, and held weekly receptions in her own house.

Rosalia's features underwent no change. Always pale and thin, she often sat musing on her misfortunes, alternately sighing and smiling, a sinister smile which did not betoken resignation, but rather a continual brooding on evil thoughts. She avoided going to church as much as possible. Sometimes she could not help going, and in order to elude inquisitive questions from the other members of the household, or observation from her mistress, she used to declare she had attended, or was going to attend, divine service, instead of which she would either take a solitary walk on the ramparts or in the country.

Meanwhile, Guido grew up a beautiful little fellow. His mother's fondness increased with his years, and her pride in him augmented daily. When he was too old for female control she had a tutor for him, to whom she gave positive injunctions not to contradict the boy, but to let him have his own way in everything that would not injure his *health* or *beauty*.

Though the Contessa Sofia Bernardi did not evince great wisdom in the bringing up of her son, she possessed, nevertheless, a good share of learning, and her opinion on some important questions of the times was much appreciated by men of learning and renown with whom she continued to correspond until the day of her death. The principal subject discussed was the religious state of the country, the efforts of foreigners to propagate their tenets, and the means resorted to by the Papal Courts to suppress any innovation they might introduce.

As the result proved, that on the score of religion the natives of the south were characterised by the same tendencies in the time of the Contessa Sofia Bernardi as they are now, it may not be uninteresting to the English reader to peruse one of the long epistles written about five years after her departure from Venice, by means of which she used to acquaint a celebrated friar of what was going on in the small town of Lucca, which, for a brief period, had made the sincere Catholic fear lest it should become the stronghold of Protestantism in Italy.

"VERY REVEREND FATHER,

"I have not answered your welcome letter so soon as I wished, having been prevented from fulfilling that pleasing task by the misfortune which has befallen our friend the Marquis ——. As I know your reverence feels great interest in that learned man's fate, I will give you a full account of what has unluckily happened."

Here follows a long narrative in which the reader would take little interest.

"The religious question is still the chief subject of discussion in some circles, but the Utopia dreamed of by some foreigners, and desired by a few deluded natives, viz., the establishment of Lutheran and Calvinistic doctrines amongst us, is as remote as ever. Though slanderous tongues have averred the contrary, both your reverence and myself are too truly devoted to the interests of our Holy Mother the Church not to rejoice heartily that such is the case.

"What makes me wonder and strengthens my former opinion, that man is apt to fancy either as accomplished, or on the point of being completed, the thing he ardently desires merely because it is his will, is the daily witnessing how distant from the longed-for goal are those very persons who have passed their whole life in endeavouring to attain it.

"If such be the condition of the people of this town, who have been instructed by the profoundly learned Ausonius Palearius, what must be the state of others who have never so much as beheld any of the champions of these strange dogmas? The failure that has attended the strenuous efforts of many is not surprising. No individual distinguished for birth or wealth has embraced the new doctrines. Human help, such as might have been truly efficacious, has been totally wanting. Your reverence knows me sufficiently well not to suppose that I consider human help as alone sufficient for the attainment of plans and attempts belonging of right to Religious Orders. I know that the first centuries of Christianity are brought forward as a proof to the contrary, but the superhuman means which worked at that time, in order to deliver mankind from the bondage and blindness of paganism, cannot be looked for now by the most ardent amongst the promoters of these new doctrines. Its main support thus coming from man, it is easy to see how weak and fragile that support must be, especially as its adherents are but a small number of very poor families, so needy that with many the hope of bettering their condition has been the sole motive of their apostasy.

"The powerful families of landed proprietors, whose vassals may be counted by hundreds, who found and maintain charitable institutions, are devoted to the Church. They may be divided into two classes.

"The first and most numerous is composed of the fanatical, who are consequently intolerant in the highest degree. With them adhesion to the new doctrines is the most heinous and unpardonable of crimes.

"The second numbers fewer families and comprises the kind and more forgiving, who cannot persecute, and will not pass harsh judgment on their neighbours, and who, in their equally intense horror of apostacy and apostates, have concluded that a person who renounces the Church, and disregards her holy ordinances, is downright mad. Both parties profess equal respect and devotion to the clergy, and are enthusiastic supporters of the monastic Orders, which they venerate. I witnessed a scene the other day, which is but one in a thousand, and which proves the truth of my assertions. The description of it may not be unpleasing to your reverence:

"The family of Count B—— is, as your reverence well knows, one of the richest and most ancient of the Peninsula.* The present count has married a most amiable woman, of a very noble family. In their intercourse with their dependents and less illustrious acquaintances, there is that perfectly polite, and yet frigid distance, which characterises some of our class. Their charities are boundless, and they are so far enlightened as to be moderate in their politics, and not exactly intolerant in their religious opinions.

* A fact.

"I had been invited to pass a day with them, at their superb villa, on the mountains that separate Lucca from that tiny place on the sea, Viareggio. Unexpectedly, Father Leonardo Caloi, of the Franciscan Order, was announced. By birth he belongs to the lower rank of society; but his reputation for sanctity, his many schemes for promoting the spiritual, mental, and temporal welfare of the poor under him render him worthy of respect and veneration. As soon as he was seated, the children were all summoned to kiss his hand. When dinner was announced he was asked to take precedence, the countess, her family, and visitors humbly following him. On entering the dining-room the count advanced towards him, bowed respectfully, and kissed his hand. At table the countess ceded her place to him, placing herself on his left hand. I was on his right. He was helped first, and during dinner the subjects discussed were only those most pleasing to him, while every one listened to what he said with religious silence and respect. It was a sight beautiful to behold! It carried my mind back to the middle ages, when the friars of the humble Order of St. Francis were the most welcome visitors at the palace and the cottage.

"Were anyone to tell the count or countess to embrace the new doctrines, to help in promoting a change, or disregard the clergy, their answer would be: 'I would sooner be reduced to beggary, see my children starved to death, and finally die on the scaffold.' Your reverence, myself, and numberless others, would, I am sure, say the same.

"I will now copy for your reverence some criticisms on the Gerusalemme Liberata, which I wrote yesterday."

[Here follows a long dissertation of little value as a criticism, and of no interest.]

"Respectfully kissing your reverence's hand,

"I remain your most faithful servant,

"SOFIA BERNARDI."

CHAPTER IX.

DEATH-BED ADVICE.

A FEW months after the mysterious disappearance of the little heir of the Centofoglias, the old patrician, Paola Centofoglia, relinquished wealth and life, and was gathered to his fathers.

Marco was now under no one's control; he no longer feared displeasing his uncle, and causing him to alter his will. He was sole master of the largest fortune in the Venetian States, and he evinced tastes and whims which no one had formerly suspected he possessed.

He began by making the tour of Italy, leaving Teresa behind to pursue the devotions and charitable occupations, to which she had vowed her life. He next discovered he had a great fondness for the equine race, and as, in Venice, the gondola replaces the brilliant equipages he wished to indulge in, he bought a beautiful estate in the environs of Rovigo, and always passed at least eight months of the year there.

It was his ardent wish to have an heir, and Teresa shared this desire, as she fancied he would then become less negligent of her, or at least save appearances, as he used to do during his uncle's lifetime. Ardently did she pray for this, and she promised to make an offering of two rich chandeliers to the cathedral of St. Mark, if her prayer were granted.

Six years after the loss of her little boy, she was again about to become a mother, and a few days before the birth of her babe she went to St. Mark's to pray for her own welfare, and that of her infant.

It happened that the Contessa Bernardi's agent had at that time an advantageous offer for the palace, and having written the conditions to the Contessa, received her answer to conclude the bargain as soon as possible; meanwhile she sent Rosalia to Venice, to see about removing the linen, and some trifles on which she set great value.

It was on this occasion that Rosalia, in crossing the Piazza St. Marco, recognised Teresa, whom she had seen but once, six years before, in the coach near Mestra. Though she was aware that Marco's wife had no share in her wretched fate—he having been the unfaithful one—still she was *his* wife, and therefore exposed to her hatred. The times conduced to the belief in predictions; no wonder, then, that unable to injure her rival in any other way, she should have recourse to the only means left her, by which she knew she could wound the poor mother to her very soul.

She therefore followed her into the cathedral, and when she saw her quietly kneeling, at a distance from other people, she gently crept behind her, and laid her hand on Teresa's shoulder. It felt as cold as ice. Teresa started, and seeing that tall, pale figure beside her—she did not so much as take her hand from off her shoulder, though she could not but be aware of the fright she had caused—she became as pale as death, and trembled all over. Rosalia bent towards her, saying:

"Wife of Marco Centofoglia, fear not. It is not my intention to harm thee. I merely wish to tell thee that thou wilt give birth to a girl, and that she will be the most unhappy of women."

She then disappeared through a side-door, and Teresa, having slightly recovered from her fright, returned home, went straight into her husband's room, and recounted to him her adventure.

Amid the turmoil of the world and the thoughtlessness which follows pleasure gratified, Marco had almost forgotten Rosalia, and hoped that she had forgotten him. The description Teresa gave of the strange apparition left him no doubt as to who it was, and reminded him she had not forgotten her threats. Teresa perceived a change in his countenance, and innocently said:

"Either you or I must have committed some great crime, since sorrow is to follow sorrow in our unhappy lives!"

"*You* are certainly guiltless," replied Marco, unawares; then recollecting himself, he continued in a hurried manner: "Let me hear no more about predictions and such like nonsense. I desire you, Teresa, not to mention the occurrence again, either to me or to others, as you would only get heartily laughed at. You will see we shall have another boy."

Instead of a boy, however, Teresa gave birth to a daughter.

"A girl is better than nothing," exclaimed Marco, endeavouring to suppress his intense disappointment, and whether from a sense of duty, or from indifference to the new-born infant, he allowed his wife to have her own way in all that concerned the child. She had it baptised Rosa after her own mother, had a wet-nurse for it in the house—nay, she never allowed it to be out of her presence a single moment, day or night.

A little happiness had entered into her desolate heart, and although Rosalia's prediction would, despite herself, cross her mind from time to time, she endeavoured to banish the thought, and determined within herself that as far as in her lay her child should shed no tears. Instead of placing her in a convent to be educated, she had masters for her in the house, and a trustworthy, superior woman besides herself to watch over her. Thus Rosa grew up alike distinguished for singular beauty, great aptness in learning, the sweetest temper, and the most affectionate heart—her mother's idol and her father's pride!

When she had attained her fifteenth year symptoms

of an alarming nature manifested themselves in her loving mother, and her physicians, desiring to avoid the responsibility of treating a disease which often ends fatally, insisted on her removal to the healthier and warmer climate of Pisa.

Marco readily complied with their advice, and though sorry to leave her native city, Teresa consented to it because she felt it was her duty to do all in her power that her daughter might not be left unsettled in life, without a mother's fond guidance. Accordingly they set out, and, travelling by short stages, reached the town of Pisa at the beginning of winter.

The palace engaged for the residence of the Centofoglia family was one of the most beautiful and ancient of the place, situated on the Lung' Arno, and known by the name of Il palazzo alla giornata, from the last two words which are to be seen in front underneath the balcony.

The change proved most beneficial to Teresa's health, and as spring advanced she began to talk of their removal to their fine estate near Rovigo, when Marco's folly about horses and his obstinacy brought her life to an untimely end.

He had bought a pair of high-mettled horses, and although he had been told they were imperfectly broken in, he insisted on their being harnessed to the carriage every day.* It must be owned that the first time they were tried he drove out alone with them, and

* A fact.

as they chose to behave properly no further apprehensions were entertained. They became great favourites, and the order was given that they were to be the horses used in the daily drive.

One beautiful afternoon, whilst Rosa was receiving some young friends, Teresa fancied she would enjoy a drive alone. She entered her carriage, elated by the sensation of returning health, and musing on her child's future, had arrived half-way down the Via S. Maria, when the horses suddenly became restive, and, disregarding bit and bridle, flew past the hospital towards the wide and shady walk of the Casina.

A lady, whose kindness led her daily to visit the sick at the hospital, and whose carriage was there waiting, learning the danger to which Teresa was exposed, requested a physician and Capuchin to accompany her, and ordering her coachman to follow the runaway horses, proceeded onwards in the hope of speedily overtaking the unhappy Teresa. They found the coachman and groom had jumped out, but had not been able to stop the horses.

By this time the whole town was in a state of commotion, and hundreds were hurrying towards the casino in order to learn the result. Marco, who by order of the kind lady had been apprised of the accident, had set off in another carriage, after desiring the maggiordomo to keep the distressing news from Rosa.

After a swift course of some miles the horses slackened their pace, and a peasant was enabled to stop them. Teresa alighted, and, although as pale as death, calmly seated herself on a stone bench. The two carriages arrived at the same time. Marco was the first to see her, and with one bound was at her side, then snatching her up in his arms, he embraced her with an affection he had never evinced before, and placed her in his carriage. The kind lady took her seat by Teresa's side, the Capuchin and Marco being opposite. The physician occupied the other carriage. As they entered the town the hundreds that had become thousands clamorously shouted their joy on seeing Teresa unhurt. The kind lady, the Capuchin, and the physician stopped at the hospital; Marco and Teresa continued their way home. The crowd would not leave the carriage, every eye was turned towards Teresa; her escape from certain death seemed a dream.

Seeing her mother did not return Rosa began to suspect some accident had befallen her, and was continually going to the window in the hope of seeing the carriage return. As it was now almost dark it was impossible clearly to discern distant objects. She saw a crowd, and her heart beat quicker, but when the crowd stopped and she recognised the carriage and her parents, she rushed downstairs before the maggiordomo had time to stop her. Just as she approached the door her mother, leaning on her father, had crossed the threshold. She threw her arms around her. Poor Teresa, who had borne up against the strongest emotions during the last hours, now lost her presence of mind, and fell fainting into her daughter's arms. She was carried upstairs and put to bed, and a month from the date of this accident her corpse was laid with pomp and splendour in the celebrated Camposanto of Pisa.

But ere she closed her eyes for ever she called her beloved child to her bedside.

"My Rosa," she said, and the tears glistened in her eyes, "we part to meet no more until you also are summoned to quit these scenes of trouble and affliction, for the peace that is only to be found above. I have endeavoured to render you good and happy, and have always implored the protection of our most Holy Mother upon you. I must now tell you what happened to me a few days before your birth." Teresa repeated Rosalia's prediction. "I should never have told you this had it been my happiness to see you settled in life before closing my eyes for ever, but as I feel I shall not behold to-morrow's sun, I have thought it my duty to tell it to you, not in order that you should make yourself unhappy, for after all we are in the hands of the Almighty, and in Him we should implicitly trust, and though that tall pale figure has often haunted me, I still pray that what I have told you may not dwell on your mind, and that it may merely serve to make you careful respecting your own happiness.

"We should accept, my dearest child, with resignation, whatever loss or trouble is sent us from on High, but we should not sport with our happiness, nor lay upon ourselves a burthen we may be too weak to bear. When God gives us trouble, He weighs our strength beforehand, and only gives us what we can sustain. But when, regardless of our weakness, we choose to lay troubles on ourselves, or allow others to place them upon us, the agony becomes twofold, and but for the mercy of God, who will still help us, we should end by becoming desperate. One of the greatest misfortunes that can befall a woman, is that of being united to a man she does not love; for then the holy tie of matrimony becomes an insupportable chain. When a woman is united to a man she loves and esteems, every affliction, every sorrow, every disappointment she may be called on to endure is rendered lighter. But when troubles visit the woman who does not love, and is not loved by the partner of her life, she feels almost crushed beneath their weight. My child, even then faith doth help—wonderfully help! but remorse assails the wretched sufferer, and whispers, 'The fault is thine.' I advise you, nay, I enjoin you, with my dying breath, to obey and respect your father's wishes in all things; but should he insist on bestowing your hand on one you feel persuaded you could never love, then humbly but firmly remonstrate, and don't be prevailed upon to yield by any argument, however plausible it may appear. The obedience a child owes her parents is a sacred duty, but as a parent has no power over his child's life, so he has none over that, the most sacred of woman's rights, not to bestow her hand on one she does not love. To insist on a marriage which your father could not approve of, would be wrong, and I forbid your ever giving him such displeasure. If, therefore, a hindrance to your marriage should arise either from him, or from yourself, choose an unmarried life devoted to God and the poor, as the best way of reconciling the reverence due to a parent's wishes, and the proper regard due to your own happiness. As a help in all the difficulties you may meet with in life, I leave you, my child, this miniature. It represents our most Holy Mother Addolorata. I have become calm and resigned, when in great trouble, by looking at the deep sorrow and heavenly resignation which her countenance expresses. Ever keep it as the most precious thing you possess. It is your mother's last gift!"

Saying this Teresa took from under her pillow a beautiful small miniature of Our Blessed Lady, in a case of black velvet and gold. Rosa took it, kissed it, and threw her arms round her dying mother's neck, and the two wept long and copiously.

That night was Teresa's last, and Rosa folded in her arms her parent's corpse.

Than this there is no greater agony on earth!

CHAPTER X.

A STORM.

INSTEAD of returning to the Venetian States, after Teresa's demise, Marco and Rosa rented a beautiful villa on the hills of Fiesole, passing their first months of mourning there. And truly and deeply did Rosa mourn her mother's loss.

During the first days after her death, Marco felt remorse for his neglect of his poor wife, and his careless obstinacy about the horses, but it soon passed away, and when Christmas came he removed with his daughter to Lucca for the winter. The palace they inhabited was near the cathedral, and thither Rosa daily resorted to pay her devotions at the famous sanctuary of the Volto Santo.

We describe it as it is now, being pretty well assured that little or no difference would be found between it as it is at the present moment, and more than two centuries ago. A peculiarity of the town of Lucca is its having preserved more than perhaps any other place the architectural features of the middle ages. Its long, narrow streets, large ancient palaces, and especially its very ancient and most interesting churches, carry the mind back to the times when Lucca was no mean though small republic. Its past history seems to be identified with the blackened walls of some of its churches, and the shadows thrown on the long, narrow streets by some of the ancient dwellings of its patrician families, so that one almost fancies one sees the ghosts of long-passed generations moving silently about.

Entering the cathedral, to the left about half-way down the nave, a small gilt chapel stands isolated. It contains an altar, and above the altar stands a crucifix as large as life. It is made of ebony. The figure of our Most Blessed Saviour is dressed, and a golden crown, studded with precious stones, encircles His head. It is exposed to public devotion twice yearly, on the 3rd of May, and on the 14th of September.

What must strike the intelligent observer, is the difference, as far as artistic worth goes, between the body and the face. The former is uncouth, stiff, almost shapeless. The latter is beautiful, perfect, and with so touching an expression that, unless blinded by prejudice, it is impossible to look at it and not be inspired with a feeling of deep devotion.

It is a production of the middle ages, and a holy legend says, that the artist who sculptured it, after having made the body, was so puzzled how to produce a face which could in any way resemble the Divine original, that he dared not begin. One day he fell asleep, and on awaking found the face carved. He concluded that an angel had taken pity on his perplexity and sculptured it, hence its name of the Volto Santo.

Splendid gifts, some of them offerings by crowned heads, adorn it, as well as the interior of the chapel. The most remarkable are two angels placed on either side. One presents to the Saviour a golden sceptre ornamented with precious stones, and the other a bunch of large golden keys. It is the very place where an aching heart would pour forth its sorrows at the foot of the Cross, and Rosa found it so.

One afternoon, whilst she was praying, the sky suddenly lowered, then a flash of lightning was seen, followed by a long, loud peal of thunder. Then the rain came pelting down, and large hailstones beat against the church windows: an awful storm had broken over the town.

It lasted some time, and when the shades of night appeared, and the church was about being closed, Rosa, followed by her maid, a superior woman who had been in the house some years, directed her steps towards a side door which was nearer the direction of her home, and had just bent her knees for the last time ere she quitted the cathedral, when a very handsome and elegant young man approached her, and after having bowed profoundly, said:

"Signora, my carriage is waiting opposite the principal door. I cannot allow you to return home on foot in such a storm. I beg of you to accept it."

"Thank you, signor," answered Rosa; "my house is close by. I always come and go on foot."

"I should deem it the greatest favour you could bestow upon me, did you accept my offer."

These words were said almost in an imploring tone; and just at that moment there came a flash of lightning that seemed to set the whole church on fire, and a peal of thunder so loud followed, that it shook all the old stained-glass windows. The young man led the way towards the principal door. Rosa followed, for she saw it was hopeless attempting to walk. The storm, which had relented a little, had set in again with redoubled force. On reaching the carriage, which approached as near as possible to the steps of the edifice, the young man handed her in, stood till she and her maid were seated; then having told the coachman where to drive to, bowed and disappeared.

It was thus that, amidst one of the wildest outbreaks of nature, Rosa Centofoglia first made the acquaintance of Count Guido Bernardi.

CHAPTER XI.

A STRANGE WILL.

AS soon as Marco heard from his daughter of the young man's politeness, he set on foot inquiries about him. He ascertained that he was the son of the learned Contessa Sofia Bernardi, who he knew had settled in Lucca, and he consequently asked for an introduction to her, in order to thank the count for his attention. The contessa did not evince great pleasure in making the acquaintance of Marco Centofoglia, but could not refuse to do so. Guido, who was delighted, apprised Marco that he could not allow him to call first, and would pay his respects to him and to his daughter. He did not let the day pass without putting his resolve into execution, for he had fallen in love, and love admits of no delay.

Marco had not been in Lucca more than a day or two, when Guido had already heard—in a small town everything that transpires is known within a few hours—that he possessed the loveliest daughter human eyes ever beheld. He contrived to see her, learned where she lived, and from that moment, at a respectful distance, in order to escape her notice, or that of her lady's-maid, he followed her in and out of church, in her walks on the ramparts, everywhere.

He vainly endeavoured to induce his mother to make the acquaintance of the Venetian nobleman and his beautiful daughter. She firmly refused, saying she had no wish to increase the number of her friends, as they were already too numerous for her literary occupations. He was obliged to submit, but hoped some opportunity would present itself of obtaining his heart's desire. The storm came to his aid. He thought, "The moment has arrived, I will not lose it," and succeeded not only in breaking the ice, but in obliging Marco to be the first to seek their acquaintance, thus depriving his mother of the possibility of refusing it.

On Guido's being announced, Marco advanced to meet him, and bowing, said:

"I have a double motive of gratitude towards you, Signor Conte; you kindly lent your carriage to my daughter, and you honour me with your most welcome acquaintance. How can I repay so much courtesy?"

"The honour the signorina did me in accepting my carriage, and the one you now confer upon me, in allowing me to make your acquaintance, demand on my part expressions of the warmest gratitude."

"If you will allow me, I will henceforth call you, Signor Conte, my friend, and I trust our friendship will be lasting and sincere," replied Marco, offering a seat to his young guest.

"It is a greater happiness than I could have aspired to, and——"

He was interrupted by Rosa's entrance; with maidenly modesty, united to the perfect self-possession generally observed in the more elevated classes of society, she came forward, and in response to Guido's submissive bow, said:

"Accept, Signor Conte, my best thanks for the kind attention shown me in the cathedral. You disappeared so quickly, I was not able to express my gratitude then."

"'Tis I who owe you thanks, noble signora. I reckon that day the happiest of my life."

By this time they had seated themselves, and Marco resumed:

"I wish to pay my respects to your noble mother. She is the most learned lady Venice can boast of. I have heard that of late her health has not been good. I trust it is only a rumour."

"Unfortunately it is but too true. She sits up reading beyond a woman's strength. To my remonstrances she answers, that it is the greatest comfort of her life. She will be charmed to number you amongst her friends; and I hope the learned conversations she will have with you and the signorina, whose fame for learning equals her fame for beauty, may have the effect of detaching her awhile from her books."

How supremely nonsensical is the complimentary talk considered necessary on making a first acquaintance! Our patience fails to follow the remainder of the conversation, and we gladly give it up.

From that day there was no more welcome guest than Guido Bernardi in Marco Contofoglia's house. They rode together, they made short excursions into the country. Sometimes Rosa accompanied them, in order to please her father, but her heart was still so afflicted she found little pleasure in society—none in the count's flattering phrases.

Upon one occasion, when Marco was expecting Guido to dine with them, he said to Rosa:

"I cannot help fancying that had my poor little boy lived, he would have been the image of Count Guido Bernardi, who is not very unlike you. I own I feel a great regard for that young man. There is some talk respecting his birth—but——" Marco recollected himself, and cut the subject short by saying: "He should be here now. He is always before his time, not behind it."

Rosa took no notice of her father's hint concerning Guido's birth, she cared little about it; and, therefore, answered indifferently:

"Yes, he is a very courteous young man."

"He is more than courteous, child; he is most amiable, noble—on his mother's side, at least—rich, highly instructed, he has every good quality."

"As to *every* good quality, papa, I do not know that; but he is certainly a great favourite of yours."

"True, so he is."

Guido's entrance at this moment put a stop to

Marco's praise of him. He apologised for having come later than usual, "Owing," added he, "to my mother's health. She is by no means well to-day, and I could not leave her until this moment."

Marco and his daughter expressed their regret; the latter could not help adding:

"It is very trying to see a mother in a precarious state, Signor Conte. You ought not to have left her, she may miss you."

Guido felt rather ashamed, but answered:

"She is not in absolute danger, therefore I felt I could not deprive myself of the pleasure of dining with you to-day."

The fact was that Guido not only could not deprive himself of the pleasure of passing a few hours in Rosa's company—for her sake he courted Marco—but since his mother's health had become so delicate, her nerves had also grown most irritable; and as for Rosalia, for some time she had been downright savage, and no one could tell the reason. She fled the company of every one, and took good care never to be in the way when Marco Centofoglia or his daughter called; besides this, her answers grew snappish. Hence Guido's home was by no means the fittest place where a lover of three-and-twenty could meditate on his lady-love; and he was glad to escape from it as frequently as possible.

When spring set in, and the ramparts were beginning to be covered with their leafy canopy, Marco and his daughter quitted Lucca for their estate near Rovigo, and Guido was left to bear the separation as well as he could.

Rosalia's temper improved a little, but the Contessa Bernardi's nerves became worse and worse with increasing illness. Her life was now fast ebbing away. She was told by a worthy priest that her days were numbered. To the surprise of her son and her female attendants, she heard the announcement with the greatest resignation; her temper became milder, her heart kindly disposed towards everyone, and her affection for her son and heir increased.

She spoke of her intention of leaving all the inmates of her household provided for during their lifetime. She continually repeated to Guido these words:

"My son, my dearest Guido, do not leave me in my last moments. Let the hands of my beloved son close my eyes in the sleep of death."

And Guido would answer:

"I will never leave you, my dearest, my beloved mother! You have been and are the best of parents." He would fondly add: "I still hope, however, to see you up and about again."

The Contessa Sofia Bernardi shook her head, and raised her eyes towards heaven. The day destined to be her last was now come. The physicians had warned Rosalia—they knew she was the contessa's principal attendant — to be watchful, for she might expire and no one be aware of it. Rosalia promised she would watch every symptom carefully, and having told Guido she meant to arrange her lady's room and bed, she shut herself up with the dying contessa.

When she again opened the door, she announced that the contessa wished to speak with her notary, and that there was not a moment to be lost. The notary was sent for. He remained in the room a short time; and when Guido, Rosalia, and the contessa's confessor entered she had already lost her speech.

Guido folded her in his arms; then putting his hand under her pillow, in order to support her head, kept saying, in his agony of grief:

"Mother, I am here; you are in my arms. Forgive all the follies of my boyish days, and whatever uneasiness I may have caused you since. Do look at me once more, once more, I implore you!"

The contessa evidently heard, for she moved. She could open her eyes, for she fixed them during a few seconds on a crucifix she held in her right hand, but never once did she turn towards her sorrowing son—never once cast her eyes on him!

That same evening she expired in his arms. Her will was read the next day. After the usual preliminaries, it ran thus:

"I leave to my son Guido Bernardi the estate of —— [the rental was not more than 7000 francs per annum]. My money invested in the Florentine bank, all my remaining property, jewels, furniture, pictures, and books, I leave to Monsignore Mariscoro di Lucca, to be equally divided by him between the Church and the poor, as he shall judge best, subject to these conditions, that as long as my servants"—here they were all named except Rosalia—"live, they shall receive yearly"—here the small allowance was certified. It amounted to about 400 francs each annually. "I desire that my body shall be laid in the Church of S. Romano, and a simple marble slab be placed over my grave."

Her household, and all who heard of it, were truly astonished. Guido was stung to the quick. The only one who appeared indifferent about it, and not in the least surprised, was Rosalia. To Guido's remark, "I cannot tell what can have made my mother treat you and me in this manner in her last moments," she calmly answered:

"You mother is not to blame."

"I dare say," retorted Guido, "her father confessor has managed it all."

Rosalia made no reply.

A few days after the funeral, the household was broken up, and Guido and Rosalia left for Venice.

As for the contessa's body, her wishes were duly attended to, and she was laid in the Church of S. Romano, where a marble slab over her grave bears this inscription:

"Here rests in peace the most noble, and most learned Contessa Sofia Bernardi."

PART II.

CHAPTER I.

KINDRED SPIRITS.

MARCO CENTOFOGLIA and Rosa passed the spring, summer, and part of the autumn at their villa near Rovigo, and about the middle of October returned to Venice for the winter. The first friend to welcome their arrival was Count Guido Bernardi. Marco received him with more than usual kindness. Rosa's manner, also, assumed a degree of interest she had never evinced for him at Lucca, and which was caused by the sympathy she felt in his loss, having herself endured the like.

Both father and daughter observed that Guido's manner had become shy, and at times quite distant. They attributed the change to his affliction, and in a measure it was so, with this difference, however, that it was not the actual loss of his poor mother, but the loss of his fortune, which made him feel he was no longer the equal of the wealthy patrician, and consequently not so likely, as he had formerly hoped, to obtain his daughter's hand.

A few days after Marco had entered on his winter residence at Venice, one of his most intimate friends, Father Pio, called on him.

"Well," said Marco, "what news, reverend Father? What is going on?"

"Nothing very particular."

"Anyone come or gone?"

"Ah, yes, Antonio Foscarini has returned."

"Has he fulfilled his mission?"

"Yes."

"I have often wished to know him. I have heard he is a noble fellow."

"So he is. His manner on first making his acquaintance does not prepossess one in his favour, there is a taciturnity and distance about him which almost inspires awe. Some say it is pride, but I say it is a certain degree of shyness in general company which is more frequently to be met with than people generally think. As soon, however, as one begins to grow intimate with him, his whole nature seems to expand, and the noble qualities of his heart and mind endear him to us for ever. I have known him long and well, and you may trust what I say."

"Would you introduce me to him? I should deem it a great favour."

"I will do so most willingly. Let us fix the day and hour."

"I shall call at the convent to-morrow, and, if it

is agreeable to you, we might then go together to his house."

"Very well."

The next day Marco Centofoglia and Father Pio called on Antonio Foscarini. On the following day he returned the visit, was introduced to Rosa, and became one of the most assiduous frequenters of the Palazzo Centofoglia.

The fact is, that as soon as he saw Rosa, he loved her, and she returned his love with all the warmth of her affectionate heart. It was a feeling quite new to her, and which she could not explain to herself. She only knew that if she heard his name mentioned her heart beat quicker: if he approached her, she felt happy. If he approved what she said, she felt an inward satisfaction unfelt before.

Antonio Foscarini was some years older than Rosa, his character and manners not such as would please every girl.

Though proud of his daughter's beauty and talents, Marco had not discovered the superiority of her mind over that of many girls of her own age; furthermore, he did not remember that the strongest love felt by man is often for a woman much younger than himself, whilst woman's deepest love is often won by a man her senior by many years. Without the slightest suspicion that they could love each other, he therefore allowed Rosa to receive Antonio Foscarini in his absence, and alone.

On one of these occasions whilst Rosa and Antonio

Foscarini were sitting in an elegant little drawing-room adjoining the reception-hall, and Rosa was admiring a lovely nosegay Foscarini had just brought her, she said, looking towards the setting sun, whose last rays were then throwing their golden light into the room :

"How lovely must the flowers be that bloom in yonder heaven !"

"And how much sweeter still the love must be that unalloyed gladdens the happy spirits who dwell there !" answered Foscarini, looking steadfastly at her, then he added : "To think it is often man's wretched lot to love—and——" he stopped.

"And what ?" said Rosa, inquiringly.

"And brood over it in silence, not daring to express it."

"Silence is the sacred token of real love—as it is of deep sorrow," replied Rosa, and sighing again, she fixed her eyes on the sky.

"Lady, you must have felt both ; you speak so truly."

"I have felt sorrow . . ." she blushed and said no more.

"I have also undergone affliction," said Foscarini, "and I have felt—I feel love intense, unconquerable——"

Rosa turned towards him. A thought passed across her mind, "Perhaps, after all, it is not me he loves." A pang shot through her heart, yet she answered sweetly :

"May you be happy. I wish it from my soul!"

"Do you really wish it, lady?" replied Foscarini, his countenance brightening. "Really? Then make me happy. Say you love me, and all my earthly wishes will be fulfilled."

Whilst saying these words he had thrown himself at Rosa's feet, clasped her hand in his, and now looked at her with eyes through which beamed the most ardent love.

"I love thee!" whispered the beautiful Rosa, bending her head downwards, whilst her cheeks became crimson.

Then by a sudden movement, as if recollecting herself, she withdrew her hand without allowing Foscarini to kiss it, rose, and going towards the door, said:

"Perhaps our guests are already arrived," and at once entered the hall. Foscarini followed her. Their countenances were beaming with joy.

Rarely had two such kindred spirits met on earth.

CHAPTER II.

THE WITCH.

JUST as Antonio Foscarini and Rosa Centofoglia were entering the reception-hall, Count Guido Bernardi was stepping from a gondola, in one of the most miserable quarters of the town. Ordering the gondolier to stop there till his return, he entered an old tumble-down palace. Hurrying through a large court-yard, he crossed the threshold of a small door, and went up a high, narrow, dark, dirty staircase, with a quickness and ease which proved he was no new visitor to the uninviting place. Having reached the fifth and last story, he knocked at a wretched door, the only one on the small landing-place.

A shrill disagreeable voice from within asked:

"Who is there?"

"Rosalia, don't keep mo waiting here," was the reply, uttered in a rather peevish tone.

In a moment the badly hinged door was thrown wide open, and the young count walked in. The door was immediately reclosed, and then Rosalia said:

"Come in, Guido; sit down and wait a moment. I have a mixture of camomile and poppy-heads simmering at the fire, and must see about it before I have a chat with you, for I own I should be sorry if it were spoiled."

"It would not be a great loss."

"You may think so, but I do not. I have promised it to a sick woman, and I shall get two eggs for it."

"What an acquisition! two eggs!" and Count Guido Bernardi laughed aloud; then added, "You must needs be always drugging people."

His laughter irritated Rosalia, and she retorted in an angry tone:

"It may be no acquisition to you; but to me who, after having served your mother nearly twenty-four years, have been left unprovided for, even two eggs are no trifle."

"Do I not provide you with what I can spare?" answered Guido in a conciliating tone.

"Poor youth! What you give me is barely enough for my daily bread."

"It is not my fault that my mother, in her last moments, chose to leave well-nigh all she possessed to the poor and the Church. I was wronged there, you know, Rosalia. But come, don't be angry with me. I will sit here without moving till your mixture is ready, so that you will neither lose it nor your two eggs."

A cloud overshadowed Rosalia's countenance. Instead of anger it seemed to betoken a feeling akin to pity.

"It is true, Guido," she replied, "it is not your fault, neither was it your mother's."

By this time Guido had seated himself on a stool near a table. Rosalia mixed her decoction, and stirred up the embers. A profound silence ensued; both were seemingly thinking on what must have greatly perplexed them, if one might judge by the contraction of the forehead, said to denote deep or vexatious thoughts.

Excepting the small entrance that led to it, the room they were in was Rosalia's sole apartment. It was very large, but lost much of its size owing to the low ceiling, which just admitted of a man of tolerable height standing upright. About a century previously the walls had been white, at the time we are writing of they were of a deep yellow colour, covered with large black and grey stains. An opening which served as a window let in little light through its broken panes, covered with paper and rags, and in bad weather admitted much rain and wind.

In the middle of the room stood a large table with four stools around it; three were unserviceable, and the fourth, now occupied by Guido, just allowed of a person's sitting on it without falling prostrate on the ground.

In one corner was a bed, the only piece of furniture in the room which, though mean enough, was not broken, and not altogether uncomfortable, and beside it was a small chest. In the opposite corner was a chimney, and on a shelf near it a few broken or cracked plates, and cups and saucers of the commonest earthenware. A few other house and kitchen utensils were placed with some pretence to order on the other side of the room, but they were blackened by long usage, or by the continual smoke which had well-nigh enveloped room, furniture, and mistress.

And this was all that Rosalia possessed after twenty-four years' work! It is true that she had saved a small sum of money, besides some very decent clothing, but hoping to better her fortune, she had invested her money at a high rate of interest, and had only succeeded in losing it all, and with it her best articles of dress. Guido gave her a small allowance, but this not being sufficient for her maintenance, she had resorted to the trade of female quack, or rather of decoction-maker, in order to secure herself a livelihood.

This occupation, added to her tall figure, large black eyes, few scattered white locks, sinister smile, or disagreeable frown, and shrill voice, had caused her to be known by no other name than that of—The Witch!

Furthermore, she was not a Venetian, and although it is the boast of several races, the Venetian amongst the rest, that they are most courteous and indulgent towards foreigners, it is no less certain that the appellation of foreigner aggravates every defect, magnifies every crime, and induces people to believe as solemn truths the most outrageous and unlikely assertions.

This happened to Rosalia.

Her denomination of foreigner, whilst it served to enhance her pretended skill in drugs—which, according to the common belief, had equal power in curing the most opposite diseases and different ailments—contributed in no small degree to give credence to the popular saying that she held communication with the devil, who visited her in person during the night; and the saying was the more readily believed as it was remarked that she never attended Divine service, or went to say the Rosary in the parish church; and the wise said she owed to him her knowledge in the medical science.

It followed, by a contradiction not uncommon even amongst the instructed, and most common amongst the ignorant and superstitious, that no sooner was anyone ill in the neighbourhood, or some unhappy infant teething, but Rosalia was sent for, received with due marks of deference, and her drugs and advice duly appreciated. But whether the sick person was obliged to go to the hospital, died at home, or by some lucky chance or other recovered, the modest fee was no sooner paid into the hands of the female practitioner, than she was declared to be nothing more nor less than a witch, and would on no account be called in, or even spoken to again.

These resolutions, however, were never carried into effect for any length of time, for the moment anyone was taken ill again, Rosalia was sent for in haste, and her mixtures most willingly swallowed.

It must also be said that, although she undertook the treatment of all kinds of diseases, she had not, hitherto at least, performed any of the charms, divinations, etc., by which witchcraft is supposed to work its cures.

Communications with the fiend, alas! she had held, but they had been of another and more serious description, as the reader will see hereafter.

Guido was the first to break the silence that had ensued:

"I suppose, Rosalia, you have already guessed the reason of my visit? It is to bring you that pittance which you say is barely enough for your daily bread."

"I guessed it, and I thank you for it. Forgive those words said in a moment of irritation. I am aware I do not deserve your kindness."

"Yes, you do! You watched over my infancy and boyhood. You were cross, and perhaps unjust, at times; but, on the whole, I owe to you the gratitude one generally pays to the person who has brought one up."

"You owe me nothing. Pray never mention it again or you will force me to refuse your bounty, and consequently to die of hunger."

These words were uttered in one of Rosalia's most disagreeable tones of voice, and a fresh and deeper cloud again hung over her countenance, forcing the young man to more moments of silence, for he now felt, as he had done all his life whenever Rosalia spoke in that determined manner, if not what is called positive fear, at least a sensation which made him most uncomfortable.

In the meantime, having put aside her decoction, carefully covered it, and extinguished the remaining embers, Rosalia drew the small chest near Guido, seated herself on it, took her knitting from off the table, and, in a softened tone, said:

"Indeed I thank you, Guido, for the allowance you bring me so regularly. It is a great comfort to me. I do not know what I should do without it. But why do you look so perplexed and sad? Has some lady-love proved unfaithful?"

"Not exactly unfaithful, for she never loved me. Say, rather, indifferent. But I suspect the cause—nay, I am sure I have accurately guessed it!—and it is this which in truth perplexes and worries me."

"They call me a witch, can I use my witchcraft on your behalf?" said Rosalia, with a slight smile on her cross countenance. "Tell me whom you suspect," she added, in a still more jesting tone and manner, showing her beautiful teeth that had not yet lost their dazzling whiteness, and which seemed to light up her whole face, "of having stolen your lady's heart?"

Guido Bernardi had been, especially of late, so little accustomed to his former nurse's smiles, that he could not help staring at her, and returning the smile, although in the oppression of his perplexing thoughts he felt Rosalia's manner jar on his sensibility at that moment, and he answered seriously:

"You must have guessed I love Marco Centofoglia's rich and lovely daughter?"

Rosalia's countenance changed again. That momentary glimpse of cheerfulness left her. Her lips quivered. She felt as though her voice would refuse its utterance. She bowed her head and knitted furiously, to gain a few minutes' silence, in order to compose her agitated feelings.

Guido, who appeared to be staring at the fireplace, but who in reality was wondering deeply whether he should or should not make his former nurse his confidante, did not observe the sudden change; and after resolving in his own mind to unburden his sorrows, he added:

"Unfortunately I have every reason to believe she does not care for me, but loves the senator Antonio Foscarini."

"So much the better for both," answered Rosalia, without so much as raising her head from her work. "You will never marry her."

"Why so? What reason can there be why I should not marry Rosa Centofoglia!" replied Guido with a painful earnestness in his voice and look.

"I do not wish to make you unhappy, Guido; I speak for your good. Don't set your mind on marrying that girl. She will never be your wife."

"Ah!" answered Guido, with an expression of countenance, and in a voice which showed too clearly the love and deep jealousy that were waging war in his troubled breast. "Ah! witch, as they call you, you have guessed there is no hope for me, that she has accepted my rival, who has possessed himself of her heart, who is greater than I am, who has therefore had better chances of success than I could possibly have; and I—I—miserable wretch, am as nothing in her eyes. If you, Rosalia, are sure of it, as your manner leads me to believe, tell me, oh! do tell me so—I would settle upon you half I possess to know it!"

Rosalia had raised her head from her work. The earnestness of Guido's manner, the pathos of his voice, the expression of sorrow and wrath which she read in his deep blue eyes, the heightened colour of his flushed cheeks, almost startled her. She gazed at him. Her hard countenance seemed to soften down to pity, as she said in an undertone:

"Are you in love, Guido? Poor young man! And you fear another is preferred before you? *It is torture!* and——"

She said no more, and fearing she had disclosed too much of her own feelings, added hastily:

"I am sorry I cannot gratify your wish. I do not know whether the lady prefers another man, or whether she has accepted his hand."

"Do you speak the truth?"

"I do."

"Then wherefore tell me in that positive manner I shall not marry her?"

"That you may not encourage a hopeless affection."

"You speak in enigmas, Rosalia. Do, pray do, explain more clearly what motives you know, or fancy exist, to prevent my obtaining the promise of Rosa's hand."

"I never said you would not obtain the promise of her hand. *That* you may obtain; but I said, and I repeat it, she will never be your wife."

"I cannot understand you, Rosalia. Be more explicit, I implore you! You torture me! but——" and his manner became almost menacing.

"Be calm, young man! You know, by experience, that violence and threats have little effect on me. When was it ever known that Rosalia Leoni feared? I repeat, Guido, be calm, and listen to me."

Here Rosalia made a movement as if to draw the chest nearer to her visitor. She put down her knitting. She arranged the black handkerchief she usually wore crossed over her bosom. She clasped her hands, and held them firmly on her knees. She gave a glance round the room, as if to see that all was in order, but only in reality to gain time, and acquire as much calmness as possible—for she determined within herself to be calm—and then fixing those large black eyes of hers on the young man, who had been watching her attentively, she continued:

"Do you remember a lovely evening at Lucca, about sixteen months ago? I was sitting on a grassy bank on the beautiful shady ramparts which surround the old town, when you happened to pass. Feeling tired, and the spot where I was inviting you to rest, you seated yourself beside me, and fell into a reflective mood, looking at the setting sun, which like a ball of fire seemed to touch the tops of the mountains that separate Lucca from Viareggio. Ah! how well I remember that evening!"

Rosalia paused a moment, and frowned. But she immediately remembered she had determined to be calm, and checking the rising feelings which in spite of her resolve made her heart beat quickly, resumed her conversation:

"It was so calm and quiet. There were only you and I in that spot. On a sudden we heard the noise of rapidly rolling wheels. A superb chariot passed by. You caught a glimpse of Rosa and of—her father, I mean, and turning to me you said: 'I never cared much for riches or titles before, but within the last few months I am glad I am a count, and still more glad that I shall be rich some day.' Guido, do you remember my answer?"

"I can't say I do, very clearly at least."

"Then I will remind you of it. I said, 'Guido, you will not be rich.' Answer me, are you rich? Did I prophesy the truth, or not?"

"And all these words are merely meant to remind me of a thorn that is in my heart, which may, perhaps, end in being the cause of my greatest misfortune—that of seeing a wealthier suitor preferred before me. I know I am not rich. I am poor. After having spoiled me with her blind fondness, my mother suddenly listens in her last moments to her covetous confessor, and bequeaths nearly all her fortune to others. I was wronged—shockingly wronged! My mother must have answered for the evil she has brought on me."

"Your mother was blameless. I have told you so, often enough."

"Have you disclosed all you wished to tell me?" asked Guido, in a peevish manner.

"Not quite," answered Rosalia, in a voice whose unnatural softness showed how far it was at variance with what she inwardly felt. "Not quite. I have not reminded you of your wrongs in order to pain you, but to warn you, that as my prophecy has once been fulfilled with regard to your fortune, it may be so now respecting your marriage."

"Yes, for once you have really been a witch; but you shall not succeed the second time. No, Rosalia, I promise you, you shall not. I would shrink from nothing to obtain Rosa's hand."

Guido spoke but too truly. There was nothing he would have shrunk from in order to become the possessor of the loveliest and richest of the daughters of Venice!

Rosalia was going to take up her knitting again, but the young man rose.

"Good-bye, witch!" said he; "as you will act like one, you may as well be called so."

"Call me what you like best, it is all the same," she answered with great composure.

By this time Guido had reached the outer door. Rosalia hastened after him, holding a flickering light in one hand, and unlatching the door with the other.

"Let me at least light you downstairs," she added.

"Don't trouble yourself. I am used to the staircase. I shall be at the foot in a minute."

Saying these words he almost pushed her inside the room, and closed the door. Then descending with singular speed, considering the total darkness, he crossed the court-yard briskly, and sprung into his gondola. He ordered the gondolier to row to the Palace Centofoglia, seated himself, leaned back, and fell into a profound reverie.

When Rosalia again found herself alone in her cheerless room, and remembered how unceremoniously her visitor had left her, she felt an inward satisfaction at his evident vexation about her prophecy, but her eyes fell on the few silver coins he had brought her, and she sighed as she said:

"Poor Guido is kinder to me than I deserve!"

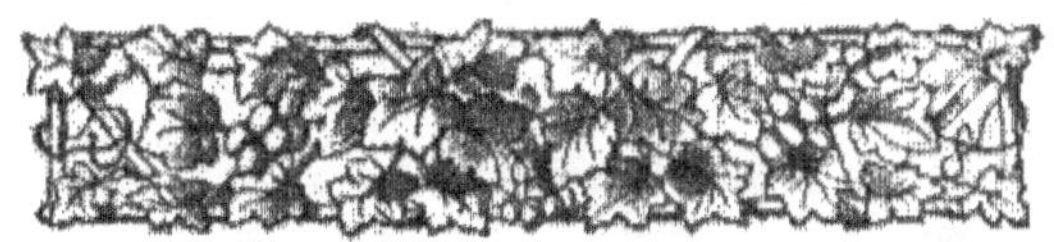

CHAPTER III.

A CONVERSATION.

IT is a well-known fact. Tell anyone, however meek, humble, and prudent he may be; tell him he cannot, or may not, act up to any long-desired or carefully-schemed plan; place before him all the trouble, the suffering, nay, the danger it will bring upon him; make use of the most persuasive arguments which affection or interest finds so readily at hand—and all will be useless. Ninety-nine times out of a hundred you will only have helped immeasurably to bring to pass the very thing you wished to prevent.

This was the case with Guido. For several weeks he had been turning over in his mind whether he should ask Rosa's hand at once. He would not have delayed so long, or revolved it so often in his mind, as he knew himself to be a favourite of her father's, had it not been for the thought, that although possessor of an illustrious name and title, he was the owner of a very moderate fortune indeed. Had he therefore the right to expect that the loveliest girl and richest heiress in Venice should bear his name? Where was the sumptuous palace to which he should conduct his bride? Where were the costly jewels he should present to her as the heirlooms destined to adorn the ladies of the noble Bernardi family? These had been once his expectation, whereas nothing but the recollection of them now remained to him. Every day, every moment as it passed, he felt more deeply how much his mother had wronged him.

It had been his ill-luck to fall in love with the rich patrician's daughter, but it was his still greater misfortune to be cursed with the most jealous of dispositions. Had no one else visited the Centofoglia family, whom he had reason to suspect of possessing a better chance than he of obtaining Rosa's hand, reflection and the fear of a refusal would at length have quelled the gentler passion of love; but jealousy having once entered into his heart, all reflection, all sense of proper and manly pride, even common justice, were impossible to him.

And now his old nurse's words, added to the fulfilment of her first prophecy, tortured him to the quick. As he leaned back in the gondola, his right hand thrust through his beautiful golden hair, he firmly resolved to make good his resolute answer to Rosalia, that he would obtain Rosa's hand, that he would shrink from nothing, literally nothing, in order to gratify his passion, or prevent another from enjoying what would in all probability be denied to him. He felt he could not support his present state much longer, and decided that, laying aside pride, he would seize the very first opportunity of seeking a private interview with Marco

Centofoglia, in order to ask him at once for his fair daughter's hand. In the event of a refusal he would then determine upon the best course to pursue, so as to thwart his rival's success.

Having thus arranged matters to his satisfaction, by a sudden reaction he felt almost light-hearted, and driving away the busy suggestions reason strove to enforce, he longed to feel the boat stop. It did stop at last, at the entrance of one of the finest palaces on the Canal Grande.

"You need not wait for me, Bartolommeo," said Guido to the sleepy gondolier.

"Signore, the other gondoliers are waiting. Why should I not wait? Do I not row as well as they?"

"I spoke thus because you seemed tired and half asleep."

"So I am. I sat up the whole of last night."

"Was there some ball which required the continual attendance of gondolas and gondoliers?"

"No, signore. My wife is ill, and——"

"What a model husband you are, Bartolommeo," replied Guido, jokingly. "Then you sat up all night with your spouse?"

"Not that either."

"You were sitting up with—I mean, making love?" and Guido cast a mischievous look on the gondolier, accompanied by the most good-humoured smile.

"Bartolommeo Reni, signore, was not making love, never has made love since his marriage," answered the gondolier, drawing himself up.

"What were you about then? Why, man, how mysterious you look!"

"First, I went and got a physician for my wife——"

"And did you find one who left his warm bed to go and visit the wife of a poor gondolier?"

"I did not go for a real physician——"

"Then you went for a quack?" And Guido laughed outright.

The gondolier by no means enjoyed Guido's laughter, and answered in a lower tone of voice, and in a very serious manner:

"In my neighbourhood—that is, at the very spot where I first conducted you this evening, there lives an old woman, who knows as much as a physician who has spent years of his life at Padua. They call her the witch——" Here Bartolommeo devoutly crossed himself, saying "St. Mark defend us!"

"Ah!" explained Guido, interrupting the boatman, then checking himself quickly, for he would not have allowed anyone, not even the humble gondolier, to know of his acquaintance with a witch, he said to himself, "It is poor Bartolommeo, after all, who is to pay the two eggs." Then added aloud:

"St. Mark defend us, indeed! And what makes you call on a witch, Bartolommeo?"

"I am poor, signore, at least I am so at present. Later on in life I shall, perhaps, not be so poor. But just now 'tis well to have a doctor who prepares his own medicines, and is pleased with a very small fee. Besides, she is clever; she has cured my sister-in-law of an incurable disease. Although a witch, it is better to employ her than go to the hospital, or die."

"So you went and got her, and then I suppose you accompanied her home, and stayed chatting with her, so that the night was passed meritoriously enough, old man, was it not?" and Guido tapped the gondolier on the shoulder.

"I did not so much as wait to see the witch. I knocked at her door, told her my wife was ill, and went away instantly," answered Bartolommeo, looking important.

"Did you go to preside at the Council of Ten, then?" replied Guido, who in the exuberance of his spirits could not help turning the gondolier's words into ridicule.

"I did not preside at the Council of Ten; but . . . Ah! Signore Conte, St. Mark help us all! I can say it with truth. Don't laugh, signore. The Council of Ten is the salvation of the State."

Guido recollected himself. Who dared so much as smile when the dreaded Council of Ten was mentioned!

"True, Bartolommeo," he added gravely. "I am not laughing. I am too good a patriot to laugh at that most honourable and honoured council—as you justly say, it is the salvation of the State. As long as it exists Venice is safe."

Guido did not think so, but he thought it wise to say so.

"After all," added he, "you have not told me where and how you passed the night."

"In serving my country, signore, for which I would

give soul and body," answered Bartolommeo, bowing his head, and speaking so low that it was hardly possible to understand him. "A relation of mine died in battle. We have all been honourable patriots," he added louder.

To speak the truth, Bartolommeo Reni was, or rather had been, an honest man. He firmly believed he served his country, for which he did risk, if not the welfare of his body, at least that of his soul. But Guido's knowledge of the laws and customs of his country, coupled with the remembrance of the gondolier's allusion that perhaps in the future he might not be so poor, awakened certain suspicions in his mind, which made him wish he had never joked with the old man, and never mentioned the Council of Ten. He took good care, however, not to let him suspect he had guessed in what his services consisted. He made up his mind to employ him more instead of less frequently, in order to make him his friend; and giving him a double fee, he said:

"Here, old man, I have made you lose time in talking, it is but fitting I should pay the penalty. Take this, it is a double fee. Wait for me if you like."

He waved his hand to the gondolier, and was already entering the stately door of the Centofoglia Palace when he heard his answer:

"Your humble servant, signore; may St. Mark grant you long life and health."

CHAPTER IV.

THE PATRICIAN'S HALL.

AS soon as Guido had crossed the threshold, a stately porter accosted him, bowing profoundly, and afterwards followed him at a respectful distance in an obsequious manner. On the approach of a man-servant in full livery, he made a motion of his hand, which was meant to signify "I consign this gentleman to your care," and forthwith retired, returning to his post.

Count Guido Bernardi walked through elegant porticoes to the foot of the princely staircase. Here another pantomimic consignment took place to another man-servant; and a third and a fourth were repeated before, having crossed several superb apartments, he was introduced into the elegant hall where Marco Centofoglia, his beautiful daughter Rosa, and two other guests were assembled.

The hall was spacious and so lofty that the beautiful paintings on the ceiling, though the production of no mean pencil, were almost invisible. On the walls hung several of Titian's and Giorgioni's masterpieces.

On one side, in the most conspicuous part of the room, between the two windows and opposite the door by which the guests entered, stood a cabinet of costly wood, inlaid with silver, and of exquisite workmanship.

Divans of rich blue damask silk were ranged round the apartment. From the ceiling hung a lighted chandelier of the cut glass for which Venice was and is still famous, which, reflecting in its many devices the several lights it bore, appeared to double and treble their splendour, and almost prevent the strongest sight from resting on it long.

As soon as the man-servant announced Count Guido Bernardi, Marco Centofoglia rose and, going towards the door, met him, shaking hands cordially with him, and saying:

"You favour us late this evening, count, with your welcome company."

By this time Rosa had also come forward to receive Guido, the guests had risen, and after the usual commonplace phrases, which all times and countries have considered, and still consider, as necessary marks of gentility and good-breeding when a visit is to be paid or received, all returned to their places.

Refusing the offered seat on the divan to the left of his host, on the plea that he would not interrupt the general conversation, Guido took a crimson velvet chair which happened to be near, and placing it between the two small groups which composed the company, sat on it, in a very different mood from that in which he had entered.

We may as well explain at once the cause of this change.

One of the guests was a venerable and learned friar of the Dominican Order (Father Pio). He was sitting next to Marco Centofoglia. The two were talking politics and theology, and discussing the famous question of the differences between the Papal Court and the Republic. What did Guido care for that? He knew Father Pio, and appreciated his talents, but cared not to enter into the intricate question which formed his favourite theme of conversation. He accordingly pretended to listen with interest, whilst his whole mind was concentrated elsewhere.

On the corner of the same divan, near one of the windows, sat Rosa. If an artist or poet had desired to behold, as in a vision, a being of unsurpassing beauty, he need only have gazed on the daughter of Marco Centofoglia.

She was of middle height, her figure slight, her complexion of marble fairness. Her features were perfectly symmetrical, her cheeks of a rosy hue. Her eyes were large, dark blue, tender, sweet, but unlike the generality of Northern blue eyes, full of expression; at times they even seemed to flash, always to reflect the splendour of her Southern clime. Her rich auburn hair was a fitting ornament to her well-shaped head. The superiority of her beauty such that she was named by universal consent the Rose of Venice!

On the corner of the divan opposite the one where she was sitting, with the embrasure of the window alone between them, the two corners of the divan forming the ends of a diagonal line of no great length, sat a man. His age was about thirty; his rank that of senator of the State, and ex-ambassador to the Court of France; his name (the reader has already guessed) Antonio Foscarini. His whole soul seemed absorbed in gazing on the wondrously beautiful face before him. Ah! Antonio Foscarini, would thou hadst never basked in the sun of those deep blue eyes! Would that thy lot had led thee anywhere rather than within the precincts of that noble palace!

Love and Death often go hand-in-hand. The one sweetens for a moment the cup of life, the other as soon embitters it. But in no instance has the one followed so closely upon the other as in that of the heroic and unfortunate Antonio Foscarini. For no sooner did the arrow of Love point its shaft to his noble heart than Death, the grim tyrant, aimed his also. The music of whispered words of love no sooner resounded in his delighted ears than the approaching sounds of death's heavy knell re-echoed them!

It was certainly not the first time Guido Bernardi beheld Rosa and Foscarini talking together. It was not the first time that jealousy of the latter had disturbed his heart, had compelled his better nature to lie dormant, and aroused his evil passions into the determination of risking all in order to frustrate his rival's success. But somehow or other he seemed never to have beheld before such evident tokens of their mutual love.

Foscarini was by habit taciturn, and was not exactly what the frivolous would have called fascinating. On that memorable evening it appeared to Guido that the few words he said were more animated than usual, and that his countenance bore an expression of unmistakable joy, almost of triumph, which made him fear, what we know had that same evening occurred, viz., that Foscarini had already superseded him, and obtained, not the hand of the fair maiden—alas! that was her father's gift alone—but the avowal of her love.

The appearance of Rosa's two lovers, to an eye experienced in such matters, showed in no small degree the jarring contrast of their feelings. Guido was sombre, jealousy supplanting love made him indulge in thoughts full of hatred, and set him against everyone and everything, not excluding the old witch Rosalia, whose ominous words the sight of his rival brought back despite himself with redoubled force to his mind.

Antonio Foscarini felt light-hearted, not because a feeling akin to jealousy never had or ever could enter his mind—we cannot say so much in man's favour, though we may be sure it never could or would have caused his noble heart to harbour one base feeling—but because, as we already know, he really had no reason to consider Guido in the light of a rival. He was certain of Rosa's affection, and that assurance made him pleased with everyone and everything; and thus, turning towards the count, he said in a most friendly tone:

"My friend, will you come and judge in this long-disputed question between the Signora Rosa and myself?"

"I am not a fit man to be a judge," was the caustic answer.

"Yes, you are," exclaimed Rosa. "It is I who say so. You are. Come nearer to us, and listen."

As Rosa uttered the last words Foscarini rose, and going to Guido, put his hand on the back of his chair, as if to force him to rise, saying, at the same time:

"Count, you must come and decide between us. You cannot refuse when a lady bids you."

Guido felt strongly inclined to persist in his refusal, and was going to say something to that effect, when he remembered he was a gentleman; a gentleman cannot refuse when a lady orders, and he rose reluctantly enough, obeying Foscarini's request to place himself on the divan next to Rosa.

The question discussed by the lovers, and which had been interrupted by Guido's entrànce, would have been an odd one in the present day, but by no means such at the time in which our interlocutors lived.

"Now, Signor Guido," said Rosa, turning towards him and looking him full in the face, "tell us if you believe in the stories that are told of prophecies respecting future happiness or unhappiness? Have you ever known any that have been fulfilled? Anto——" She checked herself and blushed. "Signor Antonio will not hear of such a thing. He says they are all old women's fables."

Guido had not failed to notice the half-pronounced word, and the blush which followed.

"Ah," thought he to himself, "she already calls him by his Christian name."

He felt more put out than before, and making no small effort to appear at ease, he replied:

"Signora, I can hardly tell you. At times they may—by chance, I mean, chance only—be fulfilled."

"That is what I have been saying," said Foscarini; "at times chance has brought to pass some strange prophecy, and that has helped to bestow credence on such nonsense. They who firmly believe in the care an All-wise Providence takes of Its children, cannot even suppose that It would allow Its will to be known beforehand by some ignorant and generally wicked old woman."

"That is true," answered the fair Rosa. "I know I ought not to believe such follies, and yet I cannot divest myself of the belief that it may—well, let us even say by chance—that it may be fulfilled."

"You were going, just before the Signor Conte favoured us with his welcome company, to tell me a story in support of your partial belief——"

"That story relates to myself," said Rosa, interrupting Foscarini, and—and certainly cannot interest Signor Guido."

Guido held down his head and bit his lips, saying to himself:

"It interests Foscarini then, and she knows *that*, and thinks it cannot interest me."

"I am sure that is the very reason it will please Signor Guido to hear it," replied Foscarini. "Is it not so, count?" he added, looking at Guido. "Besides, it may help you in your new office of judge."

"I beg," answered Guido, raising his head, but looking at neither of his two interlocutors—"I beg the Signora Rosa to believe it will interest me greatly to hear any story she may have to relate."

"In that case I will repeat it;" and Rosa related Rosalia's prediction respecting herself, adding: "And now you both see that the prophecy has in part, at least, been fulfilled, for my dearest mother's loss has caused me to shed so many bitter tears!"

"It is the course of nature," said Foscarini, looking at her tenderly. "Unless death overtakes us in youth we must mourn our parents' loss. Your sainted mother's death does not constitute you the most unhappy of mortals. Afflictions are wholesome lessons, for which we should, as Christians, be thankful. I consider death itself a blessing. The only real misfortunes in life are sin and dishonour."

"Signor Antonio, you ought to have been a priest," put in Guido, ironically; "you would have made a good preacher."

"No, thank you. I had rather be what I am," replied Foscarini, smiling, and casting a significant look at Rosa.

It did not escape Guido. But Rosa gave him little time for reflection; she turned towards him, saying:

"After all, count, you have not decided who is right and who is wrong."

"Neither can I, signora."

"Then I will pronounce the sentence myself!" exclaimed Rosa, playfully. "I will say as Signor Antonio Foscarini has just now said: I am not the most unhappy of mortals; and I will add that this evening I am one of the happiest, and so the prophecy has not been fulfilled. Is my judgment correct?" she added with almost childish complaisance, expecting her sentence would be approved.

"Most correct," said Foscarini, with love gleaming in his eyes.

"Most righteous," subjoined Guido, with hatred lurking in his heart.

So saying he rose, and having taken leave of the small party, withdrew. Father Pio and Antonio Foscarini soon after followed his example.

That evening, when Rosa entered her room, she felt happier than she had ever felt before. But joy's favourite haunts are the borders of sorrow. The greater the enjoyment of the one, the nearer the approach of the other. Not quite twenty-four hours more of happiness were to be her lot on earth, then, and for the remainder of her life, sorrow, affliction, woe!

CHAPTER V.

THE PROPOSAL.

GUIDO had not had an opportunity of executing his resolution of asking Rosa's hand. Goaded on by his increasing jealousy, he purposed doing so the next morning.

About eleven o'clock he entered Marco's private drawing-room, the owner was wont to call it his study, instead of which it resembled the luxurious saloon of an elegant lady: the predominant feature in Marco's character being a love of comfort, luxury, and show. We are apt to be very bold in soliloquy. When alone, fancying and repeating to ourselves long conversations with invisible beings, putting into their mouths the very words to which we can give an appropriate answer, we get on famously. Nothing equals the moral courage of our arguments, the clearness of our conceptions, and we fancy ourselves perfectly ready to sustain any combat, however arduous it may prove. But when reality succeeds the workings of the imagination, and instead of an invisible being a real man or woman stands before us, and to our share falls only half the conversation, and we are obliged to suit our answers to what our antagonist says, the whole affair changes its aspect. Our courage fails, and self-confidence is apt to abandon us. What is still worse, the arguments often broached are so new, the circumstances in which we are placed so unforeseen, that we find to our great regret we might as well not have passed whole hours in preparatory talk; not one word then said can we make use of now!

Thus Guido had imagined what he thought the most suitable speech possible, the most likely to influence Marco's mind in his favour, and consequently to cause him to grant his request. He thought he would be dignified, he would not sue too humbly, he would leave himself open an honourable retreat if defeated; but when he entered that elegant room, and the contrast between its costly furniture and his comparatively humble home struck him more forcibly than it had ever done before; he felt a sensation of abasement assail him, feared he had placed his hopes too high, and discovered the perfect uselessness of the flowery speech he had planned, of which he could not repeat a single word. Marco came to his aid.

"Well, my friend, you look thoughtful this morning. What is the matter?"

"I should like to——"

He hesitated; not one fine phrase would in any way enter into his mind.

"You should like to——?" answered Marco, repeating his words by way of encouragement.

"To ask you a favour."

He had no sooner uttered the words than he thought:

"What a fool I am! I have begun precisely as I did not intend. However, the die is cast; may I have courage for what is coming."

To his intense delight Marco answered:

"There is no one on earth I would oblige so willingly as you, my dear young friend."

"Suppose my request should prove fruitless, at least assure me you will not deprive me of your regard."

Guido said these last words in order, should Marco refuse him his daughter's hand, not to be obliged to consider himself, as in honour bound, banished from the palace.

"If what you mean to ask me be so entirely out of my power to bestow, be assured my friendship will never fail you."

"May I presume to nourish the fond hope of becoming your son-in-law?"

In the most hidden recesses of his heart Marco had often wished that Guido might come to this point. He therefore answered in a tone of undisguised delight:

"You may."

In Guido's countenance there gleamed a joy he had never felt before. He had attained the climax of his hopes; as for what Rosa would say, though he justly feared she did not love him, he did not care much. He knew she must obey her father, and that he should triumph over a rival, which was what he most wished for. He clasped Marco's proffered hand and exclaimed:

"You bestow life upon me?" Then, out of pretended deference for Rosa, he added: "Another's consent is needed, however."

"You mean my daughter's?"

"Of course. Is she not the principal person to be thought of?"

"Rosa will not so much as dream of contradicting *me*. You may expect it without apprehension."

"Expecting is exactly what a lover cannot submit to. I should like to know my fate as soon as possible."

"As for what you call your fate, you may take my word for it, it is settled. As for your hurry, I enter into your feelings. I shall acquaint Rosa with your proposal this very evening; if you will call a little earlier than usual, we can talk the matter over before we appoint the day of the betrothal."

Guido assented, and left. In going downstairs he almost fancied himself already master of that splendid palace; his heart beat quicker, and his cheeks flushed with elation.

Marco also felt a great inward satisfaction. He loved wealth, not so much for itself as for the comforts and luxuries it produced. He had those comforts and those luxuries in greater proportion than any other individual in Venice; it was not therefore necessary to seek a rich man as a husband for his daughter. It sufficed that he was of noble birth, and agreeable to himself. Guido possessed these qualities—he sought no further, and did not so much as think whether his daughter might not feel a positive dislike to him. In settling on a husband for her he did not reflect—too often parents who dispose tyrannically of their daughters' hands do not—on the relationship of husband, but on that of son-in-law. If the *son-in-law* was all one could wish for, it mattered little what the *husband* might be. *That* was only a secondary consideration. Full of these thoughts he entered at once into Rosa's room.

That room had been his uncle's five-and-twenty years before. When it was given to Rosa it was newly fitted up. It was a beautiful apartment. Elegance was visible in every article. The walls were hung with pink silk. The bed was of ebony and gold, the covering trimmed with rich lace. A Madonna of Raphael, some other valuable pictures, a costly cabinet, a tall looking-glass in a superb frame, a table beautifully carved, and several chairs of similar workmanship, completed the furniture.

Rosa was sitting near one of the windows embroidering an altar-cloth. She was engaged in such deep thought that she was not aware of her father's presence till he stood before her. She started, but recovering herself quickly, rose and kissed his hand.

"My dear child," said he, seating himself beside her and smiling cheerfully, "I am the bearer of most delightful news. Nothing short of an offer of marriage."

Rosa's thoughts flew to Antonio Foscarini.

"Ah!" said she to herself, "he has called this morning and spoken with papa."

Marco continued:

"Are you glad?"

Rosa did not raise her eyes from her work, but answered:

"It depends, dear papa, on who it is that is come to make this proposal."

"Oh! as for that, I am sure you will be pleased. So sure am I that I have already given my full and entire consent."

Rosa lifted her eyes from her work and fixed them on her father. Her bosom heaved tumultuously.

"It is Count Guido Bernardi."

She turned pale, her heart seemed to cease to beat, but only for a moment; her dying mother's advice flashed across her mind, and emboldened by those words that echoed in her ears, she stoutly answered:

"But, papa, I do not love Count Guido Bernardi, and I never shall. I cannot, therefore, marry him."

Marco did not expect so decided an answer. He was somewhat disconcerted, and replied with the ever-repeated and rarely-convincing maxim:

"Love will come in time. And after all, child, what do you wish for? Could you have expected better? He is one of the handsomest young men I ever saw. He is highly instructed, he is of very noble birth——"

"I remember, papa, your telling me almost these very words once in Lucca," said Rosa, interrupting her father. "But I never could see what there is so pleasing in Count Guido Bernardi."

"He has always been a great favourite of mine."

"I know that. But, dear papa, he has never been and never will be *my* favourite."

Marco here lost his patience, and answered in a hurried manner:

"Indeed, Rosa, I am not going to allow this insolence any longer. You have been a spoiled child hitherto, and have always had a will of your own. Now I will have my own way. I have pledged my word to Count Guido Bernardi that you shall be his wife, and there is nothing further to be said or done on the subject."

He then rose to leave the apartment. The words uttered in that very room five and twenty years before, "I should in duty bound respect her inclinations," were totally forgotten by him. There is not a greater destroyer of memory than selfishness!

Rosa did not lose courage, but rising also, and putting her hand on her father's arm, she calmly and firmly replied:

"Dear papa, I am sorry to displease you, but I cannot help it. I cannot marry a man I do not love. Tell him so at once, and if he be an honourable man he will be the first to ask you to retract your word. Papa, I repeat I cannot obey you. Be good to me, as you have ever been, and do not wish to seal my unhappiness."

The last words were uttered in a humble and supplicating tone. They might have had some effect on another father's heart. They had none on Marco's, for his was that perfect selfishness that nothing moves.

He was proud of Rosa, and he loved her; as far as *he* could love, viz., as far as his happiness or wishes were not interfered with. The only person he had truly loved during his whole life had been Rosalia, and the reader knows that when self-love interfered, even that love had been subdued. How much easier, then, was it now to overcome the comparatively feeble affection he felt for his daughter! He answered her harshly, as he pushed away her hand:

"It is a pretty thing to hear a daughter oppose her father's wishes in this manner! But," he added, in a cold, ironical voice, "poor child, how mistaken you are if you think I will ever give up Count Guido Bernardi!" and he left the room.

"Yes," said poor Rosa to herself, as she sat down again—"Yes, Antonio; how truly did you say, ''Tis only in heaven that love blooms unalloyed.'"

Her hands fell on her lap, and she remained some time in deep thought and in harassing perplexity.

"Shall I tell Antonio, or shall I not?" said she. "Yes, I will acquaint him with the proposal my father has had made him. He has a right to hear all from my lips ere he is told by another. My father does not suspect I love him, and together we may hit upon some plan tending to avert from me so sad a doom."

Her soliloquy was interrupted by the call to dinner. Her father did not mention their morning's talk, but his manner was cold and severe. When the repast was over she returned to her room, refused to go out in her gondola, and watched with anxious impatience for the welcome moment of Foscarini's arrival. At length he was announced. She sprang from her chair, and the next minute was seated beside him in the hall.

CHAPTER VI.

HONOUR.

WITH a lover's fond solicitude, Antonio Foscarini saw there was a change in Rosa's countenance. A melancholy agitation was but too visible in her beautiful eyes. Her manner was affectionate, yet hurried. She often looked towards the several doors, as though fearing the entrance of an intruder. It was evident she wished to say something, but did not know how to begin. He reflected that it was his duty to help her; besides, he was most anxious to know what troubled her. Taking her hand, therefore, and looking at her earnestly, he said:

"Rosa——"

"Don't call me Rosa again," she exclaimed, interrupting him. A tear glistened in her eye; then she added, with sudden vehemence: "Yes, call me so again. Call me so always, though I may not hear it."

"What has happened? Rosa, tell me—do tell me."

"But yesterday I was so happy!"

Her tears now began to fall fast.

"And you will still and ever be happy, even if I give my life for your happiness," answered Foscarini, pressing her hand to his lips.

His words encouraged her. A gleam of hope entered again into her mind, and she thought that perhaps she should still be able to call herself his wife; so without hesitation she related to him, word for word, her conversation with her father. By the time she had finished Antonio Foscarini was as pale as death. Nothing short of agony was expressed in his countenance. Rosa saw it, and her hopes faded again.

"Not twenty-four hours' happiness!" said he, with a deep, heartfelt sigh, "and then——"

He did not finish the sentence.

Rosa looked at him, but did not answer. After a short pause he continued:

"Rosa, my love, I will always call you mine, though mine you ne'er may be!"

"Never? How can anyone, even my father, oblige me to marry a man I do not love?" replied Rosa, with a resolution in her voice and manner which surprised Foscarini, and made him say to himself, "How innocent thou art! How little dost thou understand this vile world's base devices!"

"Rosa, my experience tells me that your father will never retract his word."

"Ah! he may not allow me to marry you, but he cannot force me to marry a man I could never love. I can always be faithful to you, and *I will be so.*"

That was a delicious moment in which Foscarini

heard from Rosa's lips so spontaneous a promise of everlasting love. He pressed her hand more affectionately. He kissed it with greater passion.

"And you," he said, "you will be the star whose light will be my only guide on earth! But," his countenance clouded again, "we must part. Though for ever——"

"For ever?" said Rosa, in painful astonishment.

"Yes, for ever, Rosa. You would see with what joy I would give my life for you, could you read my poor aching heart; but I cannot part with that sense of honour which alone makes me worthy of your love. Your father has accepted Count Guido Bernardi's offer. I must withdraw."

"Will you leave me alone, then? Am I to fight the battle alone?"

"My visits would only make matters worse."

"We may correspond, at least. I can find a way of having my letters conveyed to you. By this means you could advise me."

"Rosa, cease to torture me, for such it is," answered Foscarini, putting his hand to his forehead, as if to still the throbbing of his temples. "I cannot allow you to write to me in secret. It might be your ruin."

Rosa felt she could say nothing more. She thought that perhaps she had even said too much. She sighed and replied:

"Then are we to meet no more? You will often pass by this palace——"

"Never," exclaimed Foscarini, interrupting her;

"never! Do you think I could live in Venice without seeing you? No; I am but a man. I could not attain such a degree of heroism. To avoid sin we must first learn to avoid temptation."

"And you would even leave Venice?"

Rosa held down her head.

"For your sake, because my soul loves you, Rosa, with unquenchable love. I shall leave Venice to-morrow. I will carry your image engraven in my heart, and in far-off lands I shall ever think of *you* alone."

Rosa did not answer immediately. A thought had struck her. She would give him the most precious thing she possessed, the miniature of Our Blessed Lady, her mother's dying gift. It might protect him in danger, comfort him in trouble, and should his love ever begin to waver it might bring back his wandering thoughts and strengthen his fidelity.

"Will you at least," said she, after this short pause, "accept a keepsake from me? It is the most precious thing I possess."

Her voice was so sweetly supplicating that Foscarini thought his sufferings had now reached an almost insupportable height.

"Do you ask me whether I would? Let your own heart answer for me."

"If I go to fetch it now all will be discovered. I know papa is in his study, and may pass through the gallery that leads to my room. Could you not come once more? Yes, do come. Come once more?"

"I don't know what I should do were I to meet Count Guido Bernardi again," answered Foscarini, hesitatingly.

"Come into the garden a few minutes after twilight. If you enter by the small door which is quite close to the Spanish ambassador's premises no one in the palace will know. I often go at twilight to look at my favourite plants. I will take care to open the door."

Could Antonio Foscarini refuse the earnest appeal of her whom he adored? Could he deprive himself of the happiness of seeing her once more? Had he done so he would have been more than mortal.

"I will come," he therefore answered, "if you, my love, will assure me that no harm will befall you; for it is imprudent," he added, looking at her fixedly.

"Fear not, Antonio; I am sure no one will discover anything. Let us fix our meeting for the day after to-morrow."

"Very well. Need I assure you I shall be punctual? Farewell, my love."

Foscarini pressed Rosa to his heart and quitted the hall.

CHAPTER VII.

THE SPY.

TOWARDS the foot of the princely staircase he met Count Guido Bernardi. The latter's keen eye observed Foscarini's deathly paleness. The distant inclination of the head in return to his very courteous bow did not escape him. He augured success to himself; he said, "For once I have been fortunate," and he stalked up the stairs in triumph.

He found Marco Centofoglia waiting for him in his study. The wealthy patrician had been in his arm-chair for the last hour brooding over the awkwardness of the communication he was bound to make. At last he resolved he would get rid of the nuisance as quickly as possible, and inform Guido of Rosa's refusal as soon as he saw him. The moment he beheld his young friend he advanced towards him, and assuming an air of gaiety, said, taking Guido's hand in both his:

"My son, no prize worth having can be won without wrestling for."

Guido understood some difficulty had arisen to delay the speedy realisation of his ardent desire, and his elated spirits sinking, he fell into a dejected mood. Marco perceived it.

"You will only enjoy your happiness the more if you suffer a little in obtaining it. Sit down here beside me," added he, pointing to an elegant couch, "and listen to what has passed betwixt my daughter and myself. I am in honour bound to keep nothing from you, not even a single syllable."

Guido listened with intense attention. He felt assured that Rosa loved Antonio Foscarini. He knew that it was his duty to withdraw, but when and where has a jealous man had a lofty sense of honour? This basest of passions must ever lead the unhappy being possessed of it to still baser deeds. Guido felt he *would* not leave the way clear for Foscarini. He *would* not think of honour, but of thwarting his rival and gratifying himself. He accordingly answered Marco's last words: "My son, be resigned; she shall be yours. Such is my will. 'Tis only the work of a little time and patience," thus:

"I will strive to act up to your advice, though I feel resignation would be a hard task, an insupportable one did I not daily visit you and see *her*."

"You are not only to come so often, but even oftener," rejoined Marco, with warmth. "Your place is at my table. I have considered you as my son from the moment you asked my daughter's hand. Let us now go to the hall."

They both entered it.

"How strange," said Marco, "no one is here this evening. As for Father Pio, I do not wonder at his absence; he is gone into the country for a couple of days. But Rosa, and the senator Antonio Foscarini, he never misses being here at this hour."

"I met him at the foot of the stairs."

"Ah! then he is come and gone. Strange; I esteem him much. His character is noble and elevated. Do you know, Guido, I feel almost honoured by his friendship."

"I think the signorina is also pleased with his visits."

"Of course she is. Who would not be?"

Guido wished to say something as to his suspicions that Foscarini was the cause of Rosa's refusal, but he judged it prudent not to enlighten Marco's mind, for thought he, "Suppose his high opinion of my rival makes him regret his resolution to bestow his daughter on me! No; I had better say nothing. 'Il silenzio e' d'oro' (Silence is golden) says an old proverb."

At this moment a servant made his appearance, carrying a silver waiter laden with glasses filled with Cyprus wine.

"Inquire why the signorina does not come to the hall," said Marco, after the servant had handed wine to Guido and himself.

"The signorina has sent word, signor, that she feels indisposed, and cannot receive this evening."

The blood rushed to Guido's cheeks, and as suddenly left them. He called to mind Foscarini's paleness, his distant bow; he felt still surer that he and Rosa loved each other, had exchanged vows of unalterable love, and that she had acquainted him with his proposal. He felt mortified, and in a fever of impatience to discover the best way of thwarting his rival.

But Marco, who saw nothing extraordinary in Foscarini's early visit and his daughter's absence, taking for granted she did not feel very well, left Guido no time to concoct the desired scheme, and turning towards him said jocosely:

"My son, neither you nor I seem much inclined for an idle *tête-à-tête*. Suppose we play a game at chess?"

"I am at your service," replied Guido, striving to look calm.

"Let us begin, then."

Everything was soon arranged for the game. Marco played in earnest. Guido did not know what he was about. Though a good chess-player, he allowed Marco to win on, until at last he could hardly help smiling at his own ill-luck. Marco laughed, and the game being finished, said:

"This evening was not exactly well chosen for you, a lover, to win at chess!"

They soon parted, and within a few minutes Guido was reclining in his gondola, engaged in deep thought. After a little while passed in this way, having revolved in his mind every argument and plan he could devise, he came to these conclusions, viz., that Foscarini was the *sole cause* of his failure, and Foscarini must be got rid of. But how! That was the question.

"I am not," thought he, "powerful enough to induce our Government to send him again to some distant embassy. True, but if I am not, Father Pio is, and might help me; but how can I even broach the subject to him? Naturally he would say: 'Give your reasons for wishing Foscarini's absence.' Besides, he is *his* friend, and I am only an acquaintance. If I could adduce some political reason, the friar, with all his holiness, might, nay, would, I am sure, forget his friendship. But there is none I could validly prove. And, after all, would this prevent his union with Rosa? Would it not rather produce in woman's constant heart a deeper and more lasting affection? His death would be the only remedy. His death!"

Guido started as though afraid of himself, but the awful suggestion came again and again. Jealousy spoke louder still, and alas! the demoniacal thought was no difficult one to put into execution in those times, easier perhaps in Venice than elsewhere. In a moment the conversation of the evening before with the gondolier struck him with new force, and raising the curtain he had before carefully closed, he said in a familiar tone: "Bartolommeo, how is your wife getting on under the care of the female practitioner?"

"Signore, I have not seen her since yesterday evening."

"You are not then the tender husband I had judged you," said Guido, smiling.

"You judged me rightly," answered Bartolommeo with emphasis, "for my country claims the first place in my heart."

"You are right. It claims the first place in every true patriot's heart. But might I ask what are your services?"

"Though I am of no account, yet my services are perhaps more valuable, and of greater utility to my country than the heroism of a Dandolo, or the learning of Fra Paolo Sarpi."

"I am not, my good fellow, endowed with the power of divination. Unless you explain yourself better I cannot understand you."

"A good patriot, signore, must act and not speak."

Guido had guessed what Bartolommeo's services were, but he hoped to hear something more about them from his own lips. The gondolier's determination not to disclose them gave greater value to his opinion respecting him.

"Not another word shall be said on the matter, Bartolommeo. Let us speak on other subjects. You must be acquainted with many citizens. Your trade of gondolier must bring within your knowledge men and women, the rich and the poor."

"I know everyone of any note, and many of none," answered Bartolommeo, drawing himself up.

"Yes. Ah! you are the very man I want. I guessed you were a clever fellow."

"I am at your service, signore, although I am not

the clever fellow you seem to think," rejoined the gondolier, assuming an air of humility he was far from feeling.

"Do you know a senator . . . I forget his name."

"Antonio——"

"Ah! yes, truly Antonio——"

"Gradenigo?"

"No. Not like that."

"Pisani? Zeno?"

"Neither."

There ensued a short pause. After which Guido, pretending to recollect, exclaimed:

"Foscari!"

"Ah! you mean Antonio Foscarini. Of course I know him. Who does not? The best of men, the noblest, the most generous. No one in need ever asked his help in vain."

"So they say. He must be truly a noble fellow since all say it. But I have heard . . . perhaps you could assure me to the contrary, and I should be glad . . ."

"What have you heard, signore? It would be strange if you had heard what I have not."

Bartolommeo was taken by surprise, and had forgotten to show off his knowledge.

"That there is a flaw in his character."

"Everyone on earth must have a defect. He has so many good qualities, one can pass something over."

"Bartolommeo, a patriot like you ought not to say so;" and Guido grew very serious.

Bartolommeo leaned on his oars, opened his eyes wide as if he meant to hear through those organs, and said in a low, earnest voice:

"What, signore?"

"That he is not very well affected towards the illustrious Council of Ten," rejoined Guido, in a still lower voice.

"It may be only a rumour set afloat by some invidious, malignant tongue that wishes to ruin the noble signore," replied the crafty gondolier; but in his own mind he fully meant to ascertain the truth, and earn a handsome reward if he succeeded in detecting the slightest flaw in Foscarini's political opinions. He rowed with greater energy and became more cheerful.

As for Guido, the die was now cast. He knew the most remote suspicion was sufficient for the Council of Ten to condemn a man, no matter how illustrious and patriotic he might have been. He felt himself safe, being sure Bartolommeo would manage so as to claim all the glory of the discovery for himself alone, and would never dream of mentioning him. That was enough. He leaped from his gondola another man, and turning a deaf ear to the alarmed voice of conscience, enjoyed the satisfaction of a well-nigh successful plan.

CHAPTER VIII.

THE PROMISE.

HOW harassing were Rosa's thoughts as she sat watching the setting sun on that memorable evening which was to witness her last interview with her lover! She longed for the moment, and yet she dreaded it.

In seeing a young, lovely, and innocent creature—innocent at least of the crimes and vices which tarnish so great a portion of mankind—sitting brooding on the heavy woe that oppressed her, feeling how desolate and unhappy she must inevitably be for the rest of her life, resigning for ever the tender relationship of wife and mother towards which her affectionate heart forcibly inclined her; happy if allowed to give it up, and to devote her heart to the only being she felt she could ever love—it is almost impossible for man not to inquire, "Why is it so? Why is so great an injustice allowed by Providence?" The answer of the Christian must ever be, "Man is born endowed with free will. Providence interferes by means of holy inspirations, which man disregards, blinded by self-love." Were it not so, man would not be responsible for his actions. God therefore permits, but does not commit, injustice.

The sun had now set. Rosa waited a few minutes more; then, in order to prevent search being made for her, she called her maid, and having told her that if her father asked for her she was to say she had gone to look at her plants, and would be back very soon, she descended into the garden, and went straight to the small side-door. She not only unlocked it, but left it ajar, then loitered about anxiously listening for the slightest noise. She had waited about a quarter of an hour, when she perceived the door move gently, and then Foscarini entered the garden.

She did not advance towards him, but beckoned to him to follow her. He did so; and they soon reached a little nook at the opposite side of the garden. It was a retired spot, covered with thick foliage, under which there were two marble seats, and two small marble statues representing Ceres and Flora placed on high stone pedestals. These statues rested against a low wall, which separated the Centofoglia garden from a small backyard of the Spanish ambassador's residence.

As soon as the lovers had seated themselves, and Foscarini had fondly kissed Rosa's hand, she said, turning her face towards the sky, where a star or two were beginning to glimmer faintly:

"One wish alone is left me now, Antonio—one only. It is that I might meet death here on this very spot, beside you, and that you would close my eyes. I should then await you in a better land, praising God and praying for you!"

"That is my wish also, Rosa—my most ardent wish; but then it is not surprising in me. I lose my angel—the angel I had fondly hoped would have guided my thoughts, my actions, and in whose pure arms I should have breathed my last, whose tender hands would have closed my eyes. . . ."

"But you do not lose me, Antonio. We now part, 'tis true, but you do not lose me, and I do not lose you. Though death would seem to me a blessing, still at times a distant ray of hope seems suddenly to illuminate my forlorn heart. I remember that as long as there is life there is hope."

"You are young, Rosa; I am nearly twice your age . . . experience has done its work on me."

Rosa misunderstood the meaning of Foscarini's words. She thought he meant to imply that her youth prevented her from possessing firmness of character, and sufficient constancy to remain constantly faithful to him. Her cheeks grew paler, her eyes expressed the suffering she was enduring. Seizing his hand in both hers, in a faltering voice she said:

"I can—I will—be faithful—to you. How could you utter—Antonio—those cruel words! Youth is nothing. The heart is all. Besides, since the day before yesterday, it seems to me that I am become almost old. Sorrow ages more than years, and gives greater experience. How could——"

Antonio Foscarini now clasped her in his arms.

His heroic resolutions of the last forty-eight hours had vanished. For, reaching his home on the evening when Rosa had disclosed to him her father's intentions, he entered his study and passed the night in pacing up and down the room, now and then seating himself for a few minutes to endeavour to arrange some important documents prior to leaving his country, perhaps for ever. He felt like one under the weight of an irremediable and appalling affliction. His upright character, showing itself through the agonies he was enduring, suggested to him that it was cruel and selfish to bind Rosa's future to his.

"She is so young," thought he, "so artless; she will not be able to oppose her father's wishes long, neither ought I to desire it. Then, leaving her under the weight of a promise, she may, who knows . . . why should I expect her to have firmness enough? She may relent. . . . Ah! that death had overtaken me, ere I was called upon to endure this . . . that it would at least overtake me now. If her father's unbending will obliges her to forfeit her word, it may cause her pure, innocent mind afterwards to feel a remorse which it is my duty to prevent, even at the cost of my earthly happiness. Is it her fault that I love her as I never loved before—that I have thought only how to please her, and win her affection? Let me now feel the greater sorrow, and endeavour to lighten hers in the only way left me."

Encouraging the same noble resolution the two succeeding days, Foscarini had entered the garden fully meaning to induce Rosa to promise him not to sacrifice her happiness to his. And so firmly did he resolve, that he even thought he should have sufficient firmness to convince her he was utterly unworthy of her affection.

He now perceived his weakness, and felt that he could have faced death gladly, but could not relinquish Rosa's heart, and know her the wife of another.

"Forgive me, my dearest Rosa," he said, "forgive me. I know that if needed you would show the constancy of a saint, and the heroism of a martyr. I did not mean to hurt your feelings. I would rather have died——"

"Then," cried Rosa, interrupting him, "then I forgive you. But promise me you will always love me, will always think of me. And I promise you here, in presence of yonder heaven, and before this holy picture"—thus saying, she took from under the folds of a black veil, which covered her head, was crossed over her chest and tied at the back of her waist, the miniature she had brought for Antonio—"that I will always love you, always think of you, and always be faithful to you until I close my eyes in death."

She kissed the miniature and gave it to him, adding:

"May it comfort you, as it has often comforted me, and may it help to remind you of me."

The last words were said in so low a voice, they would have been inaudible to all except a lover's quick hearing.

"And I," said Antonio, reverently taking the

proffered gift and devoutly kissing it, "I swear before Heaven and our most holy Mother that I will love you, as I do now, through life; and be true to you, yes, true *even unto death!*"

There was a moment's pause. The lovers clasped each other's hands, whilst their eyes were turned towards heaven, where the stars were now appearing thick and luminous, announcing that they must soon part.

Foscarini was the first to break the solemn silence.

"The fatal moment is approaching, Rosa," said he.

"Do stay a little longer," she replied, clinging to his arm.

"Some one will come in search of you, my love. On former evenings you were already in the hall at this hour. I would remain here all night . . . but it may ruin you——"

"I left word I was going to look at my plants, so we need not fear."

At this moment a noise was heard as of cautious steps approaching from the direction of the small door. Foscarini did not lose his presence of mind. Wishing to save Rosa's honour, and knowing that if he fled the way he had entered he would be discovered, and she would suffer for it, he placed the miniature he held beneath his vest in his bosom, then folding Rosa in his arms in one last ardent embrace, he put into her hand a relic enclosed in a gold cross, studded with precious stones; and before she had time to speak, he stepped on one of the marble seats, thence on to the pedestal of one of the statues, then on the wall, and with one vigorous leap he was out of sight, in the courtyard of the Spanish ambassador's palace.

Rosa stood a moment aghast, then she went towards the small door in order to close it. As she approached it she saw a short thickset man who, judging from his dress and the baskets that hung on his arms, appeared to be a fruit-seller, leaving the garden by that same door. She was too much stunned by the sudden separation from her lover to pay much attention to anything or anyone, so she shut the door and recrossed the garden.

Before entering the palace she gave a last look to the retired corner where she had met Foscarini for the last time, and feeling it was impossible for her to sustain Count Bernardi's ceremonious talk that evening, she gave orders to her maid that she did not wish to be disturbed, as she meant to pass the evening in her room; and having closed her door, she went straight to her crucifix and threw herself on her knees before it.

Meanwhile, Foscarini found himself in no small perplexity as to how to make his exit from the courtyard. He did not like to enter the palace, for the porter and other inmates would naturally ask him whence he came, or what he wanted. He began therefore to look about for some other way of escape. It was now dark, which increased the difficulty of his search. However, he succeeded in discovering a small door, but unfortunately he found it locked. Knowing it was his only means of liberating himself he began to pull the handles towards him. He felt the door beginning to give way, and set harder to work. At length, by another energetic pull, the lock was forced, and the door thrown wide open. He quickly crossed the threshold and shut the door again as well as he could. On finishing this last operation he perceived the same listless fruit-seller Rosa had seen standing near, intent on looking at the contents of his baskets. He seemed to have heard nothing, to have been aware of nothing.

Foscarini also felt little inclined to look round, and passed by him without so much as turning his head. He went with quickened pace to the spot where he had left his gondola, stepped into it, and soon and gladly found himself at home.

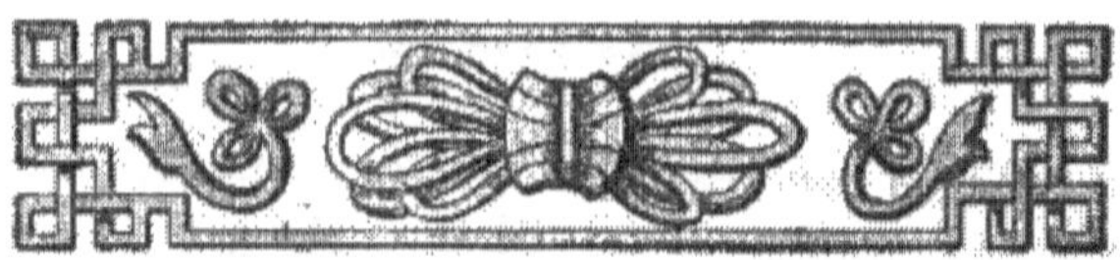

CHAPTER IX.

DENUNCIATION AND ARREST.

THE fruit-seller was the gondolier Bartolommeo Reni. No sooner was the prospect placed before him of becoming the fortunate angler of so large a fish as the senator Antonio Foscarini, than he set to work to watch him. He assumed the disguise of a fruit-seller, and posted himself near the palace where Foscarini lived. But for nearly forty-eight hours Foscarini did not leave his abode. He felt unequal to seeing anyone, or being condemned to enter into conversations in which he could now take no interest whatever.

He sent his secretary to transact all the outdoor preparations for his departure, and he himself passed his time in looking over papers of importance, and, above all, in musing on what was to be his last interview with Rosa, and on what he had determined to tell her.

When the last hues of twilight began to fade he left the palace and entered his gondola. Bartolommeo Reni saw him, and followed him at a respectful distance. He was also obliged to enter a gondola, which could not follow very close to Foscarini's; thus it happened that when the latter stepped out he lost sight of him. Nevertheless, he recognised the boat that was moored near a narrow street, and he thought of entering this street, and taking up his stand there, hoping to see something of him. After he had waited there some little time he went on a few paces, and turning to the right entered a little solitary square. He looked around and saw two small doors, of which one he knew belonged to the Spanish ambassador's premises, and the other one, left ajar, he thought he would just peep into. Discovering it was a beautiful garden, he proceeded onwards a few steps, little thinking how close he was to Foscarini. His steps were heard by Rosa and her lover, and caused the latter to leap into the small courtyard of the Spanish ambassador's residence. The spy, seeing no one, stopped a little while, looking about him; then, fearing to be caught in the garden of a patrician's palace, he retreated, and waited in the square, still hoping to see his victim. He heard a noise like a door opening, and soon, to his intense joy, he perceived Foscarini quit the prohibited premises. He pretended not to see him, but as soon as he was out of sight, he flew rather than ran home, put on better attire, and went to Vittorio Gradi, member of the Council of Ten, and his chief employer. He was instantly received.

From the joyful countenance of the well-known spy Vittoria Gradi guessed he brought good news.

"Well," said he, "what adventure are you come to relate?"

"You would never guess, illustrious signore, the service I have performed for my country."

"I suppose you have heard our just proceedings greatly condemned?"

"That would be nothing new, illustrious signore," replied Bartolommeo, thrown off his guard by the expectation of a goodly sum.

Vittoria Gradi looked at him angrily, but made no remark.

"Illustrious signore," continued Bartolommeo, touching his eyes with his right hand, "with these very eyes, which see far and well, have I, Bartolommeo Reni, your humble servant, seen the senator Antonio Foscarini steal out of a back door belonging to the Spanish ambassador's palace."

Vittorio Gradi's upper lip moved. He endeavoured to conceal a smile caused by the inward satisfaction a mean, envious mind always feels when some flaw can be detected in the character of anyone universally esteemed, but he did not entirely succeed.

"But are you sure, Bartolommeo, quite sure of what you assert?" asked he, pretending not to believe what the spy said.

"Can you doubt, signore, my patriotism? Have I not always served with zeal and fidelity the illustrious Council, whom I pray St. Mark to bless and protect for ever? By my assiduity I got to know that the senator Antonio Foscarini was not well affected towards the State" (Guido Bernardi had guessed rightly that Bartolommeo would take all the merit of the discovery to himself), "and I watched him day and night. He might have escaped everyone else, but not Bartolommeo Reni. I tell you, illustrious signore, I have seen him leave the Spanish ambassador's residence," he added forcibly.

"It is truly a grievous offence against the laws of Venice. You are a brave fellow, a true patriot. At present take this gold piece," and the inwardly delighted councillor put into Bartolommeo's hand a gold coin. "When the Council has taken proper measures you will have a recompense worthy of the service performed."

Vittorio Gradi distantly inclined his head, and Bartolommeo Reni, after having bent his person almost double, and said, "St. Mark protect your Excellency and the whole of the beneficent Council," departed to resume his occupation as gondolier.

Vittorio Gradi apprised the Council of what he had learned, and forthwith the order was issued for Antonio Foscarini's arrest.

The officers of justice sallied forth delighted. On reaching the palace where Foscarini lived, they ordered the porter to conduct them to his presence. The poor man reluctantly obeyed, and knocked at the door with a trembling hand.

He imagined, as did also the police, that all in the apartment were asleep, and that the door would not be opened so soon. They were deceived—the one to his great sorrow, the others to their great joy.

Foscarini could not sleep on that night. He had ordered his man-servant and other attendants to retire, and was pacing up and down the room, looking every now and then at the miniature he held, when he heard the knock. He thought he would not call anyone up, but would go and see who could possibly require anything of him or his household at that unusual hour.

He placed the precious miniature next his heart, and opened the door without hesitation. Seeing the porter, he kindly said:

"What is the matter, Battista? Has anything sad happened to your family that you are come at this unusual hour?"

The policemen, who had remained a little on one side, now came forward, and when the porter answered in a low voice, "These signori wish to see you," they quickly added, at the same time pushing the door wide open:

"We wish to see the senator Antonio Foscarini."

Foscarini was now aware who those men were, and calmly answered:

"I am Antonio Foscarini."

"We have orders to arrest you, senator," replied the chief officer, laying hold of him.

The others followed his example, and in one moment Foscarini was secured.

"I make no opposition," he then said, "to the

orders of the State. Let me only lock up some papers and documents I was putting in order."

"Your papers and documents now belong to the State, senator," answered the chief of the police. "Please follow us ere you oblige us to use force."

"Come, slaves!" rejoined Foscarini, severely, "I am ready."

He descended the staircase, entered the gondola, and was conducted to a narrow cell for State prisoners, and there left for the rest of the night. The next day he was summoned to appear before the Council of Ten.

CHAPTER X.

THE COUNCIL OF TEN.

THE Council of Ten was established in the fourteenth century in order to discover all the ramifications of the famous Tripolo conspiracy. For some time it so invaded all judicial and administrative powers as to depose a doge, be the arbiter of peace, and even cede provinces without asking the consent of the other authorities charged with the political interests of the State. In the course of three centuries several attempts were made to diminish its power; and during the time we speak of, its attributes were limited to the repression of crimes of high treason, conspiracies, public mutinies, and the criminal trials of politicians, etc., etc.*

Its diminished powers did not abate the tyranny and injustice of its proceedings. On the simple deposition of some low, heartless, lying spy, or even on a mere supposition, it would summon before its dreaded presence, try, and condemn to exile, imprisonment for life, or capital punishment, men perfectly innocent of

* "Histoire de la République de Venise," par P. Daru.

the crimes imputed to them, or at least not deserving the cruel sufferings and privations its severity heaped on them.

Foscarini appeared before the dreaded court calm and dignified. He knew his innocence, and was persuaded it would be easily established, but even if he had to undergo the injustice which he knew had been inflicted on others, he cared not. He was suffering inwardly more than any confinement or even execution could have caused him to endure. And, as for exile, he had already chosen it voluntarily; what, then, if it was enforced upon him by order of the State? He could neither suffer more nor less.

The councillor acting as secretary, on seeing him, felt assured that a victim stood before him. Two-thirds of the Council thought the same. Vittorio Gradi certainly did not. If the thought ever crossed his narrow, mean mind, he banished it in order not to diminish the joy he felt in seeing a noble and hitherto universally esteemed character placed on a level with a felon, and treated as such.

"Prisoner, what is your name?" asked the secretary, in a stern voice.

"Antonio Foscarini."

"Your condition?"

"Senator of the State."

"Have you ever been entrusted with any important mission for the Republic?"

"I have represented the Most Serene Republic at the French Court, and——"

"Enough. You stand arraigned on the grievous charge of conspiring against the settled government of Venice."

"Impossible! I have never conspired," answered Foscarini, warmly.

"You are charged with notorious disobedience to the salutary orders of the State."

"I have not disobeyed the orders of the State," retorted the prisoner, his countenance inflamed by just anger.

"Prisoner, be calm. Anger avails little. Can you deny having been seen secretly quitting the Spanish ambassador's palace?"

"I merely crossed a small backyard. And as for quitting it in secrecy, no such thing happened, since I was obliged to force open a door, and thereby made a great deal of noise."

"Even supposing it was a backyard, you knew you were acting against the orders of the State?"

"I know it is forbidden to a subject of the Most Serene Republic to enter within a foreign ambassador's residence, but I had a reason for doing so which certainly did not affect the security of the State."

"And what reason, unless it be a political one, could you, a senator of the State, allege for transgressing the laws of your country?"

"Illustrious councillors," answered Foscarini, turning towards all, and looking each full in the face, "I swear by St. Mark that it was not a political reason which induced me to transgress for a few seconds my beloved country's laws."

There was truth in that open, fearless countenance, in those distinctly-uttered words. The secretary felt it, as did many of the councillors also; but the evidence was not in the prisoner's favour. Besides, leniency was out of the question. Severity alone, it was thought, prevented the fall of the Republic. Clemency, nay, common justice, would have caused its ruin! O tempora! O mores!

"Prisoner, explain the reason," replied the secretary.

"I cannot."

"It is not sufficient for a criminal to declare himself innocent; he must also prove it."

"I cannot give the reason, and yet I am innocent."

"Prisoner, I tell you for the last time it is not enough. Disclose the reason. Your refusal only enhances your guilt."

"I cannot and will not," rejoined Foscarini, decidedly.

"Mind, your life is at stake."

"Let it be so."

"Have you anything else to say?"

"Nothing."

The secretary called the halberdiers, and said:

"Let the prisoner be removed from our presence."

They obeyed, and Antonio Foscarini was reconducted to his cell.

The council then retired to an adjoining room to consult on the sentence to be pronounced.

"This trial," said the secretary, "will be considered one of the most singular in the annals of history. It seems incredible that a man who has been entrusted with important missions, and has always given proofs of patriotism, who enjoys the reputation of being one of the most upright of the Venetian senators, should have allowed himself to be overcome in a moment of weakness, and have conspired against the safety of the Republic—unless," added he, holding down his head, as if ashamed of what he feared would be pronounced weakness on his part, "he be as he says, innocent."

"I am of your opinion, illustrious colleague," put in timidly a councillor who knew Foscarini well; "he must be innocent of conspiring against St. Mark, only cannot for the present proclaim the reason of his strange disobedience."

"I think also that he may not be exactly culpable," said a third, "but I think he ought to be examined by torture, that thus we may obtain the confession of the truth."

"Most illustrious colleagues," replied Vittorio Gradi, in a low, humble voice, "if my opinion has any weight in this matter I should say that it is most evident the senator Antonio Foscarini has conspired against the security of the State. 1st. He does not deny having entered a backyard of the Spanish ambassador's palace, which condemns him at once; for is it likely that a man of his standing would have stepped on forbidden ground without a political reason? 2ndly. He refuses to tell the truth. And what conspirator ever did reveal the truth unless the rack forced him to it? 3rdly. His reputation for uprightness is no proof to the contrary, since conspirators do not believe they tarnish their honour by their diabolical machinations; and although Antonio Foscarini enjoys universal esteem, are you quite sure he really deserves it?" and Vittorio Gradi grinned as much as to say: "I know to the contrary." "And lastly, the man who has denounced him is the faithful Bartolommeo Reni, one of our best employés in such matters, and who has never failed to denounce real culprits."

These words had the desired effect. The councillors feared to say anything to the contrary. There was a pause.

"What course had we best follow?" asked the secretary at length.

"Keep him in prison till we can be better assured of his guilt," answered the first councillor, timidly.

"Have him put to the rack in order to know the entire truth," said the second.

"I am of the last opinion," added three or four councillors, speaking together.

"As for me," subjoined the crafty Vittorio Gradi, raising his voice to its natural pitch, "when my country's welfare is at stake I would sacrifice myself, my wife, my children! Venice would be lost if she let conspirators live!"

"Let us judge him, then," said the secretary, more frightened than ever, "according to what the laws decree. Thus we cannot fail of being in the right. The laws of Venice," added he, in a solemn voice, "decree the punishment of death to any Venetian who without previous permission enters within a foreign ambassador's premises."

"Let it be death," re-echood all the councillors at once.

The sentence was forthwith passed that Antonio Foscarini, senator of the State, should that night die by strangulation within the precincts of the Inquisitorial Palace, and the sentence be notified to him by the Father Confessor, who was to prepare him for death.

CHAPTER XI.

DEATH.

WHEN Antonio Foscarini found himself again alone, he reflected deeply on the condition in which he was placed. He knew he could hope little or nothing either from the justice or the mercy of his accusers and judges. Two alternatives only were left him. Either to tell the reason why he had been discovered leaving the backyard of the Spanish ambassador's palace, or choose immediate death.

As to the first, independently of his intense love for Rosa, of the slur he knew would ever after be attached to her name, were it known that she had received a man alone, unknown to her father or any-one else, at dusk, the tongue of slander, envious of her beauty, would have exaggerated the event, and added lies to lies. His upright nature rebelled at the mere suggestion of preserving life by divulging a secret; it was a base act, unworthy of Antonio Foscarini! There was no other alternative left him except death, and death he willingly, unhesitatingly chose. To feel oneself, in the vigour of manhood, on the verge of

> "The undiscovered country, from whose bourn
> No traveller returns,"

though it be one's own choice, though one may feel strength and courage enough to carry the resolution into effect, "puzzles the will," and thus it was that the noble prisoner sat musing deeply. He refused the food brought to him, and would only drink a glass of water. He leant his head on his hand, and his elbow on a block of stone beside him, and now and then sighed, not from love of the world, its joys and its pleasures, not because he felt his conscience reproach him with the crimes caused by pride, hard-heartedness, or the grosser passions which debase man, but because he felt he was going to appear before a Judge in whose sight the stars themselves are not pure!

When the shadows of night had enveloped every object in darkness he was still there, in the same posture, except that within the last two hours he held in his left hand the miniature, the gift of which was to cause his death, but whose privilege it was to comfort him to the last.

The noise made by the heavy door turning on its hinges aroused him. A halberdier entered, carrying a small lantern, and followed by two other guards and a friar.

The friar belonged to the Order of the Capuchins.

He was not more than four and twenty, but he looked ten years older. He was of middle height, thin, dark, and would have been judged in a decidedly unfavourable light, but for the humble, benevolent expression of his countenance which prepossessed every one in his favour at first sight. His name was Father Paul, and his office was the difficult one of visiting and converting prisoners, and the heart-rending one of preparing them to meet death.

"Senator," said Father Paul, approaching Foscarini with a bow, "please to follow us."

Foscarini put the miniature beneath his vest, and rose instantly, saying:

"I am ready, Father, to go wherever you like."

Father Paul sighed, and followed the halberdier who led the way. The other two guards placed themselves on either side of the prisoner, and all quitted the cell.

They passed through long damp corridors, they descended narrow staircases whose only light was the small lantern carried by the first halberdier. On reaching a hall whose vaulted ceiling was covered with cobwebs, whose floor, earthy and muddy, announced that it was underground, whose only furniture was a life-size crucifix hanging on the wall, and two large high stone seats, the halberdier put the small lantern on the ground in a corner, and followed by his two comrades, left Foscarini and Father Paul alone, carefully shutting the door behind them.

The friar and the prisoner seated themselves. The latter was the first to speak.

"Father," said he, unhesitatingly, "I know enough of my country's laws and customs to be perfectly aware I have been brought into this dungeon to die——"

"Son," said Father Paul, interrupting him, "accept death as the expiation of your crime against the laws of your country, and——"

"Father," rejoined Foscarini, interrupting the friar in his turn, "I receive your reproach with humility, inasmuch as I shall soon appear before the righteous Judge; but my conscience is innocent of the crime imputed to me, so help me God," added he with energy.

"My son, I did not mean to reproach you; I am come to comfort you, to help you to meet our Judge with faith."

"Ever since I returned from the presence of the Council, I have been meditating on sin and death. I am prepared to receive the Sacrament of Penance," continued the noble prisoner, desirous to cut short at once the argument Father Paul had begun to enter upon.

"And I am ready to hear you unburthen your soul before God, for confession is made to the Almighty. Man is as nothing. I am only here in order to answer in God's stead, and to pronounce forgiveness on the Almighty's part.

Foscarini devoutly knelt before Father Paul, and made his confession. The experienced friar did not interrupt him with useless observations. Accustomed to hear confessions of rapines and murders, of treachery and tyranny even from many who enjoyed a good reputation as pious and just men, he felt an increasing interest in the man who could relate his whole life without mentioning any of the crimes which have sullied some men in all ages, and had tarnished the lives of many men in his.

When Foscarini had finished, he said kindly :

"My son, have you nothing else to say?"

"Nothing, Father."

"My son, man is imperfect. Perhaps you thought to benefit your country ultimately by having secret understandings with the ambassador of a foreign power. But though your intentions may have been good, the means were bad, and might have brought irreparable ruin on the Republic. Confess, therefore, before God, that you were wrong."

"Father, I confess that I entered for a few seconds a small backyard attached to the Spanish ambassador's palace, but that was the first time and the last. I saw no one, I spoke to no one."

"But why enter it at all, my son, since the laws forbid it?"

"Ah! Father, for a reason that God alone knows; but man shall never know. No, not even you, Father. But of one thing you may rest assured, I did not so much as dream of conspiring in any way against the government of the Republic, nor lower myself and my country by machinating against it in favour of a foreign power. And this, Father, I can assert in the presence of that crucified God," and he pointed to the crucifix, "and of His holy Mother," and he took from beneath his vest the miniature and kissed it.

"I will absolve thee, my son; it is not for me to inquire further."

Father Paul pronounced the holy words of absolution.

Foscarini rose and seated himself again on the other stone seat.

"Father," said he, "I am compelled to ask a great favour of you."

"Speak, my son; I am ready to serve you."

"I have loved and still love with a devoted attachment the lovely and virtuous daughter of the patrician Marco Centofoglia, and I am beloved in return. There was no worldly interest in our love. Mutual esteem and the same tastes inspired and fostered it. Her father promised her hand to a youth for whom he has a great regard, and I withdrew. But ere we parted for ever, Rosa gave me a keepsake—this miniature. I wish to die clasping it, and I beg of you, Father, when I am gone, to take it back to the angel, telling her it has comforted me greatly; also that I beg of her," here Foscarini's voice faltered, "that I beg of her—to mourn—as a Christian should—with fortitude and resignation, not to regret my loss too much, since I am pleased to die; and I implore you, Father, not to tell her the precise cause of my death. Let her be ignorant that I die because I entered the Spanish ambassador's palace. Trials are conducted with so much secrecy in our enslaved country, individuals disappear without others knowing what is become of them; so she will not, at least for some time, know the real cause of my death. Father, will you promise me this?"

"I will, my son; and I will promise you to go to her to-morrow morning."

"A dying man, Father, thanks you, and blesses you. I beg also that you will go about eleven o'clock, as at that hour her father does not receive visitors, and I wish the keepsake to remain a profound secret."

"I will follow your directions, and will endeavour to comfort the lady. It is a hard trial to lose those whom we love!"

Father Paul looked very sad. Painful remembrances were crowding on his mind.

Foscarini took his hand with emotion, pressed it, and kissed it.

"Father," he then said, "I have had a moment of weakness, or rather of doubt; but now I am happy. I feel reconciled to my Maker through Him," and he looked at the crucifix, "who tasted death for all, and I shall be glad to hear the steps of my executioners."

"Yes, my son," answered Father Paul, with fervour; "after all, what is the power of death? It kills the body, which is corruptible matter, but cannot destroy the soul."

"Truly. Death cannot stifle thought, and that is my comfort. The spirit, freed from the body, will be able to soar on high. All its faculties increasing by reason of its absolute freedom, it will remember more accurately, love better, and judge rightly of many events of this its nether life which during its mortal career appeared under the form of unfathomable mysteries. Exquisite and enlivening thought! A complete cessation from trouble, and yet an inconceivable increase of life. A perfect satisfaction, yet not satiety. An unlimited expanse, and no bewilderment. A great lightness, and a great strength."

"And above all, my son, the light of God."

"Ah!" exclaimed Antonio Foscarini with holy enthusiasm. "Yes, the light of God! A few pangs, and then, and for ever, the light of God! May that light shine on my poor country, and on mankind in general, and illuminate the dark paths of tyranny, that it may perceive how destructive and mistaken are its ways!"

"And may the executioner's axe and halter be for ever banished from the civilised world!" said Father Paul, looking upwards with holy earnestness. "Man, sitting in judgment, has no more real right to condemn a brother to death than the highway robber to waylay him and cut his throat."

"Father, I have often thought so, little thinking I should end my life in this manner."

"The manner of our death is as unknown to us as the hour of it."

Steps were now heard. Father Paul suddenly stopped. Presently the door opened, and the executioners appeared, accompanied by several halberdiers.

Father Paul became as pale as death. Antonio Foscarini was unmoved. He rose, and going towards the new comers, said in a clear voice:

"My friends, I know you mean to ask my forgiveness. You have it. I forgive you heartily. And," added he, turning towards Father Paul, "if by any chance you should meet with the person or persons who have been the cause of my unjust denunciation, tell them I forgive them as I hope to be forgiven."

Foscarini then approached the crucifix, kissed its holy feet devoutly, knelt before Father Paul to receive his last blessing, looked at the miniature he held, pronounced an inaudible prayer, said, "Father, remember your kind promise," and advancing to the corner where the executioners stood, wondering at the calmness with which the noble prisoner quitted life, added, smiling:

"My friends, I am ready."

Father Paul followed.

"My son," said he, "I renew the promise already made. I bless you again in God's Name. Within a few seconds you will join the song of the angels at the foot of the Almighty's throne."

The executioners began to tie his arms.

"Give us the object you are holding, prisoner," said the chief executioner.

"The only favour I ask," answered Foscarini, "is that I may be allowed to die holding this miniature of our most holy Mother."

"Don't refuse this favour to a dying man," added Father Paul.

"Be it so," answered the executioner.

"And when I am gone let the minister of God have it," said Foscarini.

"We have no wish to take it," replied the authorised murderer.

He then adjusted the rope round the victim's neck.

"Father, the light of God . . . how surpassingly glorious!" exclaimed Foscarini.

Father Paul knelt, turning his eyes towards the crucifix. He prayed earnestly. He heard the faint sound of a struggle for breath . . . then of another . . . then of a third. He prayed still more fervently. Then the harsh voice of one of the executioners said:

"Friar, the culprit is dead."

He might have added, only he knew it not, and, if he had known it he would have feared to say it, "And the most complete murder on record accomplished."

Father Paul rose from his knees.

The body lay on the ground, the muscles painfully contracted, the face livid. The executioners untied the arms, and Father Paul tried to open the hand that held the miniature. It was not so easy, for so tightly had Foscarini grasped it in the last agonies of suffocation, that the print of his fingers remained on the velvet.

When Father Paul had taken it, he cast a last affectionate and sorrowing glance on the motionless corpse, and quitted the prison to return to his cell.

CHAPTER XII.

THE KEEPSAKE RETURNED.

THE next morning, a few minutes before eleven, Father Paul entered the Centofoglia palace. The porter admitted him readily, "although," said he, "the Signora Rosa has given orders she will see no one for some days, she will not refuse to see your reverence, she is so good and charitable. Her mother was the same. . . ."

The porter would have gone on at least an hour had not Father Paul in a humble though firm tone of voice replied:

"I have heard of the many charitable acts of the late Signora Teresa Centofoglia. Would you, my son, show me upstairs, as my errand is a pressing one?"

The porter complied with no small zeal, and in a few minutes Rosa was told that a friar of the Capuchin Order earnestly desired to speak with her.

From the day of Foscarini's arrest Rosa had refused to see anyone. She even declined dining at table, knowing that Guido was there, and being quite sure he felt no sorrow respecting the sad occurrence. That was not all. She knew everybody blamed Foscarini, her father and Father Pio more than others, for his disloyal conduct. Her seclusion, and the secrecy attending political trials in Venice, prevented her from hearing that he was accused of having been seen within the precincts of the Spanish ambassador's residence. She had simply heard he was accused of disloyalty to the State.

Early in the morning succeeding his untimely end, Father Pio sent a message to his friend Marco announcing his death. Marco was beginning to suspect the *traitor*, as he called him, and his daughter loved each other. But as he was firmly determined on her marrying his favourite, Guido Bernardi, he tried, as far as he could, to render Foscarini's memory odious to her, and having learned she was already up and dressed, he entered her room, saying:

"I bring good news to a true daughter of Venice. The traitor Antonio Foscarini has paid for his crime with his life. He was executed during the night. Venice is safe again! My child, let us rejoice!"

Rosa, whose heart since the day of Foscarini's arrest had felt sad misgivings, became pale, but she had sufficient strength not to faint. She only felt she could not answer; speech was impossible. She went straight to her crucifix, and without saying a word or shedding a tear, fell on her knees before it. Even her father's callous heart felt a degree, if not of pity, of respect for a sorrow so true, so intense, and yet so nobly expressed; and without saying another word he left the room, closing the door after him.

The maid who afterwards entered, announcing the Capuchin Father, found her in the same posture. She went gently towards her. Rosa had not heard her footsteps, and started on hearing herself called.

"Signora," said the maid, "a friar of the Capuchin Order desires to have a few words with you."

"Tell him I am sorry I cannot receive him now," replied Rosa, feeling unequal to the task of receiving anyone. "If he could call in a few days I would then willingly see him."

The maid left with the message, and soon returned with the answer.

"He says he has something to tell you of the utmost importance."

"Could he not call this evening?"

"His manner is so pressing that——"

"Well," answered Rosa, in a resigned tone of voice, "perhaps some wretched creature—not more wretched than myself," thought she—"wishes for help. Tell Beppo to ask him to pass into the small drawing-room near the hall. I will be there in a minute."

And within a few minutes she entered the room in which she had first learned that Foscarini loved her, and which she had not entered since that day.

Many had been the sad and conflicting tasks which had fallen on Father Paul since he had devoted himself to the relief of the poor and afflicted. Many a wound had he healed, that but for the balm he had poured into it would have bled for years. None knew better than he how difficult it is to produce calmness during the first days of intense grief. The wind of affliction is too strong to be appeased. A little time must pass ere the mind acquire sufficient strength to be enabled to think and to listen to counsel. Religion alone, in its invisible way, softens those first hours of torture, and enables the agonised mind not to yield to despair, and to resist till the moment comes when it can regain somewhat of its accustomed power, and thus be enabled to hear and follow the holy suggestions of the ministers of religion and the thoughtful advice of devoted relations and friends.

These last kind helps are sometimes wanting, and then, though the affliction may be slightly subdued, it is still so intense as to prevent, or at least to defer for too long a time, the fulfilment of those domestic or public duties incumbent on every one.

At any other moment, notwithstanding his wide experience, Father Paul would have felt greatly embarrassed in making known to Rosa his errand, the more so as he was totally ignorant whether she knew of Foscarini's sad end. But the martyr's death had emboldened him, had elevated his thoughts still higher, had made him look on affliction and death not merely as inevitable sorrows sent to mankind for their advancement in the paths of virtue, but as blessings granted in mercy, which man ought to desire, instead of shrinking from.

As Rosa entered he advanced and bowed. She stopped, almost startled. She thought she had seen him before—and yet no, she had not seen him, but a countenance like his not long ago. Whose face it was, and where she had seen it, she could not remember; she only fancied the countenance seen previously did not evince, at least to her eyes and bewildered recollection, the celestial joy which beamed in the one before her.

She returned the bow with humility, and pointing to an armchair, said:

"Father, do be seated; excuse, nay, forgive, my not having come in as soon as I ought. But .... Father," she added, interrupting herself, and not wishing to mention her own agony, "I doubt not you wish to speak to me on behalf of some hapless person. I am ready to hear you, and to help also as far as I can."

Rosa's face was like that of a corpse, except that her eyes, though no tear glistened in them, spoke the torture she was enduring. Father Paul looked at her for a moment, then, as if moved by a holy inspiration, took the miniature from between the folds of his habit, and without saying a word, rose and put it in Rosa's hands. He then stood near her, placed his right hand on her head, and turning his eyes upwards, prayed fervently to her who had known the greatest of human sorrows to intercede for the afflicted maiden.

The prayer was no sooner heard than granted.

Rosa understood now to the full the Capuchin's mission. Foscarini had thought of her to the last, and sent her back the miniature. She burst into tears, and continued weeping for some minutes; those tears were sent in mercy, they relieved her. She now felt she could hear all about her lover's end, and speak of him. As soon, therefore, as Father Paul had returned to his seat, she said:

"Father, when did Antonio Foscarini give you this? What did he tell you? I know that last night he entered eternity. Fear not to tell me. I can bear all."

"My daughter, death is the blessed portal that leads to the presence of God. Let us therefore rejoice with those who have reached before us the happy goal, and strive to be worthy of following their footsteps."

"Yes, Father, they are happy who are gone. Would that I had met Foscarini's fate! I cannot believe he died a traitor to his country. His was an upright soul——"

"A holy soul," interrupted Father Paul, with warmth; "a soul worthy of the early martyrs. I am sure he did not die a traitor to his country. He may have mistaken the way to benefit it—in that I agree; but his intentions were pure. Besides, he ever preserved so solemn a silence on the motives that led him into that error that we cannot judge him according to justice."

"Survivors are to be pitied. Mine will ever be a life of tears."

"Tears are the best nourishment of the soul, since they lead it to heaven. Nevertheless, signora, you must not encourage tears. It is Antonio Foscarini's wish."

"He spoke, then, to you of me?"

"He did. I am the bearer of his last words and wishes to you."

"Tell me them, Father, tell me them; I can bear to hear them. Believe me, I have strength enough to hear all," added Rosa, fearing lest Father Paul should conceal something from her.

"I do not doubt it, my daughter. She whose image you are holding and pressing to your heart has interceded for you. And when was it ever known that she asked aught in vain?"

The good friar then repeated all the words Foscarini had uttered, and described all the particulars of his death, except, according to his wishes, the *real* motive of his trial and end.

Rosa listened without moving a muscle, except now and then to clasp more tightly the miniature in her right hand. When Father Paul finished she said, looking at the image, and as though talking to herself:

"He held it in his hands to the last! He expired with it there! Oh, how surpassingly dear it is to me!" and she devoutly, fondly kissed it. "But"—a dark cloud seemed to hang over her again—"but, Father, what a torturing death! What struggles for breath! Oh, Holy Mother, help me! My brain seems to give way. I cannot bear the thought."

Her face was contracted, her lips were livid.

"Hush, signora!" said Father Paul, in a firm, though kind voice. "Hush! we must not look at the kind of death. The separation of the soul from the body must inevitably be, except in very few cases, painful to the latter. But I am of opinion that so great is the comfort sent from above to the soul that quits the body reconciled to its Maker, that the physical pain is not so much felt as we fancy. The spirit is too much absorbed in the contemplation of the Deity to feel to its full extent the struggles of the body."

"Father, had he but died in his bed I fancy I should now feel almost happy. It must be immeasurably more painful to die the death those cruel men inflicted on him, than to expire on one's pillow, with tender hands to close one's eyes. I know it is more painful," she added, with energy.

"Ah, my daughter, you have not had the experience of the dying that I have. I have seen some die in their beds surrounded by every human comfort, with affectionate relatives to close their eyes, struggle for breath, and seemingly writhing in pain. I have seen others expire under the surgeon's knife in exquisite torture. Some men have met death by means of a sudden and painful accident, worse, perhaps, than the pain caused by the executioner. But let not your imagination torture you uselessly. Let not Antonio Foscarini's last words prove fruitless. Live to glorify God, and honour the martyr's memory by your resignation and by a life of good works, and always, signora, always, when it occurs to you that Foscarini's death was too cruel, remember one sort of death *alone* we should regret—the death of the impenitent sinner."

So saying, Father Paul arose to depart.

"Will you leave me so soon, Father? Oh, do stay! You do me good, and I have no one besides you to whom I can speak of Foscarini."

"My daughter, in a few days I leave Venice for ever, and retire to a convent of my Order, near the tomb of the glorious Apostles Peter and Paul. I must visit many of my children ere I depart."

"I am destined to be wretched in every way. Even your comfort is denied me."

"You have your Saviour's, my daughter. You have His Mother's. What can I do for you? Man is nothing. God is everything. Trust in Him, and He will comfort you."

"At least, come to see me once more ere you start," answered Rosa, in a supplicating tone.

"Yes, signora, I will come. I will pass the eve of my departure with you. God bless you, my daughter."

"Thank you, Father."

Rosa accompanied the friar to the door of the hall, and then retired to her room.

CHAPTER XIII.

THE FORCED CONFESSION.

FORTUNE, or the demon, as Rosalia used often to say, had helped her throughout life, and had thrown in her path Bartolommeo Reni's wife, whose medical attendant she had become. Through her she had discovered that Bartolommeo was Guido's favourite gondolier, and through her she now hoped to be freed from a thought which tormented her. Although she had assured Guido that he could never call himself the husband of Marco Centofoglia's daughter, she was, in truth, far from being sure that the marriage she dreaded would not take place. To endeavour to prevent it was now her sole aim.

On the plea of watching the result of her prescriptions, she managed to go two or three times a day to visit the sick woman. She knew that the Italian proverb "Una parole tira un altra" ("One word leads to another"), is but too true, and she hoped to learn something of Guido's goings and doings from the gondolier.

Since Bartolommeo Reni had undertaken to serve

his country and his purse in the unenviable quality of a spy, fortune had not brought to his net so important a fish as the unfortunate Antonio Foscarini. The reward he obtained for so valuable a service was adequate to its importance. It was too large a sum put into his possession at once, and Bartolommeo found moderation impossible. He determined he would for once enjoy himself, and heedless of his better half's entreaties to wait till she felt a little stronger, and could share in the projected treat, he set off, the very day succeeding Foscarini's death, to Mestra "to see something," as he said, "and enjoy myself a little," as he repeated, but in reality to have a long drive in the outskirts of the small town, and eat and drink without his wife's prudent control.

He returned the following evening in a state of absolute drunkenness, with only a few small silver coins left. He reeled about the room talking nonsense, and intermixing in his wild speeches such sentences as these:

"Bravo, Signor Conte! . . . But for you . . . I will serve you gratis for ever for the benefit you have heaped on me. . . . Poor senator! . . . He little knew that all would be discovered."

"Unhappy wretch!" said his wife turning to Rosalia, who, having offered to pass the night with the sick woman during her husband's absence, was sitting by her bedside, striving to comfort her; "the fumes of the wine are gone to his head, and he talks nonsense."

"He will be better by-and-by," answered Rosalia; "turn on your side now, and try to fall asleep. The best plan is to take no notice of him."

The woman obeyed, and soon fell into a profound sleep. When Rosalia had assured herself of it she rose gently, and taking the drunken gondolier by the arm, succeeded in pulling him out of his wife's room, and throwing him on a heap of dried maize leaves in a corner of the kitchen. She persuaded him to swallow a decoction she had brought for his wife, which lessened his excitement, and helped him to fall into a kind of fitful dozing. Rosalia then returned to the sick woman's bed, and seated herself beside it plunged in deep thought. The fact is, she had half guessed the meaning of the spy's broken sentences. A strong suspicion had entered her mind that Guido was no stranger to the unhappy fate of Foscarini, whose death had now become the common talk of all, poor and rich, noble and plebeian. She also felt assured that Bartolommeo Reni was the spy who had denounced him, especially as the sick woman, in apprising her of the sum her husband had gained, had added that he would not tell her how he had come by it.

Could Rosalia but have received from Bartolommeo himself the assurance that her suspicions were well founded, nothing would have been wanting to her happiness. Her day of triumph, longed for during twenty-five years, would have dawned at last. While her faithless lover suffered she would be left to enjoy his sufferings, and at the same time feel assured that no harm could befall her. She entered the kitchen, and gently closed the door after her.

Bartolommeo opened his eyes as she approached, upon which Rosalia, pretending to think that some ailment tormented him, said, stooping over him :

"You feel better now, do you not? Your head must have ached violently."

"It still aches. I feel an odd confusion and dizziness in it. It seems to me as if everything went round, yourself included. Besides, I feel so weak I can hardly move a finger."

Rosalia thought that his senses were now so far restored as to allow her to believe what he said. She also reflected that the slight confusion still existing in his mind, and his total prostration of strength, would enable her now better than at any other moment to extort a confession from his lips, which he would never make when strength and an entirely clear conception of things returned to him. The difficulty was how to begin. She reflected a few minutes, and then a bright idea struck her: "I am called a witch, and often treated as such. Let me for once have the benefit of it. Let me pretend to be one, and gain the information I so much desire."

She again approached Bartolommeo, and without further preliminary said to him :

"You generally serve Count Guido Bernardi——"

"I do," answered Bartolommeo, stretching himself out like one waking from sleep.

"He has also brought you luck."

"What luck? He pays for the gondola as others do—nothing more."

"No. Do you say this to me?" and Rosalia looked at him archly. "It was he who told you that the senator Antonio Foscarini was ill-affected towards the State. You believed it, and . . . and . . . in fact, got the sum——"

"Who told you so?" exclaimed the spy, entirely thrown off his guard, and ignoring that his imprudence had led Rosalia into the suspicion. "What fiend has whispered it into your ears?"

"You call me a witch, and yet you question me? Of course the demon has told me so; and mind, Bartolommeo, that you answer clearly and sincerely what I am going to ask you"—here Rosalia drew herself up to her full height, and fixed those large black eyes of hers on the bewildered man—"or else I will by means of a charm make the demon descend this chimney, and at my bidding bind you for ever to this heap of leaves."

"What is it you require of me?" said Bartolommeo, aghast, not daring to turn towards the chimney, lest the demon should already be there.

"Tell me what Count Bernardi told you. Tell me at your peril."

Had Bartolommeo Reri been less frightened and his mind less confused he would have noticed the contradiction in Rosalia's words—first assuring him that as a witch she knew everything, next threatening to call the demon unless he told her all. As it was, the gondolier had not the power of reflection, and fearing lest Rosalia should be as good as her word, overpowered also by her tall, imposing figure, he replied:

"One evening he told me he had heard that the senator Antonio Foscarini was considered not well affected towards the illustrious Council of Ten. And I . . . I . . . set about watching him, and I found out he had disobeyed the orders of the State by visiting the Spanish ambassador."

"You never suspected the senator before? No one else had ever told you to watch him?"

"How could I suspect him? He was the best of men. How could anyone else tell me to watch him? He was universally esteemed."

"It is enough."

"I have obeyed you; now promise me in your turn you will always keep the demon far from me."

"Fear not. You have complied with my request; the fiend will never molest you. I shall now go home and prepare some more decoction for yourself and your wife, and by-and-by you will be quite well."

"Thank you, Rosalia; I will repay you as well as my small means allow," and Bartolommeo sank again into a fit of dozing.

Rosalia had obtained what she wanted, and she sallied forth to her home, more light-hearted than she had felt for the last twenty-five years!

She made a jug of her decoction and took it to the gondolier. He drank some, and his wife willingly swallowed the remainder. Rosalia then put their house a little to rights, assured the gondolier he would sleep almost all the day, and by the evening be well again; went to his wife's bedside, and feeling her pulse, told her the fever had left her, and in a couple of days more she would be able to rise from bed, and again left them, hurrying to her solitary room to rest awhile.

It was now morning, and she lay down on her bed, but sleep would not visit her. Although it be but too true that

"He, like the world, his ready visit pays
Where fortune smiles; the wretched he forsakes,"

it is no less true that often when we have reached the climax of our desires, and our plans have succeeded, and we feel happy, thoroughly happy, sleep equally forsakes us—a state of total indifference being the most propitious to invite the slumber-loving god.

Rosalia was fully satisfied with the information received that morning, but when she began to think calmly she reflected that Foscarini's untimely death was not likely to have cooled Rosa's affection. Rather, on the contrary, to have increased it, and perhaps a greater impediment now existed to the full realisation of Guido's views than before; she determined, therefore, to learn something more from Guido himself. She knew she must wait at least a fortnight ere he would visit her again to bring her her small allowance. Waiting so long was out of the question. She must find some way of seeing him that very morning. She tasked her mental resources for a moment for an excuse to call on him, and finding she could not invent one, was beginning to resolve to go without accounting for her call when she remembered he was very fond of a certain kind of biscuit she alone knew the secret of making, and which she used often to make for the contessa, his mother. She instantly resolved to take him some, and having bought the necessary ingredients, set to work with uncommon alacrity. As soon as made she took them to the nearest baker's, waited there till they were baked, assured herself they had succeeded to a turn, entered a gondola, and soon reached the huge palace where Guido rented a small suite of apartments.

Guido's means were very limited, nevertheless he would have his style of life as noble as they would admit. The first requisite towards this was to inhabit a palace, not a mere house. It mattered not what part of the palace he lived in; provided he could when giving his address add the word "palace," it sufficed. The small rooms he occupied were at the back; the windows looked into a small courtyard. They were, moreover, at the very top of the edifice, but this proved far from being an inconvenience, as it enabled him to breathe purer air—no small advantage.

His suite of apartments consisted of a hall, which served as his reception-room, a small bedroom for himself, a small dining-room, a kitchen, and a tiny cabinet quite dark, which was intended for a lumber-hole, but was called the man-servant's bedroom. In it an old man who styled himself the count's man-servant, wore his livery and served him, slept. The hall was furnished with a seeming indifference to luxury and taste, the sole objects worthy of observation being two life size oil-paintings representing the contessa in her best days, dressed in gold-coloured satin—her favourite colour, and covered with costly jewels, and Guido at the age of five years.

"A more wondrously beautiful boy could not be seen," whoever saw the picture could not forbear exclaiming at his loveliness; at the same time involuntarily adding, "But how unlike his mother!"

It was about eleven o'clock when Rosalia was shown by the old man into Guido's bedroom. It was her privilege to be received without etiquette. She found the young man reclining in an easy-chair reading, or, rather, holding a book in his hand, with his eyes fixed on vacancy.

"Welcome, Rosalia," said he, as soon as he perceived her. "Come here, you shall sit in my arm-chair," he added, rising and taking another chair for himself. "What good luck brings you here?"

"I have brought you a few of your mother's favourite biscuits, which you have always said you liked." So saying, she opened a parcel she had placed on a small desk near the arm-chair. "But I will not take your easy seat; any chair is good enough for me."

"Now don't make me angry, Rosalia. The last time I saw you, you well-nigh drove me mad. Be more conciliatory."

"Very well, I will sit here. I will not make you angry. You seem very happy, happier than when we last met."

"Yes, Rosalia, I am very happy; and I am glad to say you are not a witch, although you choose to be considered one."

"It is no great detriment not to be a witch," replied Rosalia, smiling.

"You seem to be in high good humour. What luck have you had?"

"Tell me first your own good luck."

"For once you have not guessed right. You told me I should never become the husband of Centofoglia's beautiful and rich daughter, and yet my proposal for her hand has been accepted."

"Indeed! So your fears that there was a fortunate rival were unfounded?"

"No, my fears were not exactly unfounded. But that impediment is now removed."

"And is the day fixed for the wedding?"

"Not yet."

"I cannot say that I precisely understand you, Guido."

"I will explain my meaning. I have solicited Rosa's hand, and have been solemnly assured by her father that sooner or later she will be mine, but——"

Guido hesitated.

"But I suppose the lady is not willing?"

"Exactly; she is very young, and fancied herself in love with the traitor Antonio Foscarini."

Guido knew that he had been the first to awaken the spy's suspicions, and he was glad the result had proved so completely according to his wishes; still, he it remembered, he was not to blame that Foscarini was detected quitting the Spanish ambassador's premises, and he verily believed he was a traitor to his country.

"In a few weeks' time she will forget him, and then we shall be married. Her father has already given the necessary orders. Her trousseau is being prepared."

Rosalia looked thoughtful. Guido became aware of it, and added:

"Well, have you any prophetic sentence in store? Say whatever you like *now*, it cannot make me angry."

"I am in too great a hurry to think about prophecies," answered Rosalia, rising.

"You are in a hurry, indeed. You have not given me time to thank you for the biscuits," replied Guido, remembering he had omitted that politeness. "They will be quite a treat to me."

"I am glad to hear you say so," and Rosalia was already in the hall.

She glanced at her late mistress's portrait, then at Guido's, but made no remark. The latter had followed her, and on her opening the door to let her out, said:

"I hope to visit you in less than a fortnight, and I hope also to bring you a larger sum than usual. Then, as soon as I am married, I shall double your allowance, or, if you prefer it, I will procure you a suitable situation in the Centofoglia palace."

"In the Centofoglia palace!" exclaimed Rosalia.

Then, checking herself, she muttered, "I would die ten thousand times sooner!"

Guido did not understand the meaning of her exclamation, and mistook it for surprise.

"You wonder," said he. "Let me only become Centofoglia's son-in-law and you will see the change in your fortune."

"Thank you," answered Rosalia, drily. "I suppose you go there very often?"

"I dine there every day, and pass all my evenings there."

"Farewell, Guido," said Rosalia, abruptly; then, to atone for her abruptness, she added, "I hope to see you soon."

"Farewell, Rosalia, I hope so also," answered Guido, cheerfully.

Rosalia almost flew down the stairs. On reaching her home she threw herself on the chest by the side of her bed, leaned her head on her hand, and audibly, but fortunately there was no one to hear her, she said:

"This evening the queen enters her realm. This evening will see the accomplishment of twenty-five years' desires, the end of twenty-five years' sufferings. Oh that the hours would fly past!"

She arose, paced up and down the room, forgot the gondolier and his wife, and did not so much as remember the hour was past for her frugal dinner. On a sudden she stopped. Out of her wreck she had saved one good black stuff dress and a large black veil. She thought she would make herself as decent-looking as she could. It was her festival day, she would adorn herself for it. She opened the chest, took out the gown, carefully smoothed away the many creases a long laying by had caused, and laid it together with the veil ready on her bed.

She longed to be calm, but her heart beat violently; at times she spoke to herself, her eyes flashing fire; then she would try to subdue her feelings, and she partially succeeded.

As soon as it began to grow dark she dressed, put on her veil, and about eight o'clock set off for the Centofoglia palace.

Having obtained admission from the porter, she stalked proudly up the marble staircase, and earnestly asked the man-servant Beppo to allow her to speak with Rosa.

CHAPTER XIV.

FATHER PAUL'S HISTORY.

IN the superb hall of the Centofoglia palace sat its heartless owner, his afflicted daughter, Count Guido Bernardi, and Father Paul.

When Rosa found herself again alone in her room after Father Paul's visit, she returned to her crucifix, holding in her hands the precious miniature, now tenfold more priceless. She had bowed her head beneath the heavy stroke, she had embraced the cross—the only way not to sink when visited by deep affliction—and now, as the hours succeeded each other, she was enabled to sketch for herself a plan of life from which she resolved no human power should induce her to swerve. She determined to persist in her refusal of Count Bernardi's hand, or of any offer which might in future present itself, and ever remain faithful to the memory of the martyr, whose spirit she knew watched over her and prayed for her. She determined that as long as her father lived she would devote herself to him, and to the relief of the sick and needy. If she was destined to survive him, she would found a hospital in her palace, endow it richly, and, abandoning the world, take the veil and enclosing herself within its walls nurse the sick. Having settled thus far in her own mind, she became calmer, considering the severe blow she had received, than might otherwise have been expected.

A few minutes before sunset the very evening of which we are speaking, her father, who did not intend her to avoid company any longer, sent for her, and on her entering his study said, looking at her sternly:

"Rosa, I now suspect you loved the rebel. I forgive you, as you did not know what a viper he was. But I warn you, I do not mean to allow you to pass all your days shut up in your room. I insist on your dining at table, and spending the evening in the hall."

"My father," answered Rosa, in a calm, firm voice and manner, "I loved Antonio Foscarini, and I love his memory. I receive, as coming from the hands of God, the affliction his death causes me. I will obey you; I will dine at table, and pass the evening with you and our guests in the hall. I will even strive, I cannot say to be cheerful, but at least to take an interest in everything, and join in the general conversation; but, my dear father, you must first promise me that, as you cannot speak with respect of Antonio Foscarini, you will never mention him in my presence, and pray warn your friends not to speak of him when I am present."

"It is an odd request for a daughter to make to her father. I am not to speak of whom I please, and as I please! But suppose I consented; can I dictate to my friends what they are to say, or leave unsaid?"

"Dear papa, I cannot help cherishing the memory of Antonio Foscarini. If therefore I hear him called a traitor, a rebel, or by any other epithet it is thought patriotic to fling against his memory, I know what will happen: I shall either defend his cause with all my power, or be obliged to leave the room."

Marco Centofoglia knew that Rosa would be true to her word. She possessed one of those firm characters which would have preferred death to yielding when she thought herself in the right. Then, suppose a discussion really did take place in his hall, and his daughter was heard by some listening man-servant defending Antonio Foscarini's memory, might it not bring discredit on him? Might not the dreaded Council of Ten take umbrage? He decided to yield as far as he could to her wishes, and answered:

"I will humour you, spoiled child; but only, as far as lies in my power. Father Pio is gone to the country—for to him I could not have dared mention such a thing—so at least for the present you are safe on that score. There remains as our principal guest Count Guido Bernardi, and he is so obliging and amiable, takes so great an interest in you—so much greater than you deserve—that I am sure he will never consent to speak in your presence of Antonio Foscarini. Are you content?"

"Yes, dear father, I am; and I thank you. This evening I shall be the first to enter the hall."

Rosa kept her word.

As soon as twilight appeared, she called her maid to dress her.

"You will put on your usual light blue silk dress?" said the latter.

"No, Maria; I prefer wearing my black silk."

"You are not going to church. You are too young to wear black as evening-dress."

"Oh, there is not much of a party to-night in our house. This evening we shall only have one guest—perhaps two, if Father Paul comes. It suits me better."

Innocent artifice to induce her maid not to oppose her wish! She felt any other colour was not in unison with her poor aching heart, and she wished to show that little mark of respect to the memory of her lover.

The maid said nothing more, and helped her to put on the black dress. She had just entered the hall when Beppo announced Father Paul.

"Where is my father?" she asked anxiously.

"In his study, with Count Guido Bernardi, signora."

"Oh," thought Rosa, "he will be there some time. I can receive Father Paul in here."

"Show the Father into this room," she answered.

Rosa felt a great emotion on seeing Father Paul.

Her determination to be calm threatened to vanish, yet she experienced a singular comfort in the presence of the holy friar; she almost fancied herself nearer to Antonio Foscarini.

"I promised you, my daughter, to come to see you ere I left, and you see I have kept my word," said Father Paul, seating himself on a divan.

"I am truly grateful to you, Father," answered Rosa, placing herself by his side. "When do you leave?"

"To-morrow at early dawn."

"Shall you ever return again to Venice?"

"I am not quite sure; but I do not think so."

"And will you leave your native town for ever?" exclaimed Rosa in astonishment.

"My dear daughter, I do not know my native town. To me Venice is like any other place."

Rosa looked still more astonished.

"You appear surprised," continued Father Paul. "Ah! my daughter, if you knew my history, you would see you are not the only one severely afflicted in this world."

"Father, tell it to me. Do tell it to me," answered Rosa, earnestly. Then recollecting herself and reflecting Father Paul might not wish to recount his life, she added humbly, "Forgive me, Father, I ought not to have asked such a favour. But I thought it would help me to bear my own sorrow."

"It might, my daughter. I will tell you in a few

words my sorrows, and the consolations I drew from them."

Father Paul had hardly uttered the last word when Marco Centofoglia, accompanied by Count Guido Bernardi, appeared at the door of the hall.

"Alas! Father, Providence denies me the comfort of hearing you. That is my father, and the gentleman with him is a friend of his," said Rosa in a low voice.

"It makes no difference. If they do not object to hearing it, my life has no secret I wish to hide," replied Father Paul, in a reassuring tone.

Rosa was relieved; but with no small effort went forward to greet Guido Bernardi. She had not seen him for some days. He appeared to her more joyous than she had ever seen him. What a contrast between the two!

Marco Centofoglia always greeted the clergy, whether regular or secular, with uncommon civility. Father Paul accordingly thought he had never met with so courteous and amiable a person as the worthy patrician.

When Guido's turn came to be introduced, he approached, bowed, then started, and retreated a few steps backwards. The Capuchin, Marco, and Rosa looked at him astonished. He soon recovered his presence of mind, and, advancing a second time, said:

"Forgive me, reverend Father, your likeness to my dear departed mother is such that it almost seemed to me to be herself before me. I have never seen the like. I again beg your forgiveness."

"Ah!" exclaimed Rosa. "It is true—so it is. I thought Father Paul very like some one I had seen, but could not remember whom."

"Yes," put in Marco, solemnly. "The reverend Father greatly resembles the late noble and learned Contessa Sofia Bernardi."

"Such things happen," replied Father Paul, smiling kindly; "and they are strange. It is one of the caprices of nature to bestow at times the same features on persons born in the most widely different spheres of life, and certainly there could not be two persons with greater disparity in birth and circumstancos than the Contessa Sofia Bernardi and myself. I do not so much as know who my parents were!" and Father Paul sighed, bending down his head.

"Papa!" said Rosa, with an earnest, supplicating expression in her beautiful blue eyes, "this holy friar has promised to tell me the history of his life. He was just going to begin when you came in——"

"I do not wish to prevent him, my child; neither does Guido, unless his reverence prefers recounting his history to you alone. On the contrary, I should esteem myself highly favoured," he added, turning towards Father Paul, "if your reverence would allow me to be a listener."

"I can say the same for myself," said Guido; "I shall hear your reverence with great pleasure."

"I will repay your courtesy, gentlemen," answered Father Paul, "by narrating my story in as few words as possible.

"There is an insignificant country inn about a stone's-throw from the last house of a small place called Piazzola, some miles distant from the Berici hills. Early one morning, twenty-four years ago, when the innkeeper opened his door, he found on the rustic step a bundle apparently of dried leaves. He untied the handkerchief that bound it, and then discovered a little boy fast asleep, without other clothing than a thick towel, and who, he judged, could not be more than a year old. Need I say that unhappy child was myself? No one knew who had put me there, unless credit be given to an old man, fond of drink, who declared that just as it was beginning to dawn, and he was returning to his home, he saw afar off a very tall female figure carrying two bundles; he saw her stoop at the step of the small inn, then hurry away, and it then seemed to him that the two bundles were reduced to one. But as this old man was never quite sober, no one took much notice of what he said."

On hearing these words Marco Centofoglia felt an uncomfortable connection of ideas, but made no remark.

"The innkeeper was a Lombard, and had no children, so he judged Providence had sent me to him, and taking me to his wife, said he meant to adopt me. She did not oppose her husband's wishes, but was perfectly indifferent towards me. When I was five years old, my adopted father returned to his own country, much against his wife's inclination, who, being a native of the place, did not like to leave it. He had sold his house and business to a friend, a single man some years younger than himself.

"For a few months after our arrival at Monza, his native town, his affairs prospered; but afterwards things changed for the worse, and though the good man's affection for me and his tender care of me prevented my feeling the consequences of his reduced circumstances, I felt uncomfortable at seeing the privations both himself and his wife endured. I had attained my seventh year when the good and kind man died. He died in a hovel on a heap of straw, but never did the slightest complaint escape his lips, never did he regret the privations he had subjected himself to on my account. I have often reflected on the sweet and holy example of patient virtue he left me.

"No sooner had he closed his eyes than his wife returned to Piazzola. She took me with her, and after a few weeks I learned from her that I was to call father the new proprietor of the small inn, whom she had married. I felt so great a repugnance to calling that stern man—at least, stern towards me—by the same endearing appellation I used to call my adopted father, that notwithstanding my mother's threats and even blows, I never would and never once did say father to him. He hated me from the time of his marriage, and ill-treated me in every way imaginable. It was a wretched period of my wretched life!

"I was now thirteen years old. A considerable theft took place in the inn. I was accused of having helped the thieves, and though I gave a very reasonable and conclusive proof of my perfect innocence, I was arrested by order of the innkeeper and committed to the prison of Verona.

"I remained there two whole years, subjected to every species of suffering; but I bless that time, for it proved beneficial to my eternal interest, and the Christian ought to desire nothing better.

"In the same cell in which I was confined was a native of Milan, condemned for debt. He was a truly good and pious man. He suffered through the wickedness of others, for he had entrusted a large sum of money to some friends, and they had lost it, or at least had given that excuse for not returning it. In order not to deprive his family of the common necessaries of life, he had borrowed money, meaning to return the loan in a few weeks. Unfortunately his business did not prosper, and being unable to keep his promise, he was sent to prison by order of his heartless creditor.

"He took a great fancy to me, spoke to me of the blessings which sufferings borne with Christian resignation bestow on sinful man. He made me aware that the sinner ought to wish to suffer on earth in order to become like his heavenly pattern Christ, and every evening would ask me to say the Rosary with him. By a happy and certainly Providential interference, we were freed the same day.

"He insisted on taking me to his house in Verona, where he had settled. He found, alas! what a sad havoc his imprisonment and its succeeding poverty had wrought in his family. His wife and children had been obliged to sell their all; they were reduced liter ally to a state of starvation and nakedness. I saw I was a charge upon him, and offered to quit his home. He would not hear of it, and perceiving that his long confinement had brought discredit on his name, and an honourable subsistence was denied him, he left Verona for Milan, hoping to better his circumstances.

"Providence helped him, for he not only found occupation for himself, but plenty of work for me also.

"He had a large family, of whom the eldest was a beautiful girl of my own age. I loved her, and she loved me.

"It seems strange, does it not, that a friar should talk of love? But love is holy when kindred spirits meet, whose first love is their God, and I can say with truth our love was of this kind. No earthly passion marred our affection; our souls loved each other with an eternal love.

"When we were both twenty years old we married. I thought myself, and justly so, the happiest of men. I did not envy the richest and greatest patrician his wealth and his titles; I possessed a treasure which far outshone them all.

We had been married two months when the plague broke out in Milan—you know, with what intense fury. We were both attacked by it, taken to the Lazaretto. and placed in separate wards of the vast building.

We felt the separation acutely, but could not help it. I recovered, and as soon as I was able to walk a little asked to be allowed to go and inquire after my wife. I was not denied this favour, through the kind interference of a Capuchin Father; and after some difficulty and intense anxiety I found out the ward where she had been placed. But how did I find her? Breathing her last! She had just time to recognise me, and beg of me to trust in God, and be devoted to His service and that of His Holy Mother, before she expired.

"I felt stunned. I left the ward, not knowing whither I went, when my Saviour's mercy brought before me the same kind Capuchin Father. He stopped me, and hearing the sad recital of my affliction, took me with him, and endeavoured to comfort me by inspiring me with that holy faith and resignation, 'which,' said he, 'is the only fitting state of the Christian.' He partly succeeded, for he prevented my giving way to despair; but I was so truly wretched without her on whom I had centred my strongest affection, that I could not make up my mind to return to my former home and occupation.

"The same kind friar advised me to seek the counsel and assistance of the Archbishop of Milan, Federigo Borromeo, and I did so. The holy prelate received me with his accustomed unvaried kindness, and having told me how sorrow is sent in mercy, he advised me to abandon the world for a few months, and retire to a monastery. I obeyed this wholesome advice, and chose a monastery of the Capuchin Order.

"I will not trespass on your patience by telling you the reflections I made in that blessed retreat, nor how completely I felt the total nothingness of all earthly enjoyments. Within two years I entered the Order, and at my own request was appointed to the office of comforting and instructing poor prisoners, especially those condemned to death.

"Many are the consolations Providence has vouchsafed me in the performance of these holy duties.

"A twelvemonth afterwards I was sent to Venice; but whether at Milan or here I bless the hand that never strikes but in tender mercy and love, and am persuaded more and more, by all I have seen, heard, and suffered, that we ought only to regret one thing, to dread only one thing—sin.

"To-morrow I leave for Rome, having resolved to pass the rest of my life in strict penance in the Eternal City.

"Amongst the remembrances I carry with me of Venice, the courtesy I have met with in this noble house, and the patience with which you have all been pleased to listen to the history of the poor friar, will ever be a very gratifying one."

CHAPTER XV.

VENGEANCE.

N finishing the last words of his history, Father Paul looked at Rosa, as much as to say:

"My daughter, dost thou see? Thou art not the only afflicted one on earth!"

And Rosa seemed to answer:

"Father, although thy woes have been great, mine are still greater."

Marco wondered how it was possible to conceive happiness without comfort and luxury, and thanked his stars he possessed both. Guido felt a sensation steal over him which was akin to remorse, and which, unfelt before he had heard Father Paul's history, plunged him into a reflective mood.

All seemed to fear breaking the solemn silence that had ensued.

Beppo the man-servant broke it for them.

"Signora," said he in a low voice, approaching Rosa, "a respectable-looking woman earnestly desires to speak with you."

"Show her into the next room, and tell her I am coming." Then turning towards Father Paul, who had made a movement as if to take leave, she said, "I shall be back in a minute, Father, so pray do not leave till my return."

"I will obey you most willingly, my daughter," answered Father Paul.

Rosa left the hall, and in the ante-chamber found herself in the presence of Rosalia Leoni. She thought she had never seen such a singular-looking person. The sight of her impressed her with an awe she could not conquer. She almost dreaded approaching her. Rosalia became aware of it, and was the first to approach.

"Signora," she said, softening her voice, and striving to hide her tumultuous feelings, "forgive my intruding at this late hour. Untoward circumstances have forced me to it. I must say something of the utmost importance to your illustrious father. I humbly beg your kind interference in order to be permitted to see him at once."

"Could you not say it to me?" answered Rosa, with an expression of concern in her manner.

"I am sorry I cannot, signora."

"At any other hour I would at once have taken you into his presence, but now he is not alone; there are two friends with him."

"Perhaps one is Count Guido Bernardi?"

"Yes. You know him, then?"

"Very well; and I do not mind speaking before him."

"If she does not mind," thought Rosa, "speaking in the presence of so worldly a youth as Guido Bernardi, she cannot mind telling her sorrows before Father Paul."

She therefore answered:

"So much the better for you, then. As for our other guest, he is a holy friar of the Capuchin Order, a saintly man: there is no fear of his disclosing anything you may wish to say."

Rosalia would have preferred that there had been no one else present except Rosa and Guido; but she knew she could make no further objection. She feared lest Rosa should at once order her to return another time, and she was determined all should be accomplished that evening—that very evening. Consequently she replied:

"Since you give me, kind signora, such comfortable assurance of silence on the part of the holy friar, I can speak in his presence also."

"Very well; wait a moment here, whilst I apprise my father."

And Rosa re-entered the hall.

"Papa," said she, "a very respectable-looking and very strange-looking woman also, who says she knows Count Guido Bernardi, wishes to tell you something."

Guido Bernardi's thoughts flew to Rosalia, and to her prophecy respecting his marriage, and he was going to invent some pretext to hinder her being admitted, when Marco prevented his saying a word by anwering Rosa readily:

"Let her come in. I am willing to hear what she has to say."

Rosalia's heart beat as if it would leap from her bosom when Rosa, going towards her, kindly gave her permission to enter.

"Papa says he will receive you at once." And she led her into the hall.

All eyes were at once fixed upon her. Guido became as pale as death.

Rosalia bowed to no one; glanced at no one; but went straight up to Marco Contofoglia. She then untied her veil, threw back the ends to render herself — as she thought — more recognisable, and said:

"Marco Centofoglia, dost thou know me?"

Marco did not answer; he could not. Had an apparition suddenly presented itself from the regions of death, he could not have felt or looked more aghast.

Rosalia continued in a low, ironical voice, her lips white with compressed rage:

"Thou dost not know me? Am I not thy betrothed —the only woman thou hast loved? 'A queen in her realm'? Yes, truly a queen in her realm!"

In repeating the last words, Rosalia's countenance changed: her cheeks became crimson, her eyes flashed, yet she smiled—that is to say, she showed her white teeth, with that sinister grin of hers which bespoke evil. Not even Satan, when he uttered the awful sentence in Milton's sublime poem, "Evil, be thou my good," could have looked more fiendish than did at that moment the once beautiful and loving Rosalia!

"Yes, traitor," she continued, "I am come a queen in my realm, but to devastate it, to bring havoc and desolation with me. Didst thou think I should crouch quietly like a slave before thy treacherous conduct? Didst thou think my threats on that memorable evening when I met thee last would prove idle, and that I should leave thee to enjoy unmolested the fruit of thy treachery? Thou didst not know me well, alike terrible in love and in hatred. There," added she, pointing to Guido, "there is thy lost boy. There is the son thou hast mourned for. I stole him, and I deprived thee of him, but think not that I restore him again. No; he is in my power, for if thou dost denounce me I will denounce him. But ere I tell thee his crime I will relate my own."

Her hearers seemed turned into marble statues, for no one attempted to answer her; and after having stopped a moment to take breath, she continued:

"When I began to realise the magnitude of thy treachery and comprehend the abyss of my misery, I vowed my soul to the demon, if he would but help me to be revenged. My misfortunes obliged me to enter the household of the Contessa Sofia Bernardi. Before leaving Venice she sent me to the Berici Hills to fetch her little boy home. In going to the place where he was at nurse I passed near a hut. On the door step I saw a lovely boy—so lovely that I asked whose son he was. 'He is the only son and heir of the wealthy Venetian patrician, Marco Centofoglia,' was the answer. Then did the demon whisper in my ears: 'The long-desired moment has come. Steal him, and thou wilt be revenged.' I soon reached the village whither I was bound, meditating on my way how to steal the child. When the real little Count Guido Bernardi was consigned to me I retraced my steps towards the hut, devising the means to lay hold of the child unseen. The demon again helped me, for on approaching a large field I saw the little creature sitting alone near the outskirts of a wood. A woman was at a distance, and her back being turned, she could not see me. I pounced on the child, snatched him up in a moment, and retired into the wood.

"When I had reached the furthest end I decided on the course to pursue. I would not hurt an innocent child; to abandon it I knew would be useless, for although hard-hearted to me, thou wouldst have left no stone unturned to recover thy child. So I resolved to exchange the two little boys, take to the contessa—who was leaving for Lucca, and had never seen her own since she sent him to nurse—the stolen one, and leave hers near some house or cottage, where some one would doubtless take pity on him. Accordingly I undressed the two children. The clothes of the real Count Guido Bernardi I put on thy child, and his I tore up and scattered all over the wood, to make people believe some wild animal had devoured him. I then wrapped up the other poor little creature in a towel I had with me, and having gathered some dried leaves from the wood, I put them in a handkerchief, laid him on them, and made a bundle. But I did not like to leave him so near the place where he had been put out to nurse. Going out of my way, I arrived early the next morning, in fact, just at dawn, at a small place, and I deposited him on the steps of a village inn. I learned afterwards that the place is called Piazzoli."

"Oh, Father Paul!" exclaimed Rosa, as the good friar made a movement forward.

Rosalia gave neither time for further remarks, and continued:

"I met the contessa at Mestre, and there also I saw thee with the woman thou hadst preferred to me. I guessed thou wert going to seek thy child, and fearing he should be recognised I covered him till I almost smothered him, and I gloated over my revenge. My mistress sent me once to Venice. I met thy wife, and followed her into St. Mark's. I predicted evil to her expected infant; I saw her become pale, and rejoiced. I have always taken care of thy son, though at times the thought of the wrongs done me by his father may have made me cross towards him, and he would have been rich, but for thy coming to Lucca. I had become so irritable, so desperate, I could not brook the thought that the son of the traitor to his vow should become a rich man. When the contessa was declared at the point of death I shut myself up with her, and told her the truth. Thou knowest the consequences. I have suffered, but thy son has suffered also, and most of all hast thou suffered, and shalt suffer still more. A brother fell in love with his own sister! and becoming jealous of the unhappy Antonio Foscarini, whom he thought his rival, set a spy upon him, who having seen him leaving the Spanish ambassador's premises, denounced him to the Council of Ten!"

"Oh, my God! . . . Mother of my God! . . . Oh, Father Paul!" cried Rosa, in broken accents of despair. "He has died for me! . . . To save my honour! . . . A martyr! . . . How can I live, knowing this?"

Rosa recounted as well as she could her last interview with her lover in the garden, and how, hearing a noise, to save her honour he had leaped into the small courtyard attached to the Spanish ambassador's palace; then added:

"Oh, Father Paul, this is more than I can bear; it is an insupportable agony! Do *you* proclaim to the world that he died innocent . . . through me. Ah, cruel laws of my country! Ah, traitor!" and she turned towards Guido, who appeared not to have strength to answer. She suddenly checked herself, and bowing down her head, whilst big tears were trickling down her cheeks, subjoined: "and yet thou art my brother—my dearest mother's beloved child!"

At these last words the living stream rushed into Guido's brain, animation returned, and turning towards Rosalia, his cheeks and forehead scarlet, his eyes almost starting from their sockets, he cried:

"Fiend of hell! what crime had two innocent children committed that thou shouldst have wreaked thy vengeance on them? Let me fly from thy hateful sight, from the presence of man, and never behold anyone again."

Having thus spoken, he rushed from the room.

Father Paul, who during this scene had not uttered a word, and who, having abandoned the world, did not care whether he was a count or a beggar, felt no small concern for the eternal interest of his fellow-victim's soul. Seeing how he rushed out of the room, and justly fearing the awful consequences of despair caused by remorse and disappointment, he turned quickly towards Rosa, saying:

"My daughter, don't regret Foscarini's innocent death. He only resembles still more our Heavenly Pattern and the early martyrs. I shall have his innocence proclaimed, I promise you, but now I must follow your brother. *He* needs more than you the support which religion alone bestows."

In a moment he had quitted the hall in search of Gustavo Centofoglia.

Rosalia now remained alone with her former lover and Rosa. She looked around her, but did not speak. Presently she left the room without saying another word.

Anyone who had observed her ascending the staircase, and had afterwards seen her descending it, would have remarked a great difference in her mien and look. Was she satisfied with the revenge obtained?

We shall see.

CHAPTER XVI.

THE LOST SHEEP.

THE next morning all was bustle and confusion in the Centofoglia palace.

The only words the lips of the now wretched owner of so much splendour had uttered were:

"I will go to my villa near Rovigo, and there retire for the remainder of my life."

Although Rosa's affliction had been greatly increased by the agonising revelation made by Rosalia, and she was a prey to the most conflicting thoughts, she still felt a daughter's affectionate concern at the state of her father, and she wisely reflected the best thing for him was a change. She accordingly gave the most stringent orders for the preparations to be hurried, and two days after that unfortunate evening Marco, his daughter, and all his household, left for Rovigo.

But Rosa was destined to be greatly disappointed. The change so far benefited her parent that it prevented a complete paralysis of the brain, which must have taken place had he remained in his palace at Venice, where the associations had become too powerful for his poor weakened mind; but he never regained his former brilliancy of thought. Even his tastes had changed. He cared little for his horses, less for the comforts and luxury he had before doated upon. He rose late, then went out into the fields wandering about. It mattered little whether the rays of the sun scorched him, or the winds blew on him, or the rain drenched him. He generally dined alone, and retired to his room early in the evening.

Thus passed two whole years, during which Rosa endeavoured by every means in her power to shake off his torpor. She called to her aid the powerful persuasives of religion, and the advice of eminent physicians. He did not refuse to listen to the sweet comforts of the one, and followed the prescriptions of the other, more, however, like an automaton than a living being. But all proved useless. He gently faded away, and died in his loving daughter's arms at the end of two years. The only singular clause in his will—by which he left all his property to Rosa, unless his son should claim the half, which in that case he allotted him—was that he should be interred in the common churchyard, and laid in his grave without a coffin. Furthermore, no monument, not so much as a stone, was to mark the spot where he lay; a simple wooden cross, he said, was good enough for him.

From this Rosa gathered he had become convinced of the nothingness of every human comfort and joy. This inference comforted her greatly, but she felt she could, without being accused of disobedience to her parents' orders, depart from his injunctions.

She had him interred in the church of a small village near to her estate, where a noble though simple monument, erected by her orders, was placed over his grave. Having paid this last mark of respect to her father's memory, she left Rovigo, and returned to Venice in order to put into execution the plan formed on the day when she had learned her lover's sad end.

The splendid palace, of which she was left sole owner, she had fitted up as a hospital for both sexes and children, selling for that purpose all the costly furniture and works of art it contained.

The hall, and the rooms on the right hand, were changed into large airy wards for the female sex. The small drawing-room, in which Antonio Foscarini had first avowed his love for her, became her cell. Her father's study a very simple reception-room. On the left hand were the wards for the male sex. The second story was allotted to children and the other inmates of the establishment. On the ground occupied by the garden a large and handsome church was built, with an entrance on the small square.

The high altar was dedicated to the Holy Rood. The one on the right—on the very spot where Foscarini bade her farewell—to the Blessed Virgin, and the one on the left to St. Antonio of Padua, to whom, indeed, the whole establishment was dedicated.

In choosing St. Antonio as the celestial patron of

her charitable institution it must be owned Rosa thought more of honouring Foscarini's memory than that of the saint's.

No doubt the celebrated miracle-working citizen of Heaven forgave her, and blessed her good work, for the happy above excuse the frailties of an afflicted heart.

Whilst the palace was being transformed to suit its new object Rosa entered as novice a convent of the Order of St. Chiara. When it was finished she pronounced her solemn vows, and taking, by permission of the ecclesiastical authorities, a certain number of nuns of the same Order with her to help her to nurse the sick, she took up her abode in the hospital, becoming at the same time the superior of the small sisterhood.

Her total forgetfulness of self, her devotion to the sick, the kind words she alone knew how to use in order to comfort the afflicted, the noble acts of charity she continually performed, while they helped her to bear the weight of her own irreparable affliction, caused her also to be named, by the universal consent of all who saw her, by the glorious appellation of Angel of Consolation, by which she was better known than by the one of Sœur Ancilla taken in becoming a nun.

One evening, two years after she had taken the veil, an old woman, who had been attacked by the mob as a witch who had caused the death of a young girl, was brought to the hospital with several mortal wounds on her head, these had bled so profusely that the poor old creature was totally insensible. She was placed in the only empty bed in the female part of the establishment, which happened to be in the large ward that had formerly been the reception-room of the Centofoglia family.

Suor Ancilla's devoted heart prompted her to hasten to the bed of the poor woman, to help to dress her wounds, and bring her back to consciousness. Casting her eyes on her, she felt a shivering sensation creep over her, for though she had but once seen that countenance, she had never forgotten it.

The physicians told her, and her own experience assured her, the sufferer was fast approaching her end. Oh, how earnestly did Suor Ancilla pray that she might so far recover her senses as to be enabled to welcome the holy balm of charity she wished to pour into her unforgiving heart! It was not her turn to sit up, yet she said to the sister appointed to that duty that she meant to nurse the new-comer, and would consequently pass the night in that ward.

Towards midnight the invalid moved, and opened her eyes. Her kind nurse, who was watching her with the utmost solicitude, thanked God in her heart, and quickly gave her a strengthening draught. Seeing she took it willingly, and seemed sufficiently recovered to be able to hear and listen, she took her hand, and pressing it affectionately, said:

"My good woman, what is your name?"

"Rosalia Leoni," was the faint reply.

"You feel a little better now?"

"Yes, signora; but my head aches."

"No wonder. Bear it with resignation, and it will benefit you in a better world. Do you wish me to pray with you? She who is styled Health of the Sick—Salus Infirmorum—will intercede for you."

"Pray, signora, don't let me be disturbed by that nonsense," replied Rosalia, returning to her accustomed savageness.

Suor Ancilla thought that it might be advisable to let the blighted creature know with whom she was speaking. It might help to render her more humble; accordingly, she let the subject drop, and asked her in the same kind tone of voice:

"Do you know me?"

"I have never known nuns. I have never so much as spoken to one. How can I know you?"

"I was not always a nun. You have seen me before. Look at me well, and try to remember me."

Rosalia looked at her, then answered:

"I have a faint idea that I have seen you, but I cannot remember when and where. My poor brain is so confused."

"I am the daughter of Marco Centofoglia," replied Suor Ancilla at once.

To her great surprise Rosalia's countenance brightened up.

"I am glad of it," she exclaimed. "Can you tell me anything of your brother?"

"I am sorry I cannot. Both my poor father and

myself made many inquiries respecting him, but they proved of no avail. I imagine he went to some far-distant country."

"I know I am dying. It would have gladdened me in my last moments to know him well and happy."

"You loved him then?"

"No; I did not love him, neither do I love him now; but those words of his, 'Of what crime had two innocent children been guilty that thou shouldst have wreaked thy revenge on them?' have all this time been ringing in my ears, and prevented my feeling the satisfaction I should otherwise have felt after *that* evening."

"Was it ever known that revenge could produce any real satisfaction? It must always engender remorse. Forgiveness *alone* gives peace."

"Forgiveness! forgiveness!" almost screamed Rosalia, raising her head.

The effort overpowered her, and she sank back exhausted.

"Be calm!" said Suor Ancilla; "my *only* wish is to comfort you, and not to agitate you. Have you not said that you did not feel so happy after *that* evening as you had expected?"

"Yes, that is true. I ascended the staircase of your palace in triumph, fancying that the rest of my life would have felt the happy influence of that evening's joy, instead of which, no sooner had Guido—I cannot call him by his real name—uttered those words, than I felt a dejection come over me—a sensation unfelt before. . . ."

"It was remorse," put in Suor Ancilla, interrupting her. "It was sent in mercy. If you knew what the real Count Guido Bernardi had suffered!"

"No—I had been too much wronged. After such wrongs I could not feel remorse. It was unhappiness—despair."

"You are mistaken. That unhappiness was the voice of God speaking to your soul."

"No. After that evening everything continued to go wrong with me, as it has throughout my life; things went even worse also. I had no longer the little allowance Guido used to bring me regularly. My trade of making decoctions for the sick brought me in next to nothing. I could no longer pay the rent for my wretched room, and went to live in a dark hole under a staircase. I had previously been called a witch unjustly; now, to earn a crust of bread, I thought I had better be one in reality, and I began to practise on folks' credulity and tell fortunes. I also continued prescribing for the sick, but of late I have been very unfortunate, for I have lost many patients. A girl died whom I attended. Her parents set their neighbours against me as I was leaving the house. A crowd soon assembled, crying after me. I began to run away, and should have succeeded in escaping but for a gondolier, who seized me and held me whilst others beat me on the head with huge sticks. I know why that gondolier wished my death. His name is Bartolommeo Reni."

"Poor woman, how much you have suffered! But why did the gondolier wish you dead?"

"Because I drew from him a secret, and he has always feared the consequences. Signora, do you see, near that bed, the last of the row, your father is seated? Ah, no! I am mistaken, it is not he. It is Guido. Now he has disappeared."

Suor Ancilla saw that Rosalia's mind was beginning to wander. She did not answer her, and let a few minutes pass. Seeing she appeared to have regained a right conception of what was going on, she again took her hand and asked:

"Shall I now summon to you our good Father Modesto?"

"Signora, leave me to die in peace, as my father did."

"It is exactly in peace, reconciled to God, that I wish to see you die. I have sat up with you to-night in order to help as far as I can in saving your soul, which is as dear to me as my own." And Suor Ancilla warmly pressed the sinner's hand.

Rosalia was moved; and fixing her large dark eyes, rendered dim by the approach of death, on her, she said softly:

"How can you feel any concern in my soul's welfare? Have I not been in a great measure the cause of all you have suffered?"

"I do not look at the cause of my sufferings when, thanks to the Almighty's mercy, I can now bless Him for them. Will you not bless Christ with me, who has brought you into the palace, nay, into the very hall, where you enjoyed a moment's guilty triumph, and humbling yourself before him, ask pardon, and obtain mercy?"

Rosalia looked around her. She had been carried into the hospital senseless, and, although she had recovered her senses, she did not know where she was, still less could she imagine that simple ward had been once the superb reception-hall of the Centofoglia family! Those indelible words, "A queen in her realm," haunted her again; but she stifled the thought, and, fixing her eyes again on Suor Ancilla, she said:

"Signora, you do not know who I am. I am not a Christian. I am a daughter of Israel."

Suor Ancilla started. Rosalia continued:

"My real name is Rachel Levi. I was born in Palestine, at Bethlehem, and, when two years old, was taken by my father to Girgento in Sicily, where we remained some years. On coming to Venice my father passed for a native of that island. I thought I was a Sicilian by birth, and a Christian, until my father's death. In his last moments he told me his history; a history of much suffering, and much—but a daughter must be silent on a parent's faults. Poor man, he suffered much by the Christians, and——"

"Alas! not all who profess to be Christians are such in truth," replied Suor Ancilla.

The interruption obliterated from Rosalia's weakened memory the rest of the sentence. She stopped and shut her eyes. Her breathing became hard and convulsive.

Suor Ancilla prayed, and taking a small phial full of aromatic vinegar from her pocket, approached it to her nostrils.

Rosalia opened her eyes, said in a faint voice, "Marco, Marco!" shut them again aud spoke no more.

Suor Ancilla saw there was not a moment to be lost, and no time to call in a minister of religion. There was a glass of water on a stand beside the bed. She snatched it up, and pouring some of the liquid on Rosalia's head pronounced the holy words of Baptism.

Rosalia felt the water on her forehead, smiled, and died.

Was she saved? Let us hope so. The more we people Heaven, even if in no better way than by our wishes, the better it will be for our eternal interests.

CHAPTER XVII.

THE FRIAR AND THE NUN.

A TWELVEMONTH passed. A Capuchin friar was seen slowly mounting the staircase of the hospital of S. Antonio. He was tall, extremely thin, and sunburnt. His long beard was light, and though he was still very young, it was already tinged with grey. He stooped, but his stoop was evidently not caused by constitutional weakness, but by the habit of humbling himself, and of considering himself beneath others.

On reaching the first landing he asked to speak with the Superior of the sisterhood.

Suor Ancilla was in her cell musing on the past, fancying she almost saw before her Antonio Foscarini, and heard those words of love, which, though a nun, she could recall to mind without fear, because without remorse.

A young novice entered her cell.

"Mother," said she, "a Capuchin asks to speak with you."

Suor Ancilla's thoughts fled to Father Paul; she answered readily and gladly:

"Show him into the reception-room."

Her orders were instantly obeyed, and almost at the same moment she entered the room.

Imagining that it could be no other than Father Paul, she went up to him at once. Finding out her mistake, she as quickly retreated. The friar advanced towards her, and bending his head as if to hide his strong emotion, humbly said:

"Sister, do you no longer know me?"

"Oh!" exclaimed Suor Ancilla, turning pale, "it is you, Guido—I mean Gustavo?"

"Call me not," exclaimed the friar, lifting up his head, "by those names of guilt and sorrow. Call me by my name of penance—Fra Antonio."

"Oh! my brother," replied his sister with joy, "my prayers have been heard. You have chosen the path of penance, and you have been forgiven."

"I trust I have. Father Paul—may his memory be for ever blessed . . ."

"Has he gone to his rest then?" interrupted Suor Ancilla.

"He has. He showed me the way to peace; he calmed my agitated spirit; he prevented despair from taking entire possession of me. Yes, blessed be his memory!"

"How? Tell me," said Suor Ancilla, earnestly.

"When I fled from the hall on *that* evening I descended the staircase as quickly as I could, but not too quickly for that saint's solicitude. He overtook me near the porter's lodge, took my arm in his, and led me to a gondola. I allowed myself to be led, for I did not know what I was about. The gondola stopped at a monastery. He took me again by the arm and conducted me to his cell. He then spoke for the first time.

"'Brother,' said he, 'we are fellow victims. God has brought us together. Let us obey His will.'

"I am desperate," I answered, looking about me wildly; 'I cannot live. I have lost all.'

"Father Paul looked at me fixedly, nay, sternly. I felt I could not bear his look, and I bowed my head.

"'A sinner,' he said, after some minutes, 'a sinner says he cannot live! I ask that sinner whether he can die? Whether he can *now* meet, at the foot of the throne of the righteous Judge, Antonio Foscarini?'

"I did not answer. That name stunned me. Father Paul continued:

"'When man, forgetting the obedience due to his Maker's laws, insults Him by disobedience such as thine, there is but one way left him, and that is the way of repentance.'

"He was silent again.

"'I will not leave thee,' continued he after this second pause; 'I will watch over thee, and finally bring thee to the foot of the Cross. Afterwards thou mayest go wherever thou listeth; thou wilt be safe.'

"Father Paul passed the night in prayer and reading. I never moved from the place where I had first seated myself. My temples beat so that I was obliged to hold my head not to go mad; and such was the conflict and confusion of my thoughts, that to this moment I cannot well remember what I thought. I only recollect the intense suffering, both moral and physical, I underwent.

"When day began to dawn Father Paul left the cell, and presently another friar entered and stayed with me. I learned afterwards that Father Paul had taken this precaution lest my despair should lead me to attempt some rash act against my life; he passed that morning in informing the Council of Ten and the Inquisition of Foscarini's innocence, and in having it published as widely as possible.

"On his return he told me he was going to leave that evening for Rome, and that he had taken proper measures for my departure also. I was only too glad to hear this, and after a journey without incidents of any kind, we reached Rome, and went straight to a Capuchin convent.

"I had become calmer and more reconciled to life, and Father Paul judged I could have a cell to myself next his. But, although apparently calm, my very soul was tortured by remorse. I found some comfort in following the rules of the convent, and more in listening to Father Paul's holy conversations, and in the assurance he gave me of the pardon of God and of my victim.

"After a year passed in this way, one day, drawn by a force to which I could oppose no resistance, I threw myself at the foot of the Cross and wept—wept bitterly. I rose a new creature, with the full determination of passing my life in the strictest penance. I entered the Capuchin Order, endeared to me by Father Paul's holiness and the humble virtue of almost all its members.

"I took the name of Antonio in order to keep my crime ever before me. On one subject, however, I felt I had not changed. I could not think of Rosalia Leoni with that entire forgiveness a sinner who needed forgiveness so much himself should think.

"One night after the midnight devotion in common I entered Father Paul's cell, in order to pass the remainder of the night by his bedside; for, my sister, he was ill then, very ill, and I told him how I felt towards Rosalia, that I could not forgive her as a Christian should. He answered me:

"'Brother, she is the cause of all I have suffered, but I do not feel anger against her. I shall soon have ended my course, and I see more and more clearly every moment that she deserves our pity, not our anger. Let us pray for her conversion.'

"We did so, and I can now understand the fervour of the prayer Father Paul offered for her. I remember the date; it was betwixt the 29th and 30th of March last year."

"The prayers offered by victims for those who have caused their sufferings, are *always* heard," answered

Suor Ancilla, her countenance brightening with holy joy. "On that very night Rosalia died in this hospital, in my arms."

She related all the particulars of Rosalia's decease.

"I thank the Almighty for all you tell me, sister. I have returned to Venice for two reasons. One was to seek that poor woman and try to convert her. I should have come sooner, but I would not leave Father Paul in his last moments, and waited to see him fall asleep ere I came. The other was to ask your forgiveness. Oh, my sister! believe me, I have suffered in entering under our paternal roof! I know this room. It was our father's study. Here I asked . . . Let me not dwell on that. Yes, my sister, forgive all you have suffered through me. Forgive me for our mother's sake. I am now going back to Rome to end my days in penance. Oh! forgive me; I implore it, for Antonio Foscarini's sake!"

"I forgive you, my brother, with all my heart," answered Suor Ancilla in a faltering voice.

They were the last words uttered by the brother and sister, ere they parted to meet no more on earth.

Not many years after, a small marble slab at the foot of the altar of the Blessed Virgin, in the church annexed to the hospital of St. Antonio, told the faithful that beneath it Rosa's aching heart had found peace. Whilst at Rome, in the grounds of a Capuchin monastery, a black wooden cross, without name or date, marked the solitary spot where lay the last descendant of the noble Venetian family Centofoglia.

THE END.

R. WASHBOURNE, PRINTER, 18 PATERNOSTER ROW, LONDON.

Extract from the **NEW YORK CATHOLIC BOOK NEWS**, May, 1879: "No publisher does more than does Mr. Washbourne to produce a variety of excellent books, and to spread Catholic literature far and wide."

R. WASHBOURNE'S

CATALOGUE OF BOOKS,

18 PATERNOSTER ROW, LONDON

680

True Wayside Tales. By Lady Herbert. Foolscap 8vo., 3s.; or cheap edition, in 5 vols., in pretty binding, price 6d. each.
1. The Brigand Chief, and other Tales.
2. The Martyr's Children, and other Tales.
3. What a Child can do, and other Tales.
4. Sowing Wild Oats, and other Tales.
5. The Two Hosts, and other Tales.

Chats about the Commandments. By the Author of "Aunt Margaret's Little Neighbours; or, Chats about the Rosary." Fcap. 8vo., 3s. *In the Press.*

The Golden Thought of Queen Beryl, and other Stories. By Marie Cameron. 1s. 6d.; or in pretty binding, cheap edition, in 2 vols., price 6d. each.
1. The Golden Thought of Queen Beryl, and The Brother's Grave. 2. The Rod that bore Blossoms, and Patience and Impatience.

THE NEW Catechism of Christian Doctrine. No. 1, ½d. each, or 3s. a 100; No. 2, 1d. each, or 5s. a 100.

Little Books of St. Nicholas. By F. B. Drew Bickerstaffe Drew.

Oremus; or, Little Mildred. Fcap. 8vo., 1s.

To be followed by about 12 others.

Dominus Vobiscum; or, the Sailor Boy. Fcap. 8vo., 1s.

Manual of Christian Doctrine; or, Catholic Belief and Practice familiarly and explained by Question and Answer. By Rev. Daniel Ferris. 6d.

Clare's Sacrifice. An impressive little tale, for First Communicants. By C. M. O'Hara. 6d.

Revelation—ab intra et ab extra. Being the substance of several conversations on First Principles. By Henry John Pye, Esq., author of "Testimony," "The Religion of Common Sense." 6d.

The Credentials of the Catholic Church. By the Rev. J. B. Bagshawe, author of "The Threshold of the Catholic Church," "The Catechism Illustrated," 12mo., 4s.

⁂ *Though this Catalogue does not contain many of the books of other Publishers, R. W. can supply any, no matter by whom they are published. All orders, so far as possible, will be executed the same day.*

School Books, *with the usual reduction*, Copy Books, and other Stationery, Rosaries, Medals, Crucifixes, Scapulars, Incense, Candlesticks, Vases, &c., &c., supplied. Foreign Books supplied. The publications of the leading Publishers kept in stock.

A Catalogue of Books imported from the United States post free.

R. Washbourne, 18 *Paternoster Row, London.*

Lectures for Boys. By the Very Rev. Francis Cuthbert Doyle, O.S.B., Canon of Newport and Menevia. 2 Vols., cloth boards, 10s. 6d.; or separately:—Vol. I., Containing—The Sundays of the Year, and Our Lady's Festivals, etc. 6s.—Vol. II., Containing—The Passion of Our Lord, and The Sacred Heart. 6s.; or may be had separately, in cloth flush:—The Sundays of the Year, 3s. 6d.; Our Lady's Festivals, etc., 2s. 6d.; The Passion of Our Lord, 3s.; The Sacred Heart, 3s.

Indulgences, Sacramental Absolutions, and the Tax Tables of the Roman Chancery and Penitentiary considered, in reply to the charge of Venality. New Edition, with additions and Index. By the Rev. T. L. Green, D.D., 4s. 6d.

The Jesuits. By Paul Feval. 12mo., 3s. 6d.

St. Gregory's Life and Miracles of St. Benedict. Edited by Dom Edmund J. Luck, O.S.B. With 52 large Photographs. Cloth, extra gilt, 31s. 6d., or without the Photographs, 10s. 6d., 4to. Also a Small Edition Fcap. 8vo., 2s.; stronger bound, 2s. 6d.

Jack's Boy. By M. F. S., author of "Fluffy," "Tom's Crucifix, and other Tales." 3s. 6d.

Lives of the Early Popes. By Rev. Thomas Meyrick, M.A. Second Series. From the time of Constantine to Charlemagne. 8vo., 5s. 6d. The First Series is on sale. Price, 4s. 6d.

The Catholic Pilgrim's Progress—Sophia and Eulalie. Translated from the French by George Ambrose Bradbury, O.C., Permissu Superiorum. 3s. 6d.; cheaper edition, 1s. 6d.

Bellevue and its Owners. A Tale for Boys. By C. Pilley. 2s.

Nellie Gordon, the Factory Girl; or, Lost and Saved. 6d.

Bertram Eldon. By the author of "Nellie Gordon." 1s.

The Violet Sellers; or, Kindness costs Little and is worth Much. Drama in 3 Acts for Children. 6d.

The Enchanted Violin. A Comedy in 2 Acts for Boys. 6d.

What Catholics do not Believe. By the Right Rev. Bishop Ryan, Coadjutor to the Archbishop of St. Louis. 12mo., 1s.

The Faith of our Fathers: Being a Plain Exposition and Vindication of the Church founded by our Lord Jesus Christ. By Most Rev. Archbishop Gibbons. 12mo., 4s.; paper covers, 2s. nett.

OREMUS, A Liturgical Prayer Book: with the Imprimatur of the Cardinal Archbishop of Westminster. 32mo., 452 pages, paper cover, 2s.; cloth, 2s. 6d.; embossed, red edges, 3s. 6d.; French morocco, 4s. 6d.; calf or morocco, 6s.; Russia, 8s. 6d. Also in superior or more expensive bindings.

A Smaller Oremus; an abridgment of the above. Cloth, 9d.; with red edges, 1s.; roan or French morocco, 2s.; calf or morocco, 3s. Also in superior or more expensive bindings.

The Child of Mary's Manual. Compiled from the French. Second Edition, with Imprimatur. 1s.

The Fairy Ching; or the Chinese Fairies' Visit to England. By Henrica Frederic. 12mo., 1s., gilt edges, 1s. 6d.

Story of a Paper Knife. By Henrica Frederic. 1s.; gilt, 1s. 6d.

The Siege and Conquest of Grenada. Allah Akbar—God is Great. An Arab Legend. From the Spanish. By Mariana Monteiro. 12mo., 3s. 6d.

Gathered Gems from Spanish Authors. By Mariana Monteiro, author of "The Monk of the Monastery of Yuste." 3s.

ABEL ACORN: a Story of Gradual Development. By Old Oak, 1s., cloth gilt, 2s. 6d.

Adelstan (Countess), Sketch of her Life and Letters. From the French of the Rev. Père Marquigny, S.J. 1s. & 2s. 6d.

Adolphus; or, the Good Son. 18mo., 6d.

Adventures of a Protestant in Search of a Religion. By Iota. 12mo., 2s. and 3s. 6d.

AGNEW (E.), Geraldine; a Tale of Conscience. 3s. 6d.

———— **The Convent Prize Book.** 2s. 6d.

Aikenhead (Mary), Life of. Giving a History of the Foundation of the Congregation of the Irish Sisters of Charity. 8vo., 15s.

A'KEMPIS—Following of Christ. Dr. Challoner's Edition, 32mo., 1s.; embossed red edges, 1s. 6d.; roan, 2s.; French morocco, 2s. 6d.; calf or morocco, 4s. 6d.; gilt, 5s. 6d.; russia, 7s. 6d., 10s. 6d. and 12s. 6d.; ivory, with rims and clasp, 15s., 16s., 18s.; mor. antique, with corners and clasps, 17s. 6d.; russia, ditto, ditto, 16s. 20s.,

———— with Reflections. 32mo., 1s.; Persian, 3s. 6d.; 12mo., 3s. 6d.; Persian, 7s. 6d.; mor., 10s. 6d.; mor. ant. 25s.

———— **The Three Tabernacles.** 16mo., 2s. 6d.

Albertus Magnus. By Rev. Fr. Dixon. 10s. 6d.; cheap ed., 5s.

Allah Akbar—God is Great. An Arab Legend of the Siege and Conquest of Granada. From the Spanish. By Mariana Monteiro. 12mo., 3s. 6d.

ALLIES (T. W.), St. Peter; his Name and his Office. 5s.

Alphabet of Scripture Subjects. On a large sheet, 1s.; coloured, 2s., mounted to fold in a book, 3s. 6d.

ALZOG'S Church History. 8vo. Vols. I. and II., 7s. 6d. each.

AMHERST (Rt. Rev. Dr.), Lenten Thoughts. 1s. 6d., stronger bound, 2s., with red edges, 2s. 6d.

ANDERDON (Rev. W. H., S.J.), To Rome and Back. Fly-Leaves from a Flying Tour. 12mo., 2s.

ANDERSEN (Carl), Three Sketches of Life in Iceland. Translated by Myfanwy Fenton. 2s. 6d., cheap edition, 1s. 6d.

Angela Merici (S.) Her Life, her Virtues, and her Institute. From the French of the Abbé G. Beetemé. 12mo., 3s.

Angela's (S.) Manual: a Book of Devout Prayers and Exercises for Female Youth. Cloth, 2s.; Persian, 3s. 6d.; calf, 4s. 6d.

Angels (The) and the Sacraments. 16mo., 1s.

———— **Month of the Holy Angels.** By Abbê Ricard. 1s.

Anglican Orders. By Canon Williams. 12mo., 3s. 6d.

Anglicanism, Harmony of. By T. W. M. Marshall. 2s. 6d.

Are You Safe in the Church of England? A Question for Anxious Ritualists. By Charles Walker, of Brighton. 8vo., 6d.

ARNOLD (Miss M. J.), Personal Recollections of Cardinal Wiseman, with other Memories. 12mo., 2s. 6d.

ARRAS (Madame d') The Two Friends; or Marie's Self-Denial. 12mo., 1s.; gilt edges, 1s. 6d.

Artist of Collingwood. 12mo., 2s.
Association of Prayers. By Rev. C. Tondini. 3d.
Aunt Margaret's Little Neighbours; or, Chats about the Rosary. 12mo., 3s.
BAGSHAWE (Rev. J. B.), Catechism of Christian Doctrine, illustrated with passages from the Holy Scriptures. 2s. 6d.
——— **The Credentials of the Catholic Church.** 12mo., 4s.
——— **Threshold of the Catholic Church.** A Course of Plain Instructions for those entering her Communion. 12mo., 4s.
BAGSHAWE (Rt. Rev. Dr.), The Life of our Lord, commemorated in the Mass. 18mo., 1s.
BAKER (Fr., O.S.B.), The Rule of S. Benedict. From the old English edition of 1638. 12mo., 4s. 6d.
Baker (Fr. Augustine, O.S.B.), Life and Spirit of. By the Rev. Dr. Sweeney. 12mo., 2s. 6d.
Baker's Boy; or, Life of General Drouot. 18mo., 6d.
BALDESCHI. Ceremonial according to the Roman Rite. Translated by Rev. J. D. Hilarius Dale. 12mo., 6s. 6d.
BALMES (J.L.), Letters to a Sceptic. 12mo., 3s. 6d.
BAMPFIELD (Rev. G.), Sir Ælfric and other Tales. 18mo., 6d.; cloth, 1s.; gilt, 1s. 6d.
BARGE (Rev. T.), Occasional Prayers for Festivals. 32mo., 4d. and 6d.; gilt, 1s.
Battista Varani (B.), *see* Veronica (S.). 12mo., 5s.
Battle of Connemara. By Kathleen O'Meara. 12mo., 3s.
BAUGHAN (Rosa), Shakespeare. Expurgated edition. 8vo., 6s. The Comedies only, 3s. 6d.
Before the Altar. 32mo., 6d.
Beleaguered Hearth (The). A Novel. 12mo., 2s. 6d.
BELL'S Modern Reader and Speaker. 12mo., 3s. 6d.
——— **Theory of Elocution.** 3s. 6d.
BELLECIUS (Fr.), Spiritual Exercises of S. Ignatius. 2s.
——— **Solid Virtue.** 12mo., 7s. 6d.
Bellevue and its Owners. A Tale for Boys. By C. Pilley. 12mo., 2s.
BELLINGHAM (Lady Constance) The Duties of Christian Parents. Conferences by Père Matignon. Translated with a Preface by the Rt. Rev. Mgr. Capel, D.D. 12mo., 5s.
Bells of the Sanctuary,—A Daughter of St. Dominick. By Grace Ramsay. 12mo., 1s. and 1s. 6d.; stronger bound, 2s.
BENEDICT (S.), The Rule of our most Holy Father S. Benedict, Patriarch of Monks. From the old English edition of 1638, Edited in Latin and English by one of the Benedictine Fathers of St. Michael's, near Hereford. 12mo., 4s. 6d.
Benedict's (S.) Manual. 18mo., 3s.
——— **Life and Miracles.** By S. Gregory the Great. From an old English version. By P. W. (Paris, 1608). Edited by Dom E. J. Luck, O.S.B. 4to. cloth, extra gilt, with 52 large Photographs, 31s. 6d.; or without the Photos., 10s. 6d. A small edition in fcap. 8vo. 2s.; or in stronger binding, 2s. 6d.
BENNI (Most Rev. C. B.), Tradition of the Syriac Church, concerning the Primacy and Prerogatives of S. Peter. 8vo., 7s. 6d.

Benvenuto Bambozzi (Fr., O.M.C.), of the Conventual Friars Minor, Life of, from the Italian (2nd edition) of Fr. Nicholas Treggiari, D.D. 12mo., 5s.
Berchmans (Bl. John), New Miracle at Rome, through the intercession of Bl. John Berchmans. 12mo., 2d.
Bernardine (St.) of Siena, Life of. With Portrait. 12mo., 5s.
Bertram Eldon. By M. A. Pennell. 12mo., 1s.
Bessy; or, the Fatal Consequence of Telling Lies. 12mo., 1s.; stronger bound, 1s. 6d.; gilt, 2s.
BESTE (J. R. Digby), Catholic Hours. 2s. 6d.; morocco, 6s.
——— **Church Hymns.** (Latin and English.) 32mo., 6d.
——— **Holy Readings.** 32mo., 2s., 2s. 6d.; roan, 3s.; mor., 6s.
BESTE (Rev. Fr.), Victories of Rome. 8vo., 1s.
BETHELL (Rev. A.), Our Lady's Month; or, Short Lessons for the Month of May, and the Feasts of Our Lady. 18mo., 1s., stronger bound, 1s. 6d.
Bible. Douay Version. 12mo., 3s.; Persian, 8s.; morocco, 10s. 6d. 18mo., 2s. 6d.; Persian, 5s.; calf or morocco, 7s.; gilt, 8s. 6d. 8vo. with borders round pages, Persian calf, 21s.; morocco, 25s. 4to., Illustrated, cloth, 21s.; leather extra, 31s. 6d. Illustrated, morocco, £5 5s.; superior, £6 6s.
Bible History for the use of Schools. By Gilmour. 12mo., 2s.
Bible History, Catholic Child's. Old Test., 3d.; New Test., 3d.
Blessed Lord. *See* Ribadeneira; Rutter (Rev. H.).
Blessed Virgin, Devotions to. From Ancient Sources. *See* Regina Sæculorum. 12mo., 1s. and 3s.
——— **Devout Exercise in honour of.** From the Psalter and Prayers of S. Bonaventure, 32mo., 1s.
——— **History of.** By Orsini. Translated by Provost Husenbeth. Illustrated, 12mo., 3s. 6d.
——— **Life of.** In verse. By C. E. Tame, Esq. 16mo., 2s.
——— **Life of.** Proposed as a model to Christian women. 12mo., 1s.
——— **in North America, Devotion to.** By Fr. Macleod. 5s.
——— **Veneration of.** By Mrs. Stuart Laidlaw. 16mo., 4d.
——— *See* **Our Lady,** p. 22; **Leaflets,** p. 16; **May,** p. 19.
Blindness, Cure of, through the Intercession of Our Lady and S. Ignatius. 12mo., 2d.
BLOSIUS, Spiritual Works of:—The Rule of the Spiritual Life; The Spiritual Mirror; String of Spiritual Jewels. Edited by Rev. Fr. Bowden. 12mo., 3s. 6d.; red edges, 4s.
Blue Scapular, Origin of. 18mo., 1d.
BLYTH (Rev. Fr.), Devout Paraphrase on the Seven Penitential Psalms. To which is added "**Necessity of Purifying the Soul,**" by S. Francis de Sales. 18mo., 1s. stronger bound, 1s. 6d.; red edges, 2s.
BONA (Cardinal), Easy Way to God. Translated by Father Collins. 12mo., 3s.
BONAVENTURE (S.), Devout Exercise in honour of Our Lady. 32mo., 1s.
BONAVENTURE (S.), Life of St. Francis of Assisi. 3s. 6d.
Boniface (S.), Life of. By Mrs. Hope. 12mo., 6s.

BOUDON (Mgr.), **Book of Perpetual Adoration.** Translated by Rev. Dr. Redman. 12mo., 3s.; red edges, 3s. 6d.

BOUDREAUX (Rev. J., S.J.), **God our Father.** 12mo., 4s.

BOURKE (Rev. Ulick J.), **Easy Lessons in Irish.** 2s. 6d.

———— **The Last Monarch of Tara.** 6s.

BOWDEN (Rev. Fr. John), **Spiritual Works of Louis of Blois.** 12mo., 3s. 6d.; red edges, 4s.

————**Oratorian Lives of the Saints.** (Page 22).

BOWDEN (Mrs.), **Lives of the First Religious of the Visitation of Holy Mary.** 2 vols., 12mo., 10s.

BOWLES (Emily), **Eagle and Dove.** Translated from the French of Mdlle. Zénaïde Fleuriot. 12mo., 2s. 6d. and 5s.

BRADBURY (Rev. Fr.), **Sophia and Eulalie.** (The Catholic Pilgrim's Progress). 12mo., 1s. 6d.; better bound, 3s. 6d.

BRICKLEY'S Standard Table Book. 32mo., ½d.

BRIDGES (Miss), **Sir Thomas Maxwell and his Ward.** 1s.

Bridget (S.), Life of, and other Saints of Ireland. 12mo., 1s.

Brigit (S.) Life of, &c. By M. F. Cusack. 8vo., 6s.

Broken Chain. A Tale. 18mo., 6d.

BROWNE (E. G. K., Esq.), **Monastic Legends.** 8vo., 6d.

BROWNLOW (Rev. W. R. B.), **Church of England and its Defenders.** 8vo., 1st letter, 6d.; 2nd letter, 1s.

———— **"Vitis Mystica"; or, the True Vine: a** Treatise on the Passion of our Lord. 18mo., 4s.; red edges, 4s. 6d.

BUCKLEY (Rev. M.), **Sermons, Lectures, &c.** 12mo., 6s.

BURDER (Abbot), **Confidence in the Mercy of God.** By Mgr. Languet. 12mo., 3s.

———— **The Consoler**; or, Pious Readings addressed to the Sick and all who are afflicted. By Père Lambilotte., 12mo., 4s. 6d.; red ed., 5s.

———— **Souls in Purgatory.** 32mo., 3d.

———— **Novena for the Souls in Purgatory.** 32mo., 3d.

Burial of the Dead. For Children and Adults. (Latin and English.) Clear type edition, 32mo., 6d.; roan, 1s. 6d.

BURKE (Edmund), **Life of.** By Professor Robertson. 3s. 6d.

BURKE (Rev. T. N.), **Lectures and Sermons.** 2 vols., 24s.

BURKE (James), **Travels of an Irish Gentleman in search of a Religion.** 12mo., 3s. 6d.

BUTLER (Alban), **Lives of the Saints.** 2 vols., 8vo., 28s.; gilt, 34s.; 4 vols., 8vo., 32s.; gilt, 50s.; leather, 64s.

———— **One Hundred Pious Reflections.** 18mo., 1s. and 2s.

BUTLER (Dr.), **Catechisms.** 1st, ½d.; 2nd, 1d.; 3rd, 1½d.

CALIXTE—Life of the Ven. Anna Maria Taigi. Translated by A. V. Smith Sligo. 8vo., 2s. 6d. and 5s.

Callista. Dramatised by Dr. Husenbeth. 12mo., 2s.

CAMERON (Marie), **The Golden Thought,** and other Stories. 12mo. 1s. 6d.; or cheap edition, separately, 6d. each.

1. The Golden Thought of Queen Beryl, and The Brother's Grave. 2. The Rod that bore Blossoms, and Patience and Impatience.

CARAHER (Hugh), **A Month at Lourdes and its Neighbourhood.** Two Illustrations. 12mo., 2s.

Catechisms—The Catechism of Christian Doctrine. *New edition*, No. 1, ½d., or 3s. a 100; No. 2, 1d. or 5s. a 100.
———— *Old edition, Half Price*, 1d., cloth, 2d.; interleaved, 8d.
——— **Illustrated with passages from the Holy Scriptures.** By the Rev. J. B. Bagshawe. 12mo., 2s. 6d.
——— **made Easy.** By Rev. H. Gibson. Vol. III., 4s.
——— By Fr. Power. 3 vols., 10s. 6d.; 2 vols., 7s. 6d.
——— **General Catechism of the Christian Doctrine.** By the Right Rev. Bishop Poirier. 18mo., 9d.
——— By Dr. Butler. 32mo., 1st, ½d.; 18mo., 2nd, 1d.; 3rd, 1½d.
——— By Dr. Doyle. 18mo., 1½d.
——— By Bishop Challoner. Grounds of Catholic Doctrine. 4d.
——— **Fleury's Historical.** Complete Edition. 18mo., 1½d.
——— **Frassinetti's Dogmatic.** 12mo., 3s.
——— **Keenan's Controversial.** 2s.
——— **Lessons on Christian Doctrine.** 18mo., 1½d.
——— **of Mythology.** 18mo., 6d.
——— **of Perseverance.** By Gaume. Vols. I. and II., 7s. 6d. each.
——— **of the Council.** 12mo., 3d.
——— **of the History of England.** By a Lady. 18mo., 6d.
Catherine Hamilton. By M. F. S. 12mo., 2s. 6d.; gilt, 3s.
Catherine Grown Older. By M. F. S. 12mo., 2s. 6d.; gilt, 3s.
Catholic Calendar for England. 6d.; Almanack, 1d.
Catholic Directory for Scotland. 1s.
Catholic Hours. By J. R. Digby Beste. 2s. 6d.
Catholic Piety. *See* Prayer Books, page 31.
Catholic Pilgrim's Progress—The Journey of Sophia and Eulalie to the Palace of True Happiness. 2s. 6d. Popular edition, 1s. 6d.
Catholic Sick and Benefit Club. By Rev. R. Richardson. 4d.
CHALLONER (Dr.), Grounds of Catholic Doctrine. 4d.
——— **Think Well on't.** 18mo., 2d.; cloth, 6d.
Chats about the Rosary. *See* Aunt Margaret's Little Neighbours.
Chats about the Commandments. By the same. *In the Press.*
CHAUGY (Mother Frances Magdalen de), Lives of the First Religious of the Visitation. 2 vols., 12mo., 10s.
Child's Book of the Passion of Our Lord. 32mo., 6d.
Child (The) of Mary's Manual. Second edition, 32mo. 1s.
Children of Mary in the World, Association of. 32mo., 1d.
Christ bearing His Cross. A Steel Engraving from the Picture miraculously given to Blessed Colomba, with a short account of her Life. 8vo., 6d.; proofs, 1s.
CHRISTIAN BROTHERS' Reading Books.
Christian Doctrine, Lessons on. 18mo., 1½d.
Christian, Duties of a. By Ven. de la Salle. 12mo., 2s
Christian Politeness. By the same Author. 18mo., 1s.
Christian Teacher. By the same Author. 18mo., 1s. 8d.
Christmas Offering. 32mo., 1s. a 100: or 7s. 6d. for 1000.
Christmas (The First) for our dear Little Ones. 4to. 6s.
Chronological Sketches. By H. Murray Lane. 2s. 6d.
Church Defence. By T. W. M. Marshall. 2s. 6d.
Church of England and its Defenders. *See* Brownlow (Rev.).
Cistercian Legends of the XIII. Century. *See* Collins (Fr.).

Cistercian Order: its Mission and Spirit. *See* Collins (Fr.).
Clare (Sister Mary Cherubini) of S. Francis, Life of. Preface by Lady Herbert. With Portrait. 12mo., 3s. 6d.
Clare's Sacrifice. By C. M. O'Hara. A Tale for First Communicants. 6d.
Cloister Legends; or, Convents and Monasteries in the Olden Time. 12mo., 4s.
COBBETT'S History of the Protestant Reformation. 4s. 6d.
COLLINS (Rev. Fr.), Legends of the XIII. Century. 12mo., 3s., or in 3 vols., 1s. 6d. each.
——— **Cistercian Order: its Mission and Spirit.** 3s. 6d.
——— **Easy Way to God.** Translated from the Latin of Cardinal Bona. 12mo., 3s.
——— **Spiritual Conferences on the Mysteries of Faith and the Interior Life.** 12mo., 5s.
COLOMBIERE (Father Claude de la), The Sufferings of Our Lord. Sermons preached in the Chapel Royal, St. James's, in the year 1677. Preface by Fr. Doyotte, S.J. 18mo., 1s.; stronger bound, 1s. 6d.; red edges, 2s.
Colombini (B. Giovanni), Life of. By Belcari. Translated from the editions of 1541 and 1832. With Portrait. 12mo., 3s. 6d.
Columba (S.) Life of, &c. By M. F. Cusack. 8vo., 6s.
Columbkille, or Columba (S.), Life and Prophecies. 3s. 6d.
Comedy of Convocation in the English Church. Edited by Archdeacon Chasuble. 8vo., 2s. 6d. *See* page 18.
COMERFORD (Rev. P.). Month of May for all the Faithful; or, a Practical Life of the Blessed Virgin. 32mo., 1s.
——— **Pleadings of the Sacred Heart.** 18mo., 1s.; gilt, 2s.; with the Handbook of the Confraternity, 1s. 6d. Hand-book, 3d.
Communion, Prayers for, for Children. Preparation, Mass before Communion, Thanksgiving. 32mo. 1d.
Compendious Statement of the Scripture Doctrine regarding the Nature and chief Attributes of the Kingdom of Christ. By C. F. A. 8vo., 1s.
COMPTON (Herbert), Semi-Tropical Trifles. 12mo., boards, 1s.; extra cloth, 2s. 6d.
Conferences. *See* Collins, Lacordaire, Mermillod, Matignon, Ravignan.
Confession and Holy Communion: Young Catholic's Guide. By Dr. Kenny. 32mo., 4d.; cloth, 6d.; red edges, 9d., French morocco, 1s. 6d.; calf or morocco, 2s. 6d.
Confidence in the Mercy of God. By Mgr. Languet. Translated by Abbot Burder. 12mo., 3s.
Confirmation, Instructions for the Sacrament of. A very complete book. 18mo., 3d.
CONSCIENCE (Hendrick), The Amulet. 12mo., 4s.
——— **The Conscript and Blind Rosa.** 12mo., 4s.
——— **Count Hugo.** 12mo., 4s.
——— **The Fisherman's Daughter.** 12mo., 4s.
——— **Happiness of being Rich.** 12mo., 4s.
——— **Ludovic and Gertrude.** 12mo., 4s.
——— **The Village Innkeeper.** 12mo., 4s.
——— **Young Doctor.** 12mo., 4s.
Consoler (The). By Abbot Burder. 12mo., 4s. 6d. and 5s.

Contemplations on the Most Holy Sacrament of the Altar; or Devout Meditations to serve as Preparations for, and Thanksgiving after, Communion. Drawn chiefly from the Holy Scriptures. 18mo., 1s. and 2s.; red edges, 2s. 6d.
Continental Fish Cook. By M. J. N. de Frederic. 18mo., 1s.
Conversion of the Teutonic Race. By Mrs. Hope. 2 vols. 10s.
Convert Martyr; or, "Callista." By the Rev. Dr. Newman, Dramatised by the Rev. Dr. Husenbeth. 12mo., 2s.
Convocation, Comedy of. By the Author of "The Oxford Undergraduate of Twenty Years Ago." 8vo. 2s. 6d.
CORTES (John Donoso), Essays on Catholicism, Liberalism, and Socialism. 12mo., 5s.
Credentials of the Catholic Church. By Rev. J. B. Bagshawe, author of "The Threshold of the Catholic Church." 12mo., 4s.
Crests, The Book of Family. Upwards of 4,000 Engravings. 2 vols., 12mo., 24s.
Crucifixion, The. A large Picture for School walls, 1s.
CULPEPPER. Family Herbal, 3s. 6d.; coloured plates, 5s. 6d.
CUSACK (M. F.):—Sister Mary Francis Clare.
  Book of the Blessed Ones. 12mo., 4s. 6d.
  Devotions for Public and Private Use at the Way of the Cross. Illustrated. 32mo., 1s.; red edges, 1s. 6d.
  Father Matthew, Life of. 12mo., 2s. 6d.
  Good Reading for Sundays and Festivals. 2s 6d.
  Ireland, History of. 18mo., 2s.
  Knock; Apparitions, &c. 1s.
  Lives of St. Columba and St. Brigit. 8vo., 6s.
  Ned Rusheen; or, Who fired the first Shot. 5s.
  Nun's Advice to her Girls. 12mo., 2s. 6d.
  Patrick (S.), Life of. 8vo., 6s., gilt, 10s.; 32mo. 1s.
  Patrick's (S.) Manual. 18mo., 3s. 6d.
  Pilgrim's Way to Heaven. 12mo., 4s. 6d.
  The Spouse of Christ. 12mo., vol. 2, 7s. 6d.
  Tim O'Halloran's Choice. 12mo., 3s. 6d.
  Tronson's Conferences. 12mo., 4s. 6d.
DALE (Rev. J. D. H.), Sacristan's Manual. 12mo., 2s. 6d.
Dark Shadow (The). A Tale. 12mo., 3s.
Daughter (A) of S. Dominick: (Bells of the Sanctuary). By Grace Ramsay. 12mo., 1s. and 1s. 6d.; better bound, 2s.
DAVIS (Rev. R. G.) Garden of the Soul. *See* pages 30 and 32.
——— **Catechism for First Confession.** 1d
DECHAMPS (Mgr.), The Life of Pleasure. 12mo., 1s. 6d.
DEHAM (Rev. F.) Sacred Heart of Jesus, offered to the Piety of the Young engaged in Study. 32mo., 6d.
Diary of a Confessor of the Faith. 12mo., 1s.
Directorium Asceticum. By Scaramelli. 4 vols., 12mo., 24s.
DIXON (Fr., O.P.) Albert the Great: his Life and Scholastic Labours. From original documents. By Dr. Sighart. With Photographic Portrait. 8vo. 10s. 6d. Cheap edition, 5s.
——— **Life of St. Vincent Ferrer.** From the French of Rev. Fr. Pradel. With a Photograph. 12mo., 5s.
Dominican Saints, Sketches of the Lives of. By M. K. 3s. 6d.

DOWNING (Sister M. A.), **Voices from the Heart.** 2s. 6d.
DOYLE (Canon, O.S.B.), **Life of Gregory Lopez, the Hermit.** With a Photographic Portrait. 12mo., 3s. 6d.
——— **Lectures for Boys.** 2 Vols., 12mo., 10s. 6d.; or separately:—Vol. I., Containing—The Sundays of the Year, and Our Lady's Festivals, etc. 6s.—Vol. II., Containing—The Passion of Our Lord, and The Sacred Heart. 6s.; or may be had separately: The Sundays of the Year, 3s. 6d.; Our Lady's Festivals, etc., 2s. 6d.; The Passion of Our Lord, 3s.; The Sacred Heart, 3s.
——— **Rule of our holy Father St. Benedict.** Edited in Latin and English. 12mo., 4s. 6d.
DOYLE (Dr.), **Catechism.** 18mo., 1½d.
DOYOTTE (Fr., S.J.), **Elevations to the Heart of Jesus.** 3s.
——— **Sufferings of Our Lord.** *See* Columbiere (Fr.)
DRAMAS.
——— **Convert Martyr**; or, "Callista" dramatised. 2s.
——— **Darby the Dodger** (Mixed, 4 Acts). Comic Drama. 1s.
——— **The Duchess Transformed** (Girls, 1 Act). Comedy. 6d.
——— **The Enchanted Violin** (Boys, 2 Acts). Comedy. 6d.
——— **Ernscliff Hall** (Girls, 3 Acts). Drama. 12mo., 6d.
——— **Filiola** (Girls, 4 Acts). Drama. 12mo., 6d.
——— **Finola** (Moore Melodies, 4 Acts). An Opera. 1s.
——— **He would be a Lord** (Boys, 3 Acts), a Comedy. 2s.
——— **He would be a Soldier** (Boys, 2 Acts) Comedy, 6d.
——— **Reverse of the Medal** (Girls, 4 Acts). Drama. 6d.
——— **Shakespeare.** Expurgated Edition. 8vo., 6s.
——— **Shandy Maguire** (Boys, 2 Acts), a Farce. 12mo., 2s.
——— **St. Eustace** (Boys, 5 Acts). Drama. 12mo., 1s.
——— **St. William of York** (Boys, 2 Acts). Drama. 12mo., 6d.
——— **The Violet Sellers** (3 Acts). Drama for Children. 6d.
——— **Whittington and his Cat.** Drama for Children. 9 Scenes. By Henrietta Fairfield. 6d.
——— *See* R. Washbourne's **American List.**
DREW (F. B. Bickerstaffe), **Little Books of St. Nicholas.** Tales for Children, 1s. each. 1. Oremus; 2. Dominus Vobiscum; 3. Pater Noster. 4. Per Jesum Christi; 5. Veni Creator; 6. Credo; 7. Ave Maria; 8. Ora pro nobis: 9. Corpus Christi; 10. Dei Genitrix; 11. Miserere; 12. Deo Gratias; 13. Guardian Angel.
Duchess (The), **Transformed.** By W. H. A. 12mo., 6d.
DUMESNIL (Abbe), **The Reign of Terror.** 12mo., 2s. 6d.
DUPANLOUP (Mgr.), **Contemporary Prophecies.** 8vo., 1s.
——— **The Child.** Translated by Kate Anderson. 12mo., 3s. 6d.
Dusseldorf Gallery. 357 Engravings. Large 4to. Half-morocco gilt, £5 5s. nett.
——— 134 Engravings. Large 8vo. Half-morocco, gilt, 42s.
Dusseldorf Society for the Distribution of Good Religious Pictures. Subscription, 8s. 6d. a year.
Duties of Christian Parents. Conferences by R. Père Matignon. Translated from the French by Lady Constance Bellingham. 5s.
Eagle and Dove. Translated by Emily Bowles. 5s. and 2s. 6d.
E. A. M. Countess Adelstan. 12mo., 1s. and 2s. 6d.

E. A. M., Paul Seigneret. 12mo., 6d., 1s., 1s. 6d., gilt, 2s.
——— **Regina Sæculorum.** 12mo., 1s. and 3s.
——— **Rosalie.** 12mo., 1s., 1s. 6d., gilt, 2s.
Easy Way to God. By Cardinal Bona. 12mo., 3s.
Electricity and Magnetism; an Enquiry into the Nature and Results of. By Amyclanus. Illustrated. 12mo., 6s. 6d.
Enchanted Violin, The. A Comedy in 2 Acts (Boys), 6d.
England, History of. By L. Evans. 9d.
——— **A Catechism.** By a Teacher, 1s. By a Lady, 6d.
——— By W. F. Mylius. 12mo., 3s. 6d.
Epistles and Gospels. Good clear type edition, 32mo., 6d.; roan, 1s. 6d.; larger edition, 18mo., French morocco, 2s.
———, **Explanation of.** By Rev. F. Goffine. Illustrated, 8vo., 9s.
Epistles of S. Paul, Exposition of. By Dr. MacEvilly. 18s.
Ernscliff Hall. A Drama in Three Acts, for Girls. 12mo., 6d.
Eucharistic Year. 18mo., 4s.
Eucharist (The) and the Christian Life. *See* La Bouillerie.
Europe, Modern, History of. 12mo., 5s.; cloth gilt, 6s.
Eustace (St.). A Drama in 5 Acts for Boys. 12mo., 1s.
EVANS (L.), History of England, adapted for Junior Classes in Schools. 9d., or separately: Part 1 (Standard 4) 2d. Part 2 (Standard 4) 2d. Part 3 (Standard 5) 3d.
——— **Chronological Outline of English History.** 1½d.
——— **Milton's l'Allegro** (Oxford Local Exam.). 2d.
——— **Parsing and Analysis Table.** 1d.
FAIRFIELD (Henrietta), Whittington and his Cat. A Drama, in 9 Scenes, for Children. 12mo., 6d.
Fairy Ching (The); or, the Chinese Fairies' Visit to England. By Henrica Frederic. 12mo., 1s.; gilt edges, 1s. 6d.
Fairy Tales for Little Children. By Madeleine Howley Meehan, 12mo., 6d.; stronger bound, 1s. and 1s. 6d.; gilt, 2s.
Faith, Hope, and Charity; a Tale of the Reign of Terror. 2s. 6d.
Faith of Our Fathers. By Most Rev. Archbishop Gibbons. 4s.
Fall, Redemption, and Exaltation of Man. 12mo., 1s.
Familiar Instructions on Christian Truths. By a Priest. 10d.
Fardel (Sister Claude Simplicienne), Life of. With the Lives of others of the First Religious of the Visitation of Holy Mary. 12mo., 6s.
FARRELL (Rev. J.), Lectures of a certain Professor. 7s. 6d
FAVRE (Abbe), Heaven Opened by the Practice of Frequent Confession and Communion. 12mo., 2s.; stronge. bound, 3s. 6d.; red edges, 4s.
Favre (Mother Marie Jacqueline), Life of. With the Lives of others of the First Religious of the Visitation of Holy Mary. 12mo., 6s.
Feasts (The) of Camelot, with the Tales that were told there. By Mrs. E. L. Hervey. 12mo., 3s. 6d., or in 2 vols. 1s. 6d. each.
FERRIS (Rev. D.), Life of Sister Mary Frances of the Five Wounds. From the Italian. 12mo., 2s. 6d.
——— **Manual of Christian Doctrine;** or Catholic Beliet and Practice familiary explained by Question and Answer. 6d.

FEVAL (Paul), The Jesuits. 12mo., 2s. 6d.
Filiola. A Drama in Four Acts, for Girls. 12mo., 6d.
First Apostles of Europe. By Mrs. Hope. 2 vols. 10s.
First Communion and Confirmation Memorial. Beautifully printed in gold and colours, folio, 1s. each, or 9s. a dozen, nett.
First Communicants; or, Clare's Sacrifice. By M. C. O'Hara. 6d.
First Religious of the Visitation of Holy Mary, Lives of. Translated, with a Preface, by Mrs. Bowden. 2 vols., 12mo., 10s.
FLANAGAN (Rev. T.), History of the Catholic Church in England. 2 vols., 8vo., 18s.
FLEET (Charles), Tales and Sketches. 8vo., 3s. 6d.
FLEURIOT (Mlle. Zenaide), Eagle and Dove. Translated by Emily Bowles. 12mo., 2s. 6d. and 5s.
FLEURY'S Historical Catechism. Large edition, 12mo., 1½d.
Flowers of Christian Wisdom. By Henry Lucien. 2s.
Fluffy. A Tale for Boys. By M. F. S. 12mo., 3s. 6d.
Following of Christ. *See* A'Kempis.
Foreign Books. *See* R. W.'s Catalogue of Foreign Books.
FORMBY (Rev. H.), Little Book of the Martyrs. 1s. 6d.
Francis of Assisi (S.) Life of. By S. Bonaventure. Translated by Miss Lockhart. 12mo., 3s. 6d.
FRANCIS OF SALES (S.), Consoling Thoughts. 18mo., 2s.
——— **The Mystical Flora.** 4to., 8s.
——— **Necessity of Purifying the Soul.** By Fr. Blyth. 1s.
——— **Sweetness of Holy Living.** 18mo., 1s.; levant, 3s.
Franciscan Annals and Monthly Bulletin of the Third Order of St. Francis. 8vo., 6d. Vols. 1 to 3, each 6s.
FRANCO (Rev. S.) Devotions to the Sacred Heart. 4s.
FRASSINETTI—Dogmatic Catechism. 12mo., 3s.
FREDERIC (Henrica), The Fairy Ching; or, the Chinese Fairies' Visit to England. 12mo., 1s.; gilt edges, 1s. 6d.
——— **Story of a Paper Knife.** 12mo., 1s.; gilt edges, 1s. 6d.
FREDERIC (M. J. N. de), Continental Fish Cook. 1s.
From Sunrise to Sunset. By L. B. 12mo., 3s. 6d.
GALLERY (Rev. D.), Handbook of Essentials in History and Literature, Ancient and Modern. 18mo., 1s.
Garden of the Soul. *See* page 32.
Garden (Little) of the Soul. *See* page 30.
Gathered Gems from Spanish Authors. By M. Monteiro. 3s. 6d.
GAUME (Abbe), Catechism of Perseverance. 4 vols., 12mo. Vols. 1 and 2, each 7s. 6d.
GAYRARD (Mme. Paul) Harmony of the Passion. Compiled from the four Gospels, in Latin and French. 18mo., 1s. 6d.
German (S.), Life of. 12mo., 3s. 6d.
GIBBONS (Most Rev. Archbishop), The Faith of Our Fathers; Being a Plain Exposition and Vindication of the Church Founded by our Lord Jesus Christ. 12mo., 4s. Paper covers, 2s.
GIBSON (Rev. H.), Catechism made Easy. Vol. III., 4s.
GILMOUR (Rev. R.), Bible History for the Use of Schools. Illustrated. 12mo., 2s.

God our Father. By a Father of the Society of Jesus. 12mo., 4s.
GOFFINE (Rev. F.), Explanation of the Epistles and Gospels. Illustrated. 8vo., 9s.
Golden Thought of Queen Beryl, and other Stories. By Marie Cameron. 1s. 6d.; or cheap edition, in 2 vols. 6d. each.
Grace before and after Meals. 32mo., 1d.; cloth, 2d.
GRACE RAMSAY. *See* O'Meara (Kathleen).
GRACIAN (Fr. Baltasar), Sanctuary Meditations for Priests and Frequent Communicants. Translated from the Spanish by Mariana Monteiro. 12mo., 4s.
Grains of Gold. 16mo., Series 1 and 2, cloth, 2s. 6d.
GRANT (Bishop), Pastoral on St. Joseph. 32mo., 4d. & 6d.
GRAY (Mrs. C. D.), Simple Bible Stories. 1s. and 2s. 6d.
GREEN (Rev. Dr.), Indulgences, Sacramental Absolutions, and the Tax Tables of the Roman Chancery and Penitentiary considered in reply to the Charge of Venality. 12mo., 4s. 6d.
Gregory Lopez, the Hermit, Life of. By Canon Doyle, O.S.B. With a Photographic Portrait. 12mo., 3s. 6d.
Grounds of the Catholic Doctrine. By Bishop Challoner. Large type edition, 18mo., 4d.
GUERANGER (Dom), Defence of the Roman Church against F. Gratry. Translated by Canon Woods. 8vo., 1s.
HALL (E.), Munster Firesides. 12mo., 3s. 6d.
Harmony of Anglicanism. By T. W. Marshall. 8vo., 2s. 6d.
HAY (Bishop), Sincere Christian. 18mo., 2s. 6d.
——— **Devout Christian.** 18mo., 2s. 6d.
He would be a Lord. A Comedy in 3 Acts. (Boys). 12mo., 2s.
Heaven Opened by the Practice of frequent Confession and Holy Communion. By the Abbé Favre. 12mo., 2s.; stronger bound, 3s. 6d.; red edges, 4s.
HEDLEY (Bishop), Five Sermons—Light of the Holy Spirit in the World. 12mo., 1s.; cloth, 1s. 6d. Revelation, Mystery, Dogma and Creeds, Infallibility: separately, 3d. each.
HEFELE (Rev. Dr. Von), Cardinal Ximenes. 10s. 6d.
HEIGHAM (John), A Devout Exposition of the Holy Mass. Edited by Austin John Rowley, Priest. 12mo., 4s.
HENRY (Lucien), Flowers of Christian Wisdom. 18mo., 1s. and 2s.; red edges, 2s. 6d.
Herbal, Brook's Family. 12mo., 3s. 6d.; coloured, 5s. 6d.
HERBERT (Lady), True Wayside Tales. 12mo., 3s.; or in 5 vols., cheap edition, 6d. each.

1. The Brigand Chief, and other Tales. 2. The Martyr's Children, and other Tales. 3. What a Child can do, and other Tales. 4. Sowing Wild Oats, and other Tales. 5. The Two Hosts, and other Tales.

HERBERT (Wallace), My Dream and Verses Miscellaneous. With a frontispiece. 12mo., 5s.
——— **The Angels and the Sacraments.** 16mo., 1s.
HERVEY (E. L.), Stories from many Lands. 12mo., 3s. 6d.
——— **Our Legends and Lives.** 12mo., 6s.
——— **Rest, on the Cross.** 12mo., 3s. 6d.

HERVEY (E. L.) **The Feasts of Camelot, with the Tales that were told there.** 12mo., 3s. 6d.; or, separately: Christmas 1s. 6d.; Whitsuntide, 1s. 6d.

HILL (Rev. Fr.), **Elements of Philosophy,** comprising Logic and General Principles of Metaphysics. 8vo., 6s.

——— **Ethics, or Moral Philosophy.** 12mo., 6s.

HOFFMAN (Franz), **Industry and Laziness.** 12mo., 3s.

HOLLAND (Dr.), **Ulic O'Donnell.** 12mo., 2s. 6d.

Holy Childhood. A book of simple Prayers and Instructions for very little children. 32mo., 6d. or 1s.; gilt, 1s. 6d.

Holy Church the Centre of Unity. By T. H. Shaw. 1s.

Holy Communion. By Hubert Lebon. 12mo., 4s.

Holy Family Card of Membership. A beautiful design. Folio. Price 6d., or 8d., on a roller, post free; 4s. 6d. a dozen, or post free 5s.

Holy Family, Confraternity of. By Card. Manning. 3d.

Holy Places: their Sanctity and Authenticity. *See* Philpin

Holy Readings. By J. R. Digby Beste, Esq. 3s.

HOPE (Mrs.), **The First Apostles of Europe**; or, "The Conversion of the Teutonic Race." 2 vols., 12mo., 10s.

Horace. Literally translated by Smart. 18mo., 2s.

HUGUET (Pere), **The Power of S. Joseph.** Meditations and Devotions. Translated by Clara Mulholland. 1s. 6d.

——— **On Charity in Conversation.** 12mo., 2s. 6d.

HUMPHREY (Rev. W., S.J.), **The Panegyrics of Fr. Segneri, S.J.** Translated from the orignal Italian. With a Preface by the Rev. W. Humphrey, S.J. 12mo., 5s.

HUSENBETH (Rev. Dr.), **Convert Martyr.** 12mof., 2s.

——— **History of the Blessed Virgin.** Translated from Orsini. Illustrated. 12mo., 3s. 6d.

——— **Life and Sufferings of Our Lord.** By Rev. H. Rutter. Illustrated. 12mo., 5s.

——— **Life of Mgr. Weedall.** 8vo., 5s.

——— **Little Office of the Immaculate Conception.** In Latin and English. 32mo., 4d.; cloth, 6d.; roan, 1s.; calf or morocco, 2s. 6d.

——— **Our Blessed Lady of Lourdes.** 18mo., 6d.; with the Novena, 1s.; cloth, 1s. 6d. Novena, separately, 4d.; Litany, 1d.

——— **Roman Question.** 8vo., 6d.

Hymn Book (The Catholic). Edited by Rev. G. L. Vere. 32mo., 2d.; cloth, 4d.; Appendix (Hymns to Saints), 1d.

Iceland (Three Sketches of Life in). By Carl Andersen. 12mo., 2s. 6d., cheap edition, 1s. 6d.

IGNATIUS (S.), **Spiritual Exercises.** By Fr. Bellecio, S.J. Translated by Dr. Hutch. 18mo., 2s.

Ignatius (S.), Cure of Blindness through the Intercession of Our Lady and S. Ignatius. 12mo., 2d.

Imitation of Christ. *See* A'Kempis.

Immaculate Conception, Definition of. 12mo., 6d.

——— **Little Office of, Latin and English.** 32mo., 2d.

Immaculate Conception, Little Office of. By Rev. Dr. Husenbeth. 6d.
Industry and Laziness. By Franz Hoffman. From the German, by James King. 12mo., 3s.
Indulgences. *See* Green (Rev. Dr.), Maurel (Rev. F. A.).
Infallibility of the Pope. By the Author of "The Oxford Undergraduate of Twenty Years Ago." 8vo., 1s.
In Suffragiis Sanctorum. Commem. S. Joseph; Commem. S. Georgii. Set of 5 for 4d.
IOTA. The Adventures of a Protestant in Search of a Religion: being the Story of a late Student of Divinity at Bunyan Baptist College; a Nonconformist Minister, who seceded to the Catholic Church. 12mo., 3s. 6d.; cheap edition, 2s.
Ireland (History of). By Miss Cusack. 2s. By T. Young. 2s. 6d.
Ireland (Popular Poetry of). 6d.
Irish Board Reading Books.
Irish First Book. 18mo., 2d. **2nd Book,** 4d. **3rd Book,** 6d.
Irish Monthly. 8vo. Vol. 1879, cloth, 7s. 6d.
Irish Saints in Great Britain. By Bishop Moran. 5s.
Italian Revolution (The History of). The History of the Barricades. By Keyes O'Clery, M.P. 8vo., 7s. 6d. and 3s. 6d.
Jack's Boy. By M. F. S., author of "Fluffy," "Tom's Crucifix, and other Tales." 12mo, 3s. 6d.
JACOB (W. J.), Personal Recollections of Rome. 6d.
Jesuits (The). By Paul Feval, 12mo., 3s. 6d.
Jesuits (The), and other Essays. By Willis Nevin. 2s. 6d.
Jesus and Jerusalem; or, the Way Home. *See* Cusack (Miss).
Jew of Verona. 12mo., 4s. 6d.
John of God (S.), Life of. With Photographic Portrait. 12mo., 5s.
Joseph (S.), Life of. By Miss Cusack. 32mo., 6d.; cloth, 1s.
——— **Manual of a Happy Eternity.** 18mo., 2s. 6d.
——— **Novena of Meditations.** 18mo., 1s.
——— **Novena to,** with a Pastoral by the late Bishop Grant. 32mo., 4d.; cloth, 6d.
——— **Power of.** By Fr. Huguet. 1s. 6d.
——— **A Word to,** for every day in March. 4d., cloth, 1s.
——— *See* Leaflets.
Journey of Sophia and Eulalie to the Palace of True Happiness. (The Catholic Pilgrim's Progress.) From the French by Rev. Fr. Bradbury. 12mo., 1s. 6d.; better bound, 3s. 6d.
KAVANAGH (Rev. P. F.), Insurrection of '98. 2s.
KEENAN (Rev. S.), Controversial Catechism. 12mo., 2s.
Keighley Hall, and other Tales. By E. King. 18mo., 6d.; cloth, 1s.; stronger bound, 1s. 6d.; gilt, 2s.
KEMEN (Charles), The Marpingen Apparitions. 8vo., 1s.
KENNY (Dr.), Young Catholic's Guide to Confession and Holy Communion. 32mo., 4d.; cloth, 6d.; red edges, 9d. roan, 1s. 6d.; calf or morocco, 2s. 6d.
——— **New Year's Gift to our Heavenly Father.** 32mo., 4d.
Key of Heaven. *See* Prayers, page 31.
KINANE (Rev. T. H.), Angel of the Altar; or, the Love of the Most Adorable and Most Sacred Heart of Jesus. 2s. 3d.

KINANE (Rev. T. H.) Dove of the Tabernacle. 1s. 6d.
——— **Lamb of God.** 18mo., 2s.
——— **Mary Immaculate.** 2s.
KING (Elizabeth), Keighley Hall, and other Tales. 18mo., 6d.; cloth, 1s.; stronger bound, 1s. 6d.; gilt, 2s.
——— **The Silver Teapot.** 18mo., 4d.
KING (James). Industry and Laziness. 12mo., 3s.
Kishoge Papers. Tales of Devilry and Drollery. 12mo., 1s. 6d.
Knock; Apparitions and Miracles. 1s.
LA BOUILLERIE (Mgr. de), The Eucharist and the Christian Life. Translated by L. C. 12mo., 3s. 6d.
LACORDAIRE'S Conferences. 12mo., On Life, 3s. 6d.
Lacordaire. The Inner Life of Pere Lacordaire. From the French of Père Chocarne. 12mo., 6s. 6d.
Lady Mildred's Housekeeper, A Few Words from. 2d.
LAIDLAW (Mrs. Stuart), Letters to my God-child. No. 4. On the Veneration of the Blessed Virgin. 16mo., 4d.
LAING (Rev. Dr.), Blessed Virgin's Root traced in the Tribe of Ephraim. 8vo., 10s. 6d.
——— **Knight of the Faith.** 12mo., 5s.

Absurd Protestant Opinions concerning *Intention.* 4d.
Catholic, not Roman Catholic. 4d.
Challenge to the Churches. 1d.
Descriptive Guide to the Mass. 1s. and 1s. 6d.
Favourite Fallacy about Private Judgment and Inquiry. 1d.
Protestantism against the Natural Moral Law. 1d.
Shortcomings of the English Catholic Press. 6d.
What is Christianity? 6d.
Whence does the Monarch get his right to Rule? 2s. 6d.

LAMBILOTTE (Pere), The Consoler. Translated by Abbot Burder. 12mo., 4s. 6d.; red edges, 5s.
LANE-CLARKE (T. M. L.) The Violet Sellers. A Drama for Children in 3 Acts. 6d.
LANGUET (Mgr.), Confidence in the Mercy of God. Translated by Abbot Burder. 12mo., 3s.
Last of the Catholic O'Malleys. By M. Taunton. 18mo., 1s. 6d.; stronger bound, 2s.
Leaflets. 1d. each, or 1s. 2d. per 100 post free, (a single dozen 5d.).

Act of Reparation to the Sacred Heart.
Archconfraternity of the Agonising Heart of Jesus and the Compassionate Heart of Mary: Prayers for the Dying.
Archconfraternity of Our Lady of Angels.
Ditto, Rules.
Christmas Offering (or 7s. 6d. per 1000).
Devotions to S. Joseph.
Divine Praises.
Gospel according to S. John, *in Latin.* 1s. 6d. per 100.
Indulgenced Prayers for Souls in Purgatory.
Indulgences attached to Medals, Crosses, Statues, &c.
Intentions for Indulgences.
Litany of Our Lady of Angels.
Litany of S. Joseph, and Devotions.

Litany of Resignation.
Miraculous Prayer—August Queen of Angels.
Picture of Crucifixion, "I thirst" (or 5s. per 1000).
Prayer for One's Confessor.
Prayers for the Holy Souls in Purgatory. By St. Ligouri.
Reasonings of Plain Common-Sense upon the Church (2s. 10d. per 100, post free).
Union of our Life with the Passion of our Lord.
Visit to the Blessed Sacrament. 2s. 6d. per 100.

Leaflets. 1d. each, or 6s. per 100, (a single dozen 10d., post free).
Acts of Consecration to the Sacred Heart.
Concise Portrait of the Blessed Virgin.
Explanation of the Medal or Cross of St. Benedict.
Indulgenced Prayers for the Rosary of the Holy Souls.
Indulgenced Prayer before a Crucifix.
Litany of Our Lady of Lourdes.
Litany of the Seven Dolours.
Office of the Sacred Heart.
Prayer to S. Philip Neri.
Prayers before and after Holy Communion.
Why Roman Catholics disbelieve in Anglican Orders.

Lectures for Boys. By Canon Doyle. 2 vols., 12mo., 10s. 6d.
Legends of the Blessed Virgin. 12mo., 3s. 6d.
Legends of the Commandments of God. 12mo., 3s. 6d.
Legends of the Saints. By M. F. S. 16mo., 3s. 6d.
Legends of the Thirteenth Century. By Rev. H. Collins. 3s., or in 3 vols., 1s. 6d. each.
LEGUAY (Abbe), The Postulant and Novice. 2s. 6d.
Lenten Thoughts. By Bishop Amherst. 18mo., 1s. 6d.; stronger bound, 2s., with red edges, 2s. 6d.
LEO XIII., The Church and Civilisation. 8vo., 2s.
Letters to my God-child. By Mrs. Stuart Laidlaw. 16mo., 4d.
Life of Pleasure. By Mgr. Dechamps. 12mo., 1s. 6d.
Light of the Holy Spirit in the World. Five Sermons by Bishop Hedley. 12mo., 1s.; cloth, 1s. 6d.
LIGUORI (S.), Fourteen Stations of the Cross. 18mo., 1d.
——— **Selva**; or, a Collection of Matter for Sermons. 12mo., 5s.
——— **Way of Salvation.** 32mo., 1s.
Lily of S. Joseph: A little Manual of Prayers and Hymns for Mass. 64mo., 2d.; cloth, 3d., 4d., and 6d.; gilt, 8d.; roan, 1s.; French morocco, 1s. 6d.; calf or morocco, 2s.; gilt, 2s. 6d.
LINGARD (Dr.), Gunpowder Plot. 8vo., 2s. 6d.
——— **Anglo-Saxon Church.** 2 vols., 12mo., 10s.
Little Mildred, or Oremus. By F. B. Birkerstaffe Drew. 6d.
Little Prayer Book. 32mo., 3d.
Lives of the First Religious of the Visitation of Holy Mary. By Mother Frances Magdalen de Chaugy. 2 vols., 10s.
Lost Children of Mount St. Bernard. 18mo., 6d.
Lourdes, Our Blessed Lady of. By Rev. Dr. Husenbeth. 18mo., 6d.; with the Novena, 1s.; cloth, 1s. 6d.
——— **Novena of,** for the use of the Sick. 4d.

Lourdes, Litany of. 1d. each.

——— **Month at Lourdes.** By H. Caraher. 2s.

LUCK (Dom Edmund J.), Short Meditations for every Day in the Year. From the Italian. 12mo. Edition for the Regular Clergy, 2 vols., 9s.; edn. for the Secular Clergy and others, 2 vols., 9s.

——— **S. Gregory's Life and Miracles of St. Benedict.** 31s. 6d.; cheap edition, 10s. 6d.; small edition, 2s.

LYONS (C. B.), Catholic Choir Manual. 12mo., 1s.

——— **Catholic Psalmist.** 12mo., 4s.

MACDANIEL (M. A.), Month of May. 18mo., 2s.

——— **Novena to S. Joseph.** 32mo., 4d.; cloth, 6d.

——— **Road to Heaven.** A Game. 1s. and 2s.

MACEVILLY (Bishop), Exposition of the Epistles of St. Paul and of the Catholic Epistles. 2 vols., large 8vo. 18s.

——— **Exposition of the Gospels.** Large 8vo., SS. Matthew, and Mark, 12s. 6d., S. Luke, 6s.

MANAHAN (Dr.), Triumph of the Catholic Church in the Early Ages. 12mo., 5s.

MANNING (Card.) Confraternity of the Holy Family. 3d.

MANNOCK (Patrick), Origin and Progress of Religious Orders, and Happiness of a Religious State. Translated from the Latin of Rev. F. Platus. 12mo., 2s. 6d.

Manual of Catholic Devotions. *See* Prayers, page 31.

Manual of Devotions in honour of Our Lady of Sorrows. Compiled by the Clergy at St. Patrick's, Soho. 18mo., 1s. & 1s. 6d.

Manuel de Conversation. 12mo., 6d.

Map of London, with Alphabetical List of the Catholic Churches, and view of the proposed Westminster Cathedral. 6d.

Margarethe Verflassen. Translated from the German by Mrs. Smith Sligo. 12mo., 1s. 6d. and 3s.; gilt, 3s. 6d.

Marpingen Apparitions. By C. Kemen. 8vo., 1s.

MARQUIGNY (Pere), Life and Letters of Countess Adelstan. 12mo., 1s. and 2s. 6d.

MARSHALL (A. J. P., Esq.), Comedy of Convocation in the English Church. 8vo., 2s. 6d. *

——— **English Religion.** 8vo. 6d.,

——— **Infallibility of the Pope.** 8vo., 1s. *

——— **Oxford Undergraduate of Twenty Years Ago.** 8vo., 2s. 6d.; cloth, 3s. 6d. *

——— **Reply to the Bishop of Ripon's Attack on the Catholic Church.** 8vo., 6d. *

——— **Two Bibles.** A Contrast. 16mo., 1s. 6d.

MARSHALL (T. W. M., Esq.), Harmony of Anglicanism—Church Defence. 8vo., 2s. 6d. *

The 5 (*) in one Volume, 8vo., 6s.

MARSHALL (Rev. W.), The Doctrine of Purgatory. 1s.

——— **A Squib for the Saints.** 3d.

MARTIN (Rev. E. R.), Rule of the Pope-King. 8vo., 6d.

Mary Christina of Savoy (Venerable). 18mo., 6d.

Mary Immaculate, Devotion to. By Rev. T. H. Kinane. 2s.

Mary, New Mouth of. By Bishop Kenrick. 32mo., 1s. 6d.

Mary Venerated in all Ages—Regina Sæculorum. 12mo., 3s., cheap edition, 1s.
Mass, Descriptive Guide to. By Rev. Dr. Laing. 12mo., 1s., or stronger bound, 1s. 6d.
Mass, Devotions for. Very *Large type*, 18mo., 2d.
Mass (The). By Müller, 10s. 6d. Tronson, 4d. O'Brien, 9s.
Mass, A Devout Exposition of. By Rev. A. J. Rowley. 4s.
MATIGNON (Pere) The Duties of Christian Parents. 5s.
MAUREL (Rev. F. A.), Indulgences. 18mo., 2s.
Maxims of the Kingdom of Heaven. 12mo., 5s.; red edges, 5s. 6d.; calf or mor., 10s. 6d. Old Testament, 1s. 6d.; Gospels, 1s.
May, Month of. By Rev. P. Comerford. 32mo., 1s.
May, Month of. By Canon Doyle. 12mo., 2s. 6d.
May, Month of. By M. A. Macdaniel. 18mo., 2s.
May, Month of, principally for the use of Religious. 18mo., 1s. 6d.
May Readings for the Feasts of Our Lady. By Rev. A. P. Bethell. 18mo., 1s., stronger bound, 1s. 6d.
May Templeton; a Tale of Faith and Love. 12mo., 5s.
M'CORRY (Rev. Dr.), Monks of Iona. 8vo., 3s. 6d.
——— **Rome, Past, Present, Future.** 8vo., 6d.
MCNEILL (Rev. Mark), The Faith. 12mo., 5s.
Meditations for every Day in the Year. By Fr. Luck. 9s.
MEEHAN (M. H.), Fairy Tales for Little Children. 12mo., 6d. and 1s.; stronger bound, 1s. 6d.; gilt, 2s.
MELIA (Rev. Dr.), Auricular Confession. 18mo., 1s. 6d.
MERMILLOD (Mgr.), The Supernatural Life. Translated from the French, with a Preface by Lady Herbert. 12mo., 5s.
MEYRICK (Rev. T.), Life of St. Wenefred. 12mo., 2s.
——— **Lives of the Early Popes.** St. Peter to St. Sylvester. 4s. 6d. From the time of Constantine to Charlemagne. 5s. 6d.
——— **St. Eustace. A Drama (5 Acts) for Boys.** 12mo., 1s.
M. F. S., Catherine Hamilton. 12mo., 2s. 6d.; gilt, 3s.
——— **Catherine Grown Older.** 12mo., 2s. 6d.; gilt, 3s.
——— **Fluffy.** A Tale for Boys. 12mo., 3s. 6d.
——— **Jack's Boy.** 12mo., 3s. 6d.
——— **Legends of the Saints.** 16mo., 3s. 6d. [gilt, 1s. 6d.
——— **My Golden Days.** 12mo., 2s. 6d.; or in 3 vols., 1s. ea.,
——— **Stories of Holy Lives.** 12mo., 3s. 6d.
——— **Stories of Martyr Priests.** 12mo., 3s. 6d.
——— **Stories of the Saints.** Five Series, 12mo., 3s. 6d. each.
——————— First and Second Series; gilt, 4s. 6d. each.
——— **Story of the Life of S. Paul.** 2s. 6d. and 1s. 6d.
——— **The Three Wishes.** A Tale. 12mo., 2s. 6d. and 1s. 6d.
——— **Tom's Crucifix,** and other Tales. 12mo., 3s. 6d., or in 5 vols., 1s. each, gilt, 1s. 6d.
MILNER (Bishop), Devotion to the Sacred Heart of Jesus. 32mo., 3d.; cloth, 6d.; gilt, 1s. [2d.
Miracle at Rome, through the intercession of B. John Berchmans.
Miraculous Cure of Blindness, through the intercession of Our Lady and S. Ignatius. 12mo., 2d.

Misgivings—Convictions. 12mo., 6d.

Missal. *See* Prayers, page 31. [12mo., 8s.

MOEHLER (Dr.), Symbolism. Translated by Professor Robertson.

Monastic Legends. By E. G. K. Browne. 8vo., 6d.

MOHR (Rev. J., S.J.), Cantiones Sacrae. Hymns and Chants. Music and Words. 8vo., 5s.

——— **Manual of Sacred Chant.** Music and Words. 2s. 6d.

MOLLOY (Rev. Dr.), Passion Play at Ober-Ammergan. 2s.; with Photograph, 3s.

Monk of the Monastery of Yuste. By Mariana Monteiro. 2s. 6d.

Monks of Iona and the Duke of Argyll. By M'Corry. 3s. 6d.

MONSABRE (Rev. Pere), Gold and Alloy. 12mo., 2s. 6d.

MONTAGU (Lord Robert), Civilization and the See of Rome. 8vo., 6d.

Montalembert (Count de). By George White. 12mo., 6d.

MONTEIRO (Mariana), Allah Akbar—God is Great. An Arab Legend of the Siege and Conquest of Granada. 12mo., 3s. 6d.

——— **Monk of the Monastery of Yuste**; or, The Last Days of the Emperor Charles V. An Historical Legend of the 16th Century. 12mo., 2s. 6d.

——— **Gathered Gems from Spanish Authors.** 12mo., 3s.

——— **Sanctuary Meditations.** By Fr. Gracian. 4s.

MOORE'S Irish Melodies. With Symphonies and Accompaniments by John Stevenson and Sir Henry Bishop. 4to., 3s. 6d.

Mora (Ven. Elizabeth Canori), Life of. Translated from the Italian, with Preface by Lady Herbert. With Photograph. 3s. 6d.

MORAN (Rt. Rev. Dr.) Irish Saints in Great Britain. 5s.

MULHOLLAND (Rosa), Prince and Saviour: The Story of Jesus. 12mo., Coloured Illustrations, 2s. 6d.; 32mo., 6d.

MULLER (Rev. M.), The Holy Mass. 12mo., 10s. 6d.

Multiplication Table, on a sheet. 3s. per 100.

MURRAY-LANE (Chevalier H.), Chronological Sketch of the Kings of England and the Kings of France, 12mo. 2s. 6d.; or in 2 vols., 1s. 6d. each.

MUSIC: Antiphons of the B.V.M. (S. Cecilian). 3s. 6d.

Ave Maria, for Four Voices. By W. Schulthes. 1s. 3d.

Cæcilian Society. *See* Separate List.

Catholic Choralist. Monthly, 3d.

Catholic Hymnal. By Leopold de Prins. 2s.; bound, 3s.

Cor Jesu, Salus in Te sperantium. By W. Schulthes, 2s.; with Harp Accompaniment, 2s. 6d.; abridged, 3d.

Corona Lauretana. 20 Litanies by W. Schulthes. 2s.

Evening Hymn at the Oratory. By Rev. J. Nary. 3d.

Litanies (36) and Benediction Service. By W. Schulthes. 6s. Second Series (Corona Lauretana). 2s.

Litanies (6). By E. Leslie. 6d.

Litanies (18). By Rev. J. McCarthy. 1s. 6d.

Litany of the B.V.M. By Baronnesse Emma Freemantle. 6d.

Mass of St. Patrick. For three equal voices. By F. Schaller. 2s. 6d.

Mass of the Holy Child Jesus. In Unison. By W. Schulthes. 3s. The vocal part only, 4d.; or 3s. per doz. Cloth, 6d.; or 4s. 6d. per doz.
Missa, Jesu bone Pastor. By Schaller. 3s. 6d.
Moore's Irish Melodies. 4to., 3s. 6d.
Motetts (Five), S. Cecilian Society. 3s. 6d.
Ne projicias me a facie Tua. Motett for Four Voices. By W. Schulthes. 1s. 3d.
Oratory Hymns. By W. Schulthes. 2 vols., 8s.
Recordare. Oratorio Jeremiæ Prophetæ. By the same. 1s.
Regina Cœli. Motett for Four Voices. By W. Schulthes. 3s. Vocal Arrangement, 1s.
Six Sacred Vocal Pieces, for three or four equal Voices. By W. Schulthes. 4s.
Six Invocations, for four equal Voices. By W. Schulthes. 1s. 6d.
Twelve Latin Hymns. By W. Schulthes. 1s. 6d.
Veni Domine. Motett for Four Voices. By W. Schulthes. 2s. Vocal Arrangement, 6d.
Vespers and Benediction Service. Composed and harmonized by Leopold de Prins. 4to., 3s. 6d.

⁂ *All the above (music) prices are nett.*

My Conversion and Vocation. By Rev. Father Schouvaloff, 5s.
My Golden Days. By M. F. S. 12mo., 2s. 6d., or in 3 vols., 1s. each; or 1s. 6d. gilt.
NARY (Rev. J.) Evening Hymn at the Oratory. Music, 3d.
Natural Philosophy, Catechism of. 18mo., 3d.
Necessity of Enquiry as to Religion. By H. J. Pye. 6d.
Nellie Gordon, the Factory Girl; or, Lost and Saved. By M. A. Pennell. 18mo., 6d.
NEVIN (Willis, Esq.), The Jesuits, and other Essays. 2s. 6d.
NEWMAN (Rev. Dr.), Tracts, Theological and Ecclesiastical, 8s. Via Media, 2 vols., 12s. Development of Christian Doctrine, 6s.
New Testament. 12mo., 2s. 6d. Persian calf, 7s. 6d., morocco, 10s. Illustrated, large 4to., 7s. 6d.
New Year's Gift to Our Heavenly Father. 32mo., 4d.
Nicholas; or, the Reward of a Good Action. 18mo., 6d.
Nina and Pippo, the Lost Children of Mt. St. Bernard. 6d.
NOETHEN'S (Rev. T.), Good Thoughts for Priests and People; or, Short Meditations for every Day in the Year. 8s.
——— **Compendium of the History of the Catholic Church.** 12mo., 8s.
Novena to Our Blessed Lady of Lourdes for the use of the Sick. 18mo., 4d.
Novena of Grace, revealed by S. Francis Xavier. 18mo., 6d.
Novena of Meditations in honour of St. Joseph, according to the method of St. Ignatius, preceded by a new method of hearing Mass according to the intentions of the Souls in Purgatory. 18mo., 1s.
Novenas of Meditations. By Sister Mary Alphonsus. 2s. 6d.
Occasional Prayers for Festivals. *See* Prayers, page 31.

O'CLERY (**Keyes, M.P., K.S.G.**), **The History of the Italian Revolution.** First Period—The Revolution of the Barricades (1796-1849). 8vo, 7s. 6d. Cheap edition 3s. 6d.
O'GALLAGHER (Dr.), **Sermons in Irish-Gaelic**; with literal idiomatic English Translation, and a Memoir of the Bishop, by Canon U. J. Bourke. 8vo, 7s. 6d.
O'HARA (C. M.), Clare's **Sacrifice.** An impressive little Tale on First Communions. 6d.
O'KEEFFE (Rev. P.), **Moral Discourses.** 18mo, 2s.
O'MAHONY (D. P. M.), **Rome semper eadem.** 8vo, 1s. 6d.
O'MEARA (Kathleen), The **Battle of Connemara.** 12mo, 3s.
——— A Daughter of S. Dominick (Bells of the Sanctuary, No. 2). 12mo, 2s.; stronger bound, 1s. 6d. and 2s.
On what Authority do I accept Christianity? 12mo, 6d.
O[illegible] (Rev. A.), **Search the Scriptures**; or, Revelation and its Development, its Use and Abuse. 12mo, 7s. 6d.
Oratorian Lives of the Saints. With Portrait, 12mo, 5s. a vol.
I. S. Bernardine of Siena, Minor Observantine.
II. S. Philip Benizi, Fifth General of the Servites.
III. S. Veronica Giuliani, and B. Battista Varani.
IV. S. John of God. By Canon Cianfogni.
O'REILLY (Rev. Dr.), Victims of the Mamertine. 5s.
——— A Romance of Repentance. 12mo, 5s. 6d.
Oremus, A Liturgical Prayer Book. See page 31.
Our Lady: Devotion to, in N. America. By Fr. Macleod. 7s. 6d.
Our Lady's Festivals. By Canon Doyle. 2s. 6d.
Our Lady's Lament. By C. E. Tame. 2s.
Our Lady's Month. By Rev. A. P. Bethell. 18mo, 1s. and 1s. 6d.
Our Legends and Lives. By E. L. Hervey. 12mo, 6s.
Our Lord's Life, Passion, Death, and Resurrection. 1s.
——— By Rev. H. Rutter. Illustrated. 12mo, 3s.
——— Incidents. A Series of 12 Illuminations. 4to, 6s.
OXENHAM (H. N.), **Poems.** 12mo, 3s. 6d.
Oxford Undergraduate of Twenty Years Ago. By a Bachelor of Arts. 8vo, 2s. and cloth 3s. 6d.
OZANAM (A. F.), **Protestantism and Liberty.** Translated from the French by Wilfrid C. Robinson. 8vo, 1s.
PAGANI (Rev. J. B.), Science of the Saints, 4 vols, 12mo, 15s.
Panegyrics of Fr. Segneri, S.J. Translated from the original Italian. With a Preface by Rev. W. Humphrey, S.J. 12mo, 6s.
Paradise of God: or the Virtues of the Sacred Heart. By Author of "Love for Jesus," "Happiness of Heaven." 12mo, 4s.
Paray le Monial, and Bl. Margaret Mary. 18mo, 6d.
Passion of Our Lord. Sermons by Canon Doyle. 3s.
Passion of Our Lord, Harmony of. By G[illegible], 1s. 6d. [illegible] 2s.
PASSIONIST FATHERS: Sacred Eloquence. 18mo, 2s.
Manual of the Cross and Passion. 32mo, 3s.
S. Joseph's Manual of a Happy Eternity. 2s. 6d.
S. Paul of the Cross. 12mo, 3s.
School of Jesus Crucified. 18mo, 5s.
Pastor and People. By Rev. [illegible] Price. 12mo, 5s.

Path to Paradise. *See* Prayers, page 31.
Patrick (S.), Life of. 1s.; 8vo., 6s.; gilt, 10s.
Patron Saints. By E. A. Starr. Illustrated. 12mo., 10s.
Penitential Psalms. *See* Blyth (Rev. F.).
PENNELL (M. A.), Bertram Eldon. 12mo., 1s.
——— **Nellie Gordon, the Factory Girl.** 18mo., 6d.
Pens, Washbourne's Free and Easy. Fine, or Middle, or Broad Points, 1s. per gross.
Perpetual Adoration, Book of. By Boudon. 3s. and 3s. 6d.
Peter (S.), his Name and his Office. By T. W. Allies. 5s.
Peter, Years of. By an ex-Papal Zouave. 12mo., 1d.
Philip Benizi (S.), Life of. *See* Oratorian Lives of the Saints.
Philomena (S.), Life and Miracles of. 12mo., 2s. 6d.
Philosophy, Elements of. By Rev. W. H. Hill. 8vo., 6s.
PHILPIN (Rev. F.), Holy Places; their sanctity and authenticity. With three Maps. 12mo., 2s. 6d. and 6s.
Photographs (10) illustrating the History of the Miraculous Hosts, called the Blessed Sacrament of the Miracle. (S. Gudule's, Bruges). 2s. 6d. the set.
PILLEY (C.), Bellevue and its Owners. 12mo., 2s.
Pius IX., from his Birth to his Death. By G. White. 4d.
Pius IX. By J. F. Maguire. 12mo., 6s.
Plain Chant. (Gregorian), and Modern Music. 2s. 6d.
——— The Cecilian Society Music kept in stock.
PLATUS (Rev. F.), Origin and Progress of Religious Orders, and Happiness of a Religious State. 12mo., 2s. 6d.
PLAYS. *See* Dramas, page 10.
POIRIER (Bishop), A General Catechism of the Christian Doctrine. 18mo., 9d.
POOR CLARES OF KENMARE. *See* Cusack (Miss).
Pope-King, Rule of. By Rev. E. R. Martin. 8vo., 6d.
Popes of Rome. By Rev. C. Tondini. 3s. 6d.
Popes, Lives of the Early. By Rev. T. Meyrick. 2 vols. 10s.
POTTER (Rev. T. J.), Extemporary Preaching. 5s.
——— **Farleyes of Farleye.** 12mo., 2s. 6d.
——— **Pastor and People.** 12mo., 5s.
——— **Percy Grange.** 12mo., 3s.
——— **Rupert Aubrey.** 12mo., 3s.
——— **Sir Humphrey's Trial.** 16mo., 2s. 6d.
POWELL (J., Esq.), Two Years in the Pontifical Zouaves. Illustrated. 8vo., 3s. 6d.
POWER (Rev. P.) Catechism. 3 vols., 10s. 6d.; 2 vols. 7s. 6d.
PRADEL (Fr., O. P.), Life of St. Vincent Ferrer. Translated by Rev. Fr. Dixon. With a Photograph. 12mo., 5s.
PRAYER BOOKS. *See* page 31.
PRICE (Rev. E.), Sick Calls. From the Diary of a Missionary Priest. 12mo., 3s. 6d.
PRINS (Leopold de). *See* Music.
Pro-Cathedral, Kensington. Tinted View of the Interior; 11 × 15 inches, 1s.; Proofs, on larger paper, 2s.
Prophecies, Contemporary. By Mgr. Dupanloup. 8vo., 1s.

Protestantism and Liberty. By F. Ozanam. 1s.
Protestant Principles examined by the Written Word. 1s.
Prussian Spy. A Novel. By V. Valmont. 12mo., 4s.
Purgatory, A Novena in favour of the Souls in. 32mo., 3d.
Purgatory, Month of the Souls in Purgatory. By Ricard, 1s.
Purgatory, The Doctrine of. By Rev. W. Marshall. 12mo., 1s.
Purgatory, Souls in. By Abbot Burder. 32mo., 3d.
PYE (Henry John, M.A.), Necessity of Enquiry as to Religion. 32mo., 4d.; cloth, 6d.
—— **Revelation.** Being the substance of several conversations on First Principles. 6d.
—— **The Religion of Common Sense.** New Edition. 1s.
RAMIERE (Rev. H.), Apostleship of Prayer. 12mo., 6s.
RAVIGNAN (Pere), The Spiritual Life, Conferences. Translated by Mrs. Abel Ram. 12mo., 5s.
Ravignan (Pere), Life of. 12mo., 9s.
RAWES (Rev. F.). Sursum. 1s.
Reading Books, by the Marist Brothers. 12mo., 1st, 4d.; 2nd, 7d.
Reasonings of Plain Common-Sense upon the Church. 2s. 10d. a 100, post free.
REDMAN (Rev. Dr.), Book of Perpetual Adoration. By Mgr. Boudon. 12mo., 3s.; red edges, 3s. 6d.
REDMOND (Rev. Dr.), Sermon Essays. 18mo., 1s.
REEVES' History of the Bible. 12mo., 3s. 6d. 18mo., 1s.
Reflections, One Hundred Pious. By Alban Butler. 1s.
Regina Sæculorum; or, Mary Venerated in all Ages. Devotions to the Blessed Virgin from Ancient Sources. 12mo., 1s. and 3s.
Rejection of Catholic Doctrines attributable to the Non-Realization of Primary Truths. 8vo., 1s.
Religion of Common Sense. By H. J. Pye, M.A. 12mo., 1s.
Religious Orders. By Rev. F. Platus. 2s. 6d.
Rest, on the Cross. By Eleanora Louisa Hervey. 12mo., 3s. 6d.
Revelation. By Henry John Pye, Esq. 6d.
Reverse of the Medal. A Drama for Girls. 12mo., 6d.
RIBADENEIRA—Life, Passion, Death, and Resurrection of Our Lord. 12mo., 1s.
RICARD (Abbe), Month of the Holy Angels. 18mo., 1s.
—— **Month of the Souls in Purgatory.** 18mo., 1s.
RICHARDSON (Rev. Fr.), Catholic Sick and Benefit Club; or, the Guild of our Lady; and St. Joseph's Catholic Burial Society. 32mo., 4d.
—— **Holy War against Drunkenness.** Manual 6d. a dozen, Cards 2d. each.
—— **Little by Little**; or, the Penny Bank. 32mo., 1d.
—— **Shamrocks.** 6s. 2d. a gross (144), post free.
—— **S. Joseph's Catholic Burial Society.** 2d.
—— **The Crusade.** For the Suppression of Drunkenness. 1d.
Ritus Servandus in Expositione et Benedictione. 10s. 6d.
Road to Heaven. A Game. By Miss M. A. Macdaniel. 3s. 6d.
ROBERTSON (Professor), Edmund Burke. 12mo., 3s. 6d.

ROBINSON (Wilfrid C.), Protestantism and Liberty. Translated from the French of Professor Ozanam. 8vo., 1s.

Roman Question, The. By Rev. Dr. Husenbeth. 8vo., 6d.

Rome and her Captors: Letters collected and edited by Count Henri d'Ideville, and Translated by F. R. Wegg-Prosser. 4s.

Rome, Past, Present, and Future. By Dr. M'Corry. 8vo., 6d.

—— **Personal Recollections of.** By W. J. Jacob, 8vo., 6d.

—— **The Victories of.** By Rev. F. Beste. 8vo., 1s.

—— **(To) and Back.** Fly-Leaves from a Flying Tour. Edited by Rev. W. H. Anderdon, S.J., 12mo., 2s.

Rosalie; or, the Memoir of a French Child, told by herself. 12mo., 1s.; stronger bound, 1s. 6d.; gilt, 2s.

Rosary, Fifteen Mysteries of, and Fourteen Stations of the Cross. In One Volume, 32 Illustrations. 16mo., 2s.

Rosary for the Souls in Purgatory, with Indulgenced Prayer. 6d. and 9d. Medals separately, 1d. each, or 9s. gross. Prayers separately, 1d. each, 9d. a dozen, or 6s. for 100.

Rosary, Chats about the; Aunt Margaret's Little Neighbours. 3s.

ROWLEY (Rev. Austin John), A Devout Exposition of the Holy Mass. Composed by John Heigham. 12mo., 4s.

RUSSELL (Rev. M.), Emmanuel. 2s.; cheap edition, 6d.

—— **Madonna.** Verses on Our Lady and the Saints, 1s. 6d.

RUTTER (Rev. H.) Life and Sufferings of Our Lord, with Introduction by Rev. Dr. Husenbeth. Illustrated. 12mo., 5s.

RYAN (Bishop). What Catholics do not Believe. 12mo., 1s.

Sacred Heart. By Canon Doyle. 3s.

——, **Act of Consecration to.** 1d.; or 6s. per 100.

——, **Act of Reparation to.** 1s. 2d. per 100.

——, **A Novena.** 1s.

——, **A Spiritual Banquet.** 6d.

——, **Devotions to.** By Rev. S. Franco. 12mo., 4s.; cheap edition, 2s.

——, **Devotions to.** By Bishop Milner. 3d.; cloth, 6d.

——, **Elevations to the.** By Rev. Fr. Doyotte, S.J. 3s.

——, **Golden Treasury.** 48mo., 1s. 6d.; French morocco, 2s. 6d.; calf or morocco, 3s. 6d.

——, **Handbook of the Confraternity.** 18mo., 3d.

——, **Little Treasury of.** 32mo., 2s.; French morocco, 2s. 6d.; calf, 5s.; morocco, 6s.

——, **Manual of Devotions to the,** from the writings of Blessed Margaret Mary. 32mo., 3d.

—— **offered to the Piety of the Young engaged in Study.** By Rev. F. Deham. 32mo., 6d.

——, **Office.** 1d.

—— *See* Paradise of God; Kinane (Rev. T. H.).

—— **Pleadings of.** By Rev. M. Comerford. 18mo., 1s.; gilt edges, 2s.; Handbook of the Confraternity, 3d.

——, **Treasury of.** 18mo., 3s. 6d.; roan, 4s.

Sacred History in Forty Pictures. Plain, 5s.; coloured, 7s. 6d.; mounted on cardboard, coloured, 18s. 6d. and 22s.

Saints, Lives of, for every day in the Year. Beautifully printed, within illustrated borders from ancient sources, on thick toned paper. 4to., gilt, 25s.

ST. JURE (S.J.) Knowledge and Love of Jesus Christ. 3 vols., 8vo., 31s. 6d.

——— **The Spiritual Man.** 12mo., 6s.

Sanctuary Meditations for Priests and Frequent Communicants. Translated from the Spanish of Fr. Baltasar Gracian, by Mariana Monteiro. 12mo., 4s.

SCARAMELLI—Directorium Asceticum; or, Guide to the Spiritual Life. 4 vols. 12mo., 24s.

SCHMID (Canon), Tales. Illustrated. 12mo., 3s. 6d. Separately :—The Canary Bird, The Dove, The Inundation, The Rose Tree, The Water Jug, The Wooden Cross. 6d. each; gilt, 1s.

SCHOOL BOOKS. Supplied according to order.

School of Jesus Crucified. By the Passionist Fathers. 18mo., 5s.

SCHOUVALOFF (Rev. Father, Barnabite), My Conversion and Vocation. Translated from the French, with an Appendix, by Fr. C. Tondini. 12mo., 5s.

SCHULTHES (William). *See* Music.

SEGNERI (Fr., S.J.), Panegyrics. Translated from the original Italian. With a Preface, by Rev. W. Humphrey. 12mo., 6s.

SEGUR (Mgr.), Books for Little Children. Translated. 32mo., 3d. each. Confession, Holy Communion, Child Jesus, Piety, Prayer, Temptation and Sin. In one volume, cloth, 2s.

——— **Three Roses of the Elect.** 16mo., 1s. 6d.

SEGUR (Countess de), The Little Hunchback. 12mo., 3s.

Seigneret (Paul), Life of. 12mo., 6d., 1s., and 1s. 6d.; gilt, 2s.

Selva; a Collection of Matter for Sermons. By St. Liguori. 12mo., 5s.

Semi-Tropical Trifles. By H. Compton. 12mo., 1s.; cloth, 2s. 6d.

Sermon Essays. By Rev. Dr. Redmond. 12mo., 1s.

Sermons. Irish and English. By Dr. O'Gallagher. 8vo., 7s. 6d.

——— *See* Doyle, 2 vols., 10s. 6d.; Scaramelli, 4 vols., 24s.; Segneri, 6s.; O'Keeffe, 2s.; Buckley, 6ds.

——— By Rev. J. Perry. First Series, 3s. 6d. Second Series, 3s. 6d.

——— **The Light of the Holy Spirit in the World.** By Bishop Hedley. 1s.; cloth, 1s. 6d.

Serving Boy's Manual, and Book of Public Devotions. Containing all those prayers and devotions for Sundays and Holydays, usually divided in their recitation between the Priest and the Congregation. Compiled from approved sources, and adapted to Churches, served either by the Secular or Regular Clergy. 32mo., embossed, 1s.; French morocco, 2s.; calf, 4s.; with Epistles and Gospels, 6d. extra.

SHAKESPEARE. Expurgated edition. By Rosa Baughan. 8vo., 6s. The Comedies only, 3s. 6d.

Shandy Maguire. A Farce for Boys. 2 Acts. 12mo., 2s.

SHAW (T. H.), Holy Church the Centre of Unity; or, Ritualism compared with Catholicism. 8vo., 1s.

——— **The McPhersons,** to which is added "England's Glory; the Roll of Honour." 8vo., 2s. 6d.

Shilling Fund, The. By Canon Sing. 8vo., 6d.

SIGHART (Dr.) Albertus Magnus. 10s. 6d. Cheap edition, 5s.
Silver Teapot. By Elizabeth King. 18mo., 4d.
Simple Tales—Waiting for Father, &c., &c. 16mo., 2s. 6d.
Sir Ælfric and other Tales. *See* Bampfield (Rev. G.).
Sir Thomas Maxwell and his Ward. By Miss Bridges. 12mo, 1s. and 2s.
Sisters of Charity, Manual of. 18mo. 6s.
SMITH-SLIGO (A. V., Esq.), Life of the Ven. Anna Maria Taigi. Translated from French of Calixte. 8vo., 2s. 6d. and 5s.
— **(Mrs.) Margarethe Verflassen.** 12mo., 1s. 6d., 3s., and 3s. 6d.
Sophia and Eulalie. (The Catholic Pilgrim's Progress.) From the French by Rev. Fr. Bradbury. 12mo., 1s. 6d., better bound, 3s. 6d.
SPALDING'S (Abp.) Works. 5 vols., 52s. 6d.; or separately: Evidences of Catholicity, 12s.; Miscellanea, 2 vols., 21s.; Protestant Reformation, 2 vols., 21s.; cheap edition, 1 vol., 14s.
Spalding (Archbishop), Life of. 8vo., 10s. 6d.
——— **Sermon at the Month's Mind.** 8vo., 1s.
Spiritual Conferences on the Mysteries of Faith and the Interior Life. By Father Collins. 12mo., 5s.
Spiritual Life. Conferences by Père Ravignan. Translated by Mrs. Abel Ram. 12mo., 5s.
Spiritual Life of Fr. Schouvaloff. 12mo., 5s.
Spiritual Works of Louis of Blois. Edited by Rev. F. John Bowden. 12mo., 3s. 6d.; red edges, 4s.
STARR (Eliza Allen), Patron Saints. Illustrated. 12mo., 10s.
Stations of the Cross, Devotions for Public and Private Use at the. By Miss Cusack. Illustrated. 16mo., 1s. and 1s. 6d.
Stations of the Cross. By S. Liguori. 18mo., 1d.
Stations, and Mysteries of the Rosary. Illustrated, 2s.
STEWART (A. M.)
——— **St. Angela's Manual.** 2s.
——— **Biographical Readings.** 12mo., 3s.
——— **Cardinal Wolsey.** 12mo., 6s. 6d.
——— **Sir Thomas More.** Illustrated, 10s. 6d.; gilt, 11s. 6d.
——— **Life of S. Angela Merici.** 12mo., 3s.
——— **Life of Bishop Fisher.** 12mo., 7s. 6d.
——— **Life in the Cloister.** 12mo., 3s. 6d.
——— **Limerick Veteran**; or, the Foster Sisters. 5s. and 6s.
——— **Yorkshire Plot.** 6s. 6d.
Stonyhurst College, Present and Past. By A. Hewitson. cash 10s. 6d., postage 7d. [1s.
Stories for my Children—The Angels and the Sacraments.
Stories of Holy Lives. By M. F. S. 12mo., 3s. 6d.
Stories of Martyr Priests. By M. F. S. 12mo., 3s. 6d.
Stories of the Saints. By M. F. S. 12mo., Five Series, each 3s. 6d.; 1st and 2nd Series, gilt, 4s. 6d.
Stories from many Lands. Compiled by E. L. Hervey. 3s. 6d.
Story of a Paper Knife. 12mo., 1s.; gilt edges, 1s. 6d.
Story of Marie and other Tales. 12mo., 2s. 6d.; gilt, 3s.; or separately:—The Story of Marie, 2d.; Nelly Blane, and a Contrast, 2d.; A Conversion and a Death-bed, 2d.; Herbert Montagu, 2d.; Jane Murphy, the Dying Gipsy, and the Nameless Grave, 2d.; The Beggars, and True and False Riches, 2d.; Pat and his Friend, 2d.

Story of the Life of St. Paul. By M. F. S., author of "Stories of the Saints." 12mo., 2s. 6d., cheap edition, 1s. 6d.
Sufferings of our Lord. Sermons preached by Father Claude de la Colombière, S.J., in the Chapel Royal, St. James's, in the year 1677. 18mo., 1s.; stronger bound, 1s. 6d.; red edges, 2s.
Supernatural Life, The. By Mgr. Mermillod. Translated from the French, with a Preface by Lady Herbert. 12mo., 5s.
Supremacy of the Roman See. By C. E. Tame, Esq. 8vo., 6d.
Sure Way to Heaven. A Little Manual for Confession and Holy Communion. 32mo., 6d.; persian, 2s. 6d.; calf or morocco, 3s. 6d.
Sweetness of Holy Living; or, Honey culled from the Flower Garden of S. Francis of Sales. 18mo., 1s.; French morocco, 3s.
Sydenhams of Beechwood; or, the Two Espousals. 3s. 6d.
Taigi (Anna Maria), Life of. Translated from the French of Calixte by A. V. Smith-Sligo, Esq. 8vo., 2s. 6d. and 5s.
Tales and Sketches. By Charles Fleet. 3s. 6d.
Tales of the Jewish Church. By Charles Walker. 12mo., 2s. 6d., cheap edition, 1s. 6d.
TAME (C. E., Esq.), Early English Literature. 16mo., 2s. a vol. I. Our Lady's Lament, and the Lamentation of S. Mary Magdalene. II. Life of Our Lady, in verse.
——— **Supremacy of the Roman See.** 8vo., 6d.
TANDY (Rev. Dr.), Terry O'Flinn. 12mo., 1s.; stronger bound, 1s. 6d.; gilt, 2s.
TAUNTON (M.), Last of the Catholic O'Malleys. 18mo., 1s. 6d.; stronger bound, 2s.
——— **One Hundred Pious Reflections,** from Alban Butler's Lives of the Saints. 18mo., 1s.; stronger bound, 2s.
TERESA (S.), Book of the Foundations. Translated by Canon Dalton. 12mo., 3s. 6d.
——— **Letters of.** Translated by Canon Dalton. 12mo., 3s. 6d.
——— **Way of Perfection.** 12mo., 3s. 6d.
——— **The Interior Castle.** 12mo., 3s. 6d.
Terry O'Flinn. By Rev. Dr. Tandy. 12mo., 1s., 1s. 6d. and 2s.
Testimony; or, the Necessity of Enquiry as to Religion. By John Henry Pye, M.A. 32mo., 4d.; cloth, 6d.
Theobald; or, The Triumph of Charity. 12mo., 2s. 6d.
Three Wishes. A Tale. By M. F. S. 2s. 6d., cheap edition, 1s. 6d.
Threshold of the Catholic Church. By Fr. Bagshawe. 4s.
Tim O'Halloran's Choice. By Miss Cusack. 3s. 6d.
Tom's Crucifix, and other Tales. By M. F. S. 12mo., 3s. 6d., or in 5 vols., 1s. each; gilt, 1s. 6d.
TONDINI (Rev. Cæsarius), My Conversion and Vocation. By Rev. Fr. Schouvaloff. 12mo., 5s.
——— **The Pope of Rome and the Popes of the Oriental Orthodox Church.** An essay on Monarchy in the Church, with special reference to Russia. Second Edition. 12mo., 3s. 6d.
——— **Association Prayers in Honour of Mary Immaculate.** 12mo., 3d.
Transubstantiation, Catholic Doctrine of. 12mo., 6d.
TRONSON (Abbe), The Mass: a devout Method. 32mo., 4d.
TRONSON'S Conferences for Ecclesiastical Students and Religious. By Sister M. F. Clare. 12mo., 4s. 6d.

True Wayside Tales. By Ladv ' 'erbert. 12mo., 3s., or cheap edition, in 5 vols., 6d. each.
Two Colonels. By Father Thomas. 12mo., 6s. [gilt, 1s. 6d.
Two Friends; or Marie's Self-Denial. By Madame d'Arras. 1s., or
Ursuline Manual. *See* Prayers, page 32.
VALMONT (V.), The Prussian Spy. A Novel. 12mo., 4s.
VAUGHAN (Bishop of Salford), The Mass. 2d.; cloth, 6d.
——— **Love and Passion of Jesus Christ.** 2d.
VERE (Rev. G. L.), The Catholic Hymn Book. 32mo., 2d.; cloth, 4d. Appendix containing Hymns in honour of Saints. 1d.
Veronica Giuliani (S.), Life of, and B. Battista Varani. With a Photographic Portrait. 12mo., 5s.
Village Lily. A Tale. 12mo., 1s.; gilt, 1s. 6d.
Vincent Ferrer (S.), of the Order of Friar Preachers; his Life, Spiritual Teaching, and Practical Devotion. By Rev. Fr. Andrew Pradel, O.P. Translated from the French by the Rev. Fr. T. A. Dixon, O.P., with a Photograph. 12mo., 5s.
VINCENT OF LIRINS (S.). Commonitory. 12mo., 1s. 3d.
Violet Sellers, The; a Drama in 3 Acts, for Children. 12mo., 6d.
VIRGIL. Literally translated by Davidson. 12mo., 2s. 6d.
"Vitis Mystica"; or, the True Vine. By Canon Brownlow. 4s.
WALKER (Charles), Are You Safe in the Church of England? 8vo., 6d.
——— **Maggie Wilson,** 2d.; **Joe Marks,** 2d.
——— **Tales of the Jewish Church.** 12mo., 2s. 6d. and 1s. 6d.
——— **Why Roman Catholics disbelieve in Anglican Orders,** 1d.
WALLER (J. F., Esq.), Festival Tales. 12mo., 3s 6d.
WALSH (Rev. Dr.), Harmony of Gospel Narrative. 2s.
Weedall (Mgr.), Life of. By Rev. Dr. Husenbeth. 8vo., 5s.
WEGG-PROSSER (F. R.), Rome and her Captors. 4s.
Wenefred (St.), Life of. By Rev. T. Meyrick. 12mo., 2s.
What Catholics do not Believe. By Bishop Ryan. 12mo., 1s.
WHITE (George), Cardinal Wiseman. 12mo., 1s. and 1s. 6d.
——— **Comte de Montalembert.** 12mo., 6d.
——— **Life of S. Edmund of Canterbury.** 1s. and 1s. 6d.
——— **Pius IX., from his Birth to his Death.** 12mo., 4d.
——— **Queens and Princesses of France.** 12mo., 3s. 6d.
William (St.), of York. A Drama in Two Acts. (Boys.) 12mo., 6d.
WILLIAMS (Canon), Anglican Orders. 12mo., 3s. 6d.
WISEMAN (Cardinal), Doctrines and Practices of the Catholic Church. 12mo., 3s. 6d.
——— **Science and Religion.** 12mo., 5s.
Wiseman (Cardinal), Life and Obsequies. 1s., cloth, 1s. 6d.
——— **Recollections of.** By M. J. Arnold. 12mo., 2s. 6d.
WOODS (Canon), Defence of the Roman Church against F. Gratry. Translated from the French of Gueranger. 1s. 6d.
Young Catholic's Guide to Confession and Holy Communion. By Dr. Kenny. 32mo., 4d.; cloth, 6d.; red edges, 9d., French morocco, 1s. 6d.; calf or morocco, 2s. 6d.
YOUNG (T., Esq.), History of Ireland. 18mo., 2s. 6d.
Zouaves, Pontifical, Two Years in. By Joseph Powell, Z.P. Illustrated. 8vo., 3s. 6d.

Garden, Little, of the Soul. Edited by the Rev. R. G. Davis. *With Imprimatur of the Cardinal Archbishop of Westminster.* This book, as its name imports, contains a selection from the "Garden of the Soul" of the Prayers and Devotions of most general use. Whilst it will serve as a *Pocket Prayer Book* for all, it is, by its low price, *par excellence*, the Prayer Book for children and for the very poor. In it are to be found the old familiar Devotions of the "Garden o, the Soul," as well as many important additions, such as the Devotions to the Sacred Heart, to Saint Joseph, to the Guardian Angels, and others. The omissions are mainly the Forms of administering the Sacraments, and Devotions that are not of very general use. It is printed in a clear type, on a good paper, both especially selected, for the purpose of obviating the disagreeableness of small type and inferior paper. Twentieth Thousand.

32mo., price, **cloth, 6d.**; with rims, 1s.; with Epistles and Gospels, 8d.; with clasp, 1s.; Superior, 1s. Strong roan, 1s.; with E. and G, 1s. 6d.; with rims and clasp, 1s. 6d. and 2s.; French morocco, 1s. 6d.; with E. and G., 2s. 6d.; with rims and clasps, 2s. and 2s. 6d. French morocco extra gilt, 2s.; with E. and G., 2s. 6d.; with rims and clasp, 2s. 6d. and 3s. Calf or morocco, 3s.; with rims and clasp, 4s. Calf or morocco, extra gilt, 4s.; with rims and clasp, 5s. Morocco antique, 7s. 6d., 10s. 6d., 12s., 16s. Velvet, rims and clasp, 5s., 8s. 6d., and 10s. 6d. Russia, 5s.; with clasp, &c., 8s.; Russia antique, 17s. 6d. Ivory, with rims and clasp. 10s. 6d., 13s., 15s., 17s. 6d. Imitation ivory, with rims and clasp, 2s. 6d. With oxydized silver or gilt mountings, in morocco case, 25s. Cheap edition with Epistles and Gospels, 6d.; stronger, 8d.; with clasp, 1s.; or better bound, 1s.; roan, 1s. 6d.; french mor., 2s.; ex. gilt, 2s. 6d.

Catholic Hours: a Manual of Prayer, including Mass and Vespers. By J. R. Digby Beste, Esq. 32mo., cloth, 2s.; red edges, 2s. 6d.; roan, 3s.; morocco, 6s.

Catholic Piety; with Epistles and Gospels. Large 32mo., roan, 1s. 6d. and 2s.; French morocco, with rims and clasp, 2s. 6d.; extra gilt, 3s.; with rims and clasp, 3s. 6d.

Key of Heaven, same prices as above.

Catholic Piety. 32mo., 6d.; rims and clasp, 1s.; French morocco, 1s.; velvet, with rims and clasp, 2s. 6d. With Epistles and Gospels, roan, 1s.; French morocco, 1s. 6d.; with rims and clasp, 2s.; extra gilt, 2s.; Persian, 2s. 6d.; morocco, 3s. 6d.; velvet, rims and clasp, 3s. 6d.

Key of Heaven, same prices as above.

Crown of Jesus. 18mo., Persian calf, 6s. Calf or Morocco, 7s. 6d. and 8s. 6d.; with rims and clasp, 10s. 6d. Calf or morocco, extra gilt, 10s. 6d.; with rims and clasp, 12s. 6d; with turn-over edges, 10s. 6d. Ivory, with rims and clasp, 21s., 25s., 27s. 6d. and 30s.

Devotions for Mass. Very large type, 12mo., 2d.

Garden of the Soul. Very large Type. 18mo., cloth, 1s.; with Epistles and Gospels, 1s. 6d.; French morocco, 2s. 6d.; with E. and G., 3s. 6d. Best edition, without E. and G., 3s. 6d.; with E. and G., morocco circuit, 7s. 6d.; calf antique, with clasp, 8s.; French morocco, antique, with clasp, 6s. 6d.

Epistles and Gospels, in French morocco, 2s.

Golden Treasury of the Sacred Heart. 48mo., 1s. 6d.; French morocco, 2s. 6d.; calf or morocco, 3s. 6d.
Holy Childhood Simple Prayers for very little children. 32mo., 1s.; gilt, 1s. 6d.; cheap edition, 6d.; roan, 1s.
Key of Heaven. *Very large type.* 18mo., 1s.; leather, 2s. 6d.
Lily of St. Joseph, The; a little Manual of Prayers and Hymns for Mass. 64mo., price 2d.; cloth, 3d., 4d., 6d., or 8d.; roan, 1s.; French morocco, 1s. 6d.; calf or morocco, 2s.; gilt, 2s. 6d.
Little Prayer Book, The, for Ordinary Catholic Devotions. 3d.
Manual of Catholic Devotions. Small, for the waistcoat pocket. 64mo., 4d.; with Epistles and Gospels, cloth, 6d.; with rims, 1s.; roan, 1s.; with tuck, 2s.; calf or morocco, 2s. 6d.; ivorine, 2s. 6d.
Manual of Devotions in Honour of our Lady of Sorrows. 18mo., 1s. 6d.; cheaper binding, 1s.
Missal (Complete). 18mo., roan, 5s.; Persian, 8s. 6d.; calf or morocco, 10s. 6d.; with rims and clasp, 13s. 6d.; calf or mor., extra gilt, 12s. 6d., with rims and clasp, 15s. 6d.; morocco, with turn-over edges, 13s. 6d.; morocco antique, 15s.; velvet, 20s.; Russia, 20s.; ivory, with rims and clasp, 31s. 6d. and 35s. A very beautiful edition, handsomely bound in morocco, gilt mountings, silk linings, edges red on gold, in a morocco case. Illustrated, £5.
Missal and Vesper Book, in one vol. 32mo., morocco, 6s.; with clasp, 8s.
Occasional Prayers for Festivals. 4d. and 6d.; gilt, 1s.
Ordinary of the Mass. 32mo., 2d.; cloth, 6d.
Oremus, A Liturgical Prayer Book: with the Imprimatur of the Cardinal Archbishop of Westminster. An adaptation of the Church Offices: containing Morning and Evening Devotions; Devotion for Mass, Confession, and Communion, and various other Devotions; Common and Proper, Hymns, Lessons, Collects, Epistles and Gospels for Sundays, Feasts, and Week Days; and short notices of over 200 Saints' Days. 32mo., 452 pages, 2s.; cloth, 2s. 6d.; embossed, red edges, 3s. 6d.; French morocco, 4s. 6d.; calf or morocco, 6s.; Russia, 8s. 6d., &c., &c., &c.
A Smaller Oremus. An abridgment of the above. Cloth, 9d., with red edges, 1s.; roan or French morocco, 2s.; calf or morocco, 3s.
Path to Paradise. 32 full-page Illustrations. 32mo., cloth, 3d. With 50 Illustrations, cloth, 4d. Superior edition, 6d. and 1s.
Serving Boy's Manual and Book of Catholic Devotions, containing all those Prayers and Devotions for Sundays and Holidays, usually divided in their recitation between the Priest and the Congregation. Compiled from approved sources, and adapted to Churches served either by the Secular or the Regular Clergy, 32mo., Embossed, 1s.; with Epistles and Gospels, 1s. 6d.; French morocco, 2s., with Epistles and Gospels, 2s. 6d.; calf, 4s., with Epistles and Gospels, 4s. 6d.
Soul united to Jesus in the Adorable Sacrament. 1s. 6d.
S. Patrick's Manual. Compiled by Sister Mary Frances Clare. 3s. 6d.
Sure Way to Heaven. Cloth, 6d.: Persian, 2s. 6d.; morocco, 3s. 6d.
Treasury of the Sacred Heart. 18mo., 3s. 6d.; roan, 4s. 6d. 32mo., 2s.; French morocco, 2s. 6d.; calf 5s.; morocco, 6s.
Ursuline Manual. 18mo., 4s.; Persian calf, 7s. 6d.; morocco, 10s.

Garden of the Soul. (WASHBOURNE'S EDITION.) Edited by the Rev. R. G. Davis. *With Imprimatur of the Cardinal Abp. of Westminster.* Twenty-third Thousand. This Edition retains all the Devotions that have made the GARDEN OF THE SOUL, now for many generations, the well-known Prayer-book for English Catholics. During many years various Devotions have been introduced, and, in the form of appendices, have been added to other editions. These have now been incorporated into the body of the work, and, together with the Devotions to the Sacred Heart, to Saint Joseph, to the Guardian Angels, the Itinerarium, and other important additions, render this edition pre-eminently the Manual of Prayer, for both public and private use. The version of the Psalms has been carefully revised, and strictly conformed to the Douay translation of the Bible, published with the approbation of the LATE CARDINAL WISEMAN. The Forms of administering the Sacraments have been carefully translated, *as also the rubrical directions*, from the Ordo Administrandi Sacramenta. To enable all present, either at baptisms or other public administrations of the Sacraments, to pay due attention to the sacred rites, the Forms are inserted without any curtailment, both in Latin and English. The Devotions at Mass have been carefully revised, and enriched by copious adaptations from the prayers of the Missal. The preparation for the Sacraments of Penance and the Holy Eucharist have been the objects of especial care, to adapt them to the wants of those whose religious instruction may be deficient. Great attention has been paid to the quality of the paper and to the size of type used in the printing, to obviate that weariness so distressing to the eyes, caused by the use of books printed in small close type and on inferior paper.

32mo. Embossed, 1s.; with rims and clasp, 1s. 6d.; with Epistles and Gospels, 1s. 6d.; with rims and clasp, 2s. French morocco, 2s.; with rims and clasp, 2s. 6d.; with E. and G., 2s. 6d.; with rims and clasp, 3s. French morocco extra gilt, 2s. 6d.; with rims and clasp, 3s.; with E. and G., 3s.; with rims and clasp, 3s. 6d. Calf, or morocco 4s.; with rims and clasp, 5s. 6d.; with E. and G., 4s. 6d., with rims and clasp, 6s. Calf or morocco extra gilt, 5s.; with rims and clasp, 6s. 6d.; with E. and G., 5s. 6d.; with rims and clasp, 7s. Velvet, with rims and clasp, 7s. 6d., 10s. 6d., and 13s.; with E. and G., 8s., 11s., and 13s. 6d. Russia, antique, with clasp, 8s. 6d., 10s., 12s. 6d.; with E. and G., 9s. 10s. 6d., 13s., with corners and clasps, 20s.; with E. and G., 20s. 6d. Ivory 14s., 16s., 18s., and 20s., with E. and G., 14s. 6d., 16s. 6d., 18s. 6d., and 20s. 6d. Morocco antique, 8s. 6d.; with 2 patent clasps, 12s.; with E. and G., 9s. and 12s. 6d.; with corners and clasps, 18s.; with E. and G., 18s. 6d.; morocco, with turn-over edges, 7s. 6d.

The Epistles and Gospels. *Complete*, cloth, 6d.; roan, 1s. 6d.

"This is one of the best editions we have seen of one of the best of all our Prayer Books. It is well printed in clear, large type, on good paper."—*Catholic Opinion* "A very complete arrangement of this which is emphatically the Prayer Book of every Catholic household. It is as cheap as it is good, and we heartily recommend it."—*Universe.* "Two striking features are the admirable order displayed throughout the book, and the insertion of the Indulgences in small type above Indulgenced Prayers. In the Devotions for Mass, the editor has, with great discrimination, drawn largely on the Church's Prayers, as given us in the Missal."—*Weekly Register.*

www.ingramcontent.com/pod-product-compliance
Lightning Source LLC
Chambersburg PA
CBHW031333230426
43670CB00006B/331

* 9 7 8 3 7 4 1 1 6 3 6 5 4 *